To Understand the Future Management: Managing through Digital Transformation

Yavuz Tansoy Yıldırım (ed.)

To Understand the Future Management: Managing through Digital Transformation

PETER LANG

Bibliographic Information published by the Deutsche Nationalbibliothek

The Deutsche Nationalbibliothek lists this publication in the Deutsche Nationalbibliografie; detailed bibliographic data is available online at http://dnb.d-nb.de.

Library of Congress Cataloging-in-Publication Data

A CIP catalog record for this book has been applied for at the Library of Congress.

This book project has been carried out under callforchapter.com editorial process

ISBN 978-3-631-83885-3 (Print)
E-ISBN 978-3-631-87027-3 (E-PDF)
E-ISBN 978-3-631-87028-0 (EPUB)
10.3726/b19302

Peter Lang – Berlin · Bern · Bruxelles · Istanbul · New York · Oxford · Warszawa · Wien

This publication has been peer reviewed.

www.peterlang.com

Table of Contents

List of Figures 7

List of Tables 9

List of Contributors 11

Preface and Acknowledgments 13

Senem NART & Yavuz Tansoy YILDIRIM
Artificial Intelligence in Management 17

Tuğba ERHAN
Digital Leadership: The Competencies of Leaders (Managers) in the Digital Age 29

İlksun Didem ÜLBEĞİ
Digitalization and Stress: Further Validation of the Technostress Scale 41

Fatma ZEYBEK & Hatice BATMANTAŞ
The Impact of Digitalization on Human Resource Management 57

Zümrüt Hatun DEMİREL
Artificial Intelligence Applications in Human Resource Management 71

Volkan TEMİZKAN & Abdülkadir ÖZTÜRK
Digital Public Relations as a Marketing Communication Tool: Examining Five Brands with High Interaction on Facebook 83

Elif KOÇ
Digital Marketing 95

İbrahim Tolga ÇOŞKUN
Finance Management and Digitalization 117

Arda TOYGAR & Senem NART
Requirements of Digital Management in the Global Supply Chain: The Case of Container Logistics 133

Emre İPEKÇİ
Digital Transformation in Logistics Activities 143

Oğuzhan KIVRAK, Mustafa Zahid GÜRBÜZ & Aysun GÜRAN
Management and Digitalization in the Service Industry 155

Umut YILDIRIM & Arda TOYGAR
An Evaluation of the Factors Affecting Risk Management Processes in the Maritime Sector 165

Aysun KANBUR & Ibrahim A. H. MOHAMED
The Path to Innovation: Discovering Intellectual Capital 177

Maruf GÖGEBAKAN & Serkan AKOĞUL
A New Approach to Clustering the Human Development Index in Terms of Business Management Using Gaussian Mixture Models 191

Remzi GÖK, Aviral Kumar TİWARİ & Şener İLTER
International Co-movement of Stock Markets during Crisis and Non-crisis Periods 215

List of Figures

İlksun Didem ÜLBEĞİ
Digitalization and Stress: Further Validation of the Technostress Scale
Figure 1. Technostress scale confirmatory factor analysis results 50

Fatma ZEYBEK & Hatice BATMANTAŞ
The Impact of Digitalization on Human Resource Management
Figure 1. HR 4.0 conceptual framework in the impact of digitalization 63

Elif KOÇ
Digital Marketing
Figure 1. Stages of web development 97
Figure 2. The framework of digital marketing 99
Figure 3. Sources of primary and secondary data 101
Figure 4. Digital marketing planning framework 111

Oğuzhan KIVRAK, Mustafa Zahid GÜRBÜZ & Aysun GÜRAN
Management and Digitalization in the Service Industry
Figure 1. Test page of the proposed integrated video conferencing application 160
Figure 2. UML diagram of the proposed system 160

Maruf GÖGEBAKAN & Serkan AKOĞUL
A New Approach to Clustering the Human Development Index in Terms of Business Management Using Gaussian Mixture Models
Figure 1. For the LEB variable: (a) BIC values based on component numbers, (b) 3-component GMM chart 198
Figure 2. For the EYS variable: (a) BIC values according to the number of components, (b) GMM graph with 1 component 199
Figure 3. For MYS: (a) BIC values based on component numbers, (b) 2-component GMM chart 199
Figure 4. For GNI variable: (a) BIC values based on component numbers, (b) 3-component GMM chart 200
Figure 5. BIC values for different types of covariance matrices for HDI data according to the number of components 202
Figure 6. Dispersion chart of four clusters of countries in terms of variables 203

Figure 7. A graph of BIC values according to the component number of the HDI score is shown in Figure 7(a) and a plot of the 3-component GMM is shown in Figure 7(b). 204
Figure 8. BIC values based on component numbers for HDI data 205
Figure 9. Scattering graph of three sets in terms of variables of countries 206

Remzi GÖK, Aviral Kumar TİWARİ & Şener İLTER
International Co-movement of Stock Markets during Crisis and Non-crisis Periods
Figure 1. Wavelet coherence analysis of market stock returns (CWT) 229
Figure 2. Wavelet coherence analysis of market stock returns (CWT) 230
Figure 3. Wavelet coherence analysis of market stock returns (CWT) 230

List of Tables

İlksun Didem ÜLBEĞİ
Digitalization and Stress: Further Validation of the Technostress Scale
Table 1. Factor loadings of the technostress scale 46
Table 2. Reliability analysis of the technostress scale 47
Table 3. Confirmatory factor analysis model fit results 48
Table 4. Means, standard deviations, Cronbach's alphas, McDonald's omegas, composite reliabilities, AVEs, and MSVs of the scales used 49
Table 5. Correlations of the scales used 49

Volkan TEMİZKAN & Abdülkadir ÖZTÜRK
Digital Public Relations as a Marketing Communication Tool: Examining Five Brands with High Interaction on Facebook
Table 1. Brands with successful Facebook accounts 88
Table 2. Information on the gift draw organized by brands on Facebook between 1 and 31 May 88
Table 3. Information on shares of brands on Facebook between 1 and 31 May 89
Table 4. Content analysis of the sample according to Wilcox and Cameron public relations goals variables 90
Table 5. Information on shares of brands on Instagram and Twitter between 1 and 31 May 90

Emre İPEKÇİ
Digital Transformation in Logistics Activities
Table 1. Significant developments in logistics and supply chain from past to present 145
Table 2. Logistics information systems 145

Maruf GÖGEBAKAN & Serkan AKOĞUL
A New Approach to Clustering the Human Development Index in Terms of Business Management Using Gaussian Mixture Models
Table 1. Mclust model V (univariate, unequal variance) with 3 components for LEB variable 198
Table 2. Mclust model V with 1 component for MYS variable 198

Table 3. Mclust model V with 2 components for average training time variable 199
Table 4. Mclust model V with 3 components for GNI variable 200
Table 5. All possible mixture model and appropriate mixture model numbers based on the number of components in variables 201
Table 6. Log-L, BIC, ICL, CCR and Adjusted Rand Index (Adj RI) values for four classes (Mclust model EVI (diagonal, equal volume, varying shape) with 4 components) 202
Table 7. Cross-correctness of countries according to four classes 203
Table 8. Log-L, BIC and ICL values of HDI score for U-GMM (Mclust V model with 3 components) 204
Table 9. Observation numbers falling into three classes in HDI data set 204
Table 10. Log-L, BIC, ICL, CCR and Adj Ri values for three classes (Mclust VVV ellipsoidal, varying volume, shape, and orientation model with 3 components) 205
Table 11. Cross-accuracy of countries according to three classes 206

Remzi GÖK, Aviral Kumar TİWARİ & Şener İLTER
International Co-movement of Stock Markets during Crisis and Non-crisis Periods
Table 1. Descriptive statistics 222
Table 2. Kapetanios unit root test (2005) – Model C (break in intercept & trend) 224
Table 3. Maki cointegration test (2012) 225
Table.4 . Granger causality test results based on VECM 226

List of Contributors

Assoc. Prof. Senem NART
Bandırma Onyedi Eylül University, Bandırma, Balıkesir, Turkey

Assoc. Prof. Yavuz Tansoy YILDIRIM
Bandırma Onyedi Eylül University, Bandırma, Balıkesir, Turkey

Asst. Prof. Tuğba ERHAN
Süleyman Demirel University, Isparta, Turkey

Assoc. Prof. İlksun Didem ÜLBEĞİ
Çukurova University, Adana, Turkey

Fatma ZEYBEK
Bandırma Onyedi Eylül University, Bandırma, Balıkesir, Turkey

Lect. Hatice BATMANTAŞ
Bandırma Onyedi Eylül University, Bandırma, Balıkesir, Turkey

Asst. Prof. Zümrüt Hatun DEMİREL
Yıldırım Beyazıt University, Ankara, Turkey

Asst. Prof. Volkan TEMİZKAN
Karabük University, Karabük, Turkey

Asst. Prof. Abdülkadir ÖZTÜRK
Recep Tayyib Erdoğan University, Rize, Turkey

Res. Asst. Dr. Elif Koç
Bandırma Onyedi Eylül University, Bandırma, Balıkesir, Turkey

Res Asst. İbrahim Tolga ÇOŞKUN
Çukurova University, Adana, Turkey

Lect. Arda TOYGAR
Artvin Çoruh University, Artvin, Turkey

Lect. Emre İPEKÇİ
Artvin Çoruh University, Artvin, Turkey

Asst. Prof. Oğuzhan KIVRAK
Bandırma Onyedi Eylül University, Bandırma, Balıkesir, Turkey

Asst. Prof. Mustafa Zahid GÜRBÜZ
Doğuş University, İstanbul, Turkey

Asst. Prof. Aysun GÜRAN
Doğuş University, İstanbul, Turkey

Asst. Prof. Umut YILDIRIM
Karadeniz Teknik University, Trabzon, Turkey

Assoc. Prof. Aysun KANBUR
Kastamonu University, Kastamonu, Turkey

Ibrahim A. H. MOHAMED
Higher Institute of Tourism and Hospitality, Benghazi, Libya

Asst. Prof. Maruf GÖGEBAKAN
Bandırma Onyedi Eylül University, Bandırma, Balıkesir, Turkey

Asst. Prof. Serkan AKOĞUL
Pamukkale University, Denizli, Turkey

Res. Asst. Dr. Remzi GÖK
Dicle University, Diyarbakır, Turkey

Dr. Aviral Kumar TİWARİ
Rajagiri Business School, Rajagiri, Valley Campus, Kochi, India

Şener İLTER
Anadolu University, Eskişehir, Turkey

Preface and Acknowledgments

Technology, which has gained a different meaning today, rapidly penetrate every aspect of our lives and reshape both our social and business life. Especially the advances in the field of information technologies affect all sectors from the industrial to the health sector. Companies try to keep up with the developments and to improve their processes. With our digitalized lives, many organizations have started to be involved in the digital transformation process in order to renew themselves and improve their current situation. The "transformation process" that emerged in this context requires organizations to build new practices instead of traditional methods. In this process, organizations develop a new management approach by integrating the ever-developing technology and digitalization into their activities. This approach is based on managing the changes and creates new strategies that integrate all business functions, such as production, finance, marketing, accounting, human resources, public relations, research and development, into the digitalization process. The main objective of these strategies is to increase the success of the organization by operating business functions in harmony with technology and information processing systems. In line with this goal, the digitalized business structure improves its processes and productivity, provides better customer and employee experiences, manages business risk, controls its costs and ultimately provides the highest benefit from management practices.

Organizations using the right strategies and processes in digitalization not only increase their performance but also increase their productivity, thus providing a significant competitive advantage in their sector. Therefore, digital transformation is a necessary tool for an organization to grow the business and keep up with the developing technologies of our time. The management, who understands the importance of digitalization, should first start by bringing a digital culture understanding to their organizations in order to gain effectiveness in processes such as strategic decision-making, execution and control. Transformation in organizations can only be possible with a corporate culture that believes and supports these changes. A successful digital transformation strategy depends on developing the necessary skills for digitalization in management. The main factor of this ability is a management approach that encourages keeping up with digitalized technology and allows employees to increase their skills and productivity under the umbrella of digital culture.

This book, which takes into account the issue of digitalization in management, consists of 15 chapters. In the first chapter, Senem Nart and Yavuz Tansoy Yıldırım seek artificial intelligence in management. The main objective of this study is to present the recommendations regarding how organizations can provide the exchange so that they can adopt to the artificial intelligence technology. In the second chapter, Tuğba Erhan explains the competencies of leaders in the digital age. In the twenty-first century, definitions of leader and leadership have been shaped. Changing developments force to adopt new leadership style in organizations. The organizations that adapt themselves to the new technological developments rapidly increase their chances to obtain competitive advantage. In the third chapter, İlksun Didem Ülbeği examines the validity and reliability of the technostress instrument. This study shows that technostress instrument is valid as well as reliable to utilize in Turkish studies. Fatma Zeybek and Hatice Batmantaş explain the digitalization in Human Resource Management in an organization. Zümrüt H. Demirel explains artificial intelligence in human resource management implementations. In the sixth chapter, Volkan Temizkan ve Abdülkadir Öztürk examined brand share made through social networks which would be one of the most effective tools of digital public relations. As a result of this study, they noticed brands that respond quickly and attentively to the customers' question through their social media accounts have high interaction rates. In chapter "Digital Marketing", Elif Koç presents digitalization in marketing. This study explains that when companies define digital marketing strategies with their mission, vision and targets, the starting point should be the information obtained from data-related customers, markets and competitors. In chapter "Finance Management and Digitalization", İbrahim Tolga Coşkun examined the effects of new financial instruments and technologies on financial management. According to this study, innovative services offered by financial institutions and organizations play an active role in solving many problems faced by companies in financial management.

Arda Toygar and Senem Nart present digitalization practices in supply chain management and container logistics management in chapter "Requirements of Digital Management in the Global Supply Chain: The Case of Container Logistics". Emre İpekçi explained Digital Transformation in Logistics activities in chapter "Digital Transformation in Logistics Activities". This study points that the existence of digital technologies in logistics has become a necessity. "Management and Digitalization in the Service Industry" is studied by Oğuzhan Kıvrak, Mustafa Zahid Gürbüz and Aysun Güran in chapter "Management and Digitalization in the Service Industry". This study points out that companies which want to take advantage in the competition must adopt new technologies such as the integrated video conferencing application. In chapter "An Evaluation of the Factors Affecting Risk Management Processes in the Maritime Sector", Umut Yıldırım and Arda Toygar studied an evaluation of the factors affecting risk management processes in the maritime sector. In this study, it is determined that human factor and financial uncertainties are the most threatening risk factors for maritime transport and ship management. Aysun Kanbur and İbrahim A. H. Mohamed present discovering intellectual capital which is the path to innovation in chapter "The Path to Innovation: Discovering Intellectual Capital". In the study, intellectual capital is determined as a critical factor for performance, innovation and value. In chapter "A New Approach to Clustering the Human Development Index in Terms of Business Management Using Gaussian Mixture Models", Maruf Gögebakan and Serkan Akoğul proposed a new model for the Human Development Index in terms of business management. Remzi Gür, Aviral Kumar Tivari and Şener İlter examine stock markets of both developed and developing countries in chapter "International Co-movement of Stock Markets during Crisis and Non-crisis Periods". At the end of this study, they expressed significant implications for investors in building international portfolio diversification, hedging and arbitrage opportunities as well as for policy makers in constructing monetary policies to attain financial stability.

Editor; Assoc. Prof. Yavuz Tansoy YILDIRIM

Senem NART & Yavuz Tansoy YILDIRIM

Artificial Intelligence in Management

1. Introduction

At the "International Robotics Festival", which was held in 2017, there happened a very interesting development; the philharmonic orchestra, in which the famous tenor Andrea Bocelli is the soloist, performed with an artificial intelligence orchestra conductor. Thus, for the first time, an orchestra was led by artificial intelligence (Kaya, 2017). Another interesting development in the realm of artificial intelligence occurred in Japan in 2018. An artificial intelligence-powered robot ran for mayor in local elections. AI did not win the election. But for the first time, the systems necessary for artificial intelligence to take part in political governance have become developable (Kahraman, 2019). The local government, continuing its activities in Amsterdam, has implemented in 2019 a 'Supervised Artificial Intelligence' model to find solutions to the problems faced by the city's population in public spaces. This model has begun to help the government make real-time decisions thanks to learning algorithms and efficient data processing technologies (Mutlu, 2020). Furthermore, in a study on "Automation and the Pace of Technological Change" conducted across Europe in 2019, a quarter of respondents said they would prefer artificial intelligence to be involved in the country's governance. In this study, carried out with the participation of 2,500 citizens of 7 European countries (Great Britain, Spain, Germany, France, Ireland, Italy, the Netherlands), 1 in 4 participants stated that they wanted artificial intelligence to be active in political decisions (Bischof, 2019). In fact, long before all these developments, Holloway (1983) had stated in his article "Strategic Management and Artificial Intelligence" that artificial intelligence could be predicted to be employed in senior management. This situation, which used to be viewed as not quite probable, has been occupying the agenda in recent years. Therefore, given the fact that discussions about the involvement of artificial intelligence in management have existed in every period, the answer to the question "Can artificial intelligence be a manager in the near future?" will give an idea of the real impact of artificial intelligence in business life.

According to the theory of "technological singularity" developed by Raymond Kurzweil, known for his work in the field of technology, by surpassing human intelligence artificial intelligence has evolved into something that can radically change all of humanity. Kurzweil predicts that the "singularity" will occur from the year 2045 onwards. Thus, when this phase is reached, the human brain and artificial intelligence will be able to merge (Hochman, 2016). If these developments reach the predicted dimensions, it will be inevitable that the business world will undergo a radical change. A large-scale study on "The Future of Artificial Intelligence" conducted by Oxford University and Yale University academics on academics in 2017 offers an idea of how developments in artificial intelligence technology reflect on the business world. In this study, which included 352 academics, participants were asked about their "predictions for when various capabilities in the field of Artificial Intelligence will be realized." The study revealed that participants believed that within 45 years, artificial intelligence would largely replace humans in all lines of work, and within 120 years, the entire workforce would be replaced by artificial intelligence (Grace, 2018).

All these studies also indicate that artificial intelligence will take on most administrative, bureaucratic, routine, chore and repetitive tasks; it will take the workload away from the workforce (Aksu, 2019a). Brynjolfsson and McAfee's book *The Second Machine Age* also explains this in detail. The authors note that there will be significant innovations, from robots in the production process to software that evaluates a job application or can propose a corporate strategy, and that "thinking machines" will thus supersede (Frick, 2015). Moreover, the study titled "The Impact of Cognitive Computing in Management" carried out by the Research Institute of Accenture Institute for High Performance (AIHP) and Accenture Strategy on 1,770 management staff and employees covering 14 countries has provided an important contribution to the literature about the place of artificial intelligence in management. As a result of the study, it was determined that in the near future, artificial intelligence applications will assume routine tasks such as planning, programming and optimization, and, herein, will assume their place in management activities (Shanks et al., 2016). Also, according to a report published by the "World Economic Forum" in 2017, it is estimated that developments in artificial intelligence technology will concern senior management by 2026 (World Economic Forum, 2015).

Considering all these studies, it appears to be a strong possibility that artificial intelligence managers and employees will be present in business life in the near future (Avansas, 2018). Studies give important clues especially about artificial intelligence managers replacing middle managers (Aksu, 2019b). On the other hand, it is extremely important that the business community provides the necessary restructuring now to keep up with this change. For, it is only expected that all these developments will lead to both structural and cultural changes in organizations. Therefore, in-depth research is needed to determine the possible effects of artificial intelligence technology on businesses, which will reshape working life, and to make various recommendations accordingly (Unal & Kılınç, 2020). Thus, this section of the book attempts to explain the impact of artificial intelligence on business management. In the first part, information is provided about the concept of artificial intelligence, its historical development, and the theoretical foundations of the discipline of artificial intelligence. In the second part, assessments are made on the impact of artificial intelligence in management. The widespread belief that the success of organizations in the near future could be achieved by artificial intelligence has made it crucial to address this issue.

2. Artificial Intelligence

Artificial intelligence is a field of study that aims to examine the mental functions that determine human intelligence through computer models and transfer them to artificial systems (Russell & Norvig, 1995). This field of study is based on philosophy, mathematics, psychology, linguistics, and computer science (McCorduck et al., 1977). According to Boden (2014), artificial intelligence is a branch of science, and activities aimed at illuminating the powers of the mind, rather than the development of intelligent machines, are carried out in this branch of science to generate commercial revenue. Accordingly, *Oxford Dictionary* defines the concept of artificial intelligence as the "theory of computing systems" forming human intelligence and performing actions such as perception, speech recognition, analysis, problem solving and decision making (Kahraman, 2019). This branch of science creates opportunities for the development of software and robots that can develop themselves, even design themselves and make decisions without being dependent on the human factor (OECD, 2016).

When we examine the historical process, the first ideas about artificial intelligence were put forth in the 1940s. The "Boolean Circuit Model of the Brain", developed by McCulloch and Pitts in 1943, attempted to mathematically explain the way neurons work in the brain using simple assumptions. Therefore, this model is considered to be one of the most important steps of artificial intelligence. By 1948, Shannon had suggested that several algorithms could be developed to prove complex mathematical theorems and play chess. Following this, in 1950, the famous British mathematician Alan Turing, in an article titled "Computing Machinery and Intelligence" published in a philosophy journal called *Mind*, looked for an answer to the question "If a human can hack the skills such as decision-making and problem-solving by using logic as much as current knowledge, why can't machines?" In this quest, he developed a test to determine whether a machine is intelligent or not. In an imitation created for this test, referred to as the "Turing Test", the machine tries to convince the interrogator, positioned in a separate section, that it is also human. Accordingly, the machine that can pass this test were considered "intelligent" (Russel & Norvig, 1995). Thus, the study became the source of a strategy for producing intelligent machines (Nilsson, 2010).

Later, the establishment of artificial intelligence as a discipline was achieved by a proposal presented by McCarthy and his colleagues at the Dortmund conference in 1956. However, the first person to bring this concept to the literature and become a reference point for the work carried out in this field was John Mccharty (McCorduck, 1977). The researcher referred to artificial intelligence as "human-like intelligent machines, especially the science and engineering of making intelligent computer programs" (McCarthy, 2007:7). Thereafter, the topic of the ability of a computer to display humanoid behaviors such as reasoning, problem solving, meaning extraction and generalization has been conceptualized as "artificial intelligence" (Arslan, 2020). At the same time, a program called "the Logic Theory Machine" was developed in 1956 by Newell and Simon to solve a mathematical problem. This software is the first artificial intelligence program designed to mimic humans' problem-solving abilities.

By the 1960s, the U.S. Department of Defense began to focus on studies related to artificial intelligence and to develop computer programs to mimic human-reasoning activity. As a result of these studies, machines imitating human biology using technology were developed in the 1990s inspired by neural and genetic structures. For example, in 1997, a computer program called "Deep Blue" was developed for chess experts to process chess moves. This significant development was the reference for a software called "AlphaGo", developed in 2016. This strategy game managed to defeat the world champion in the game Go. Unlike the previous software, a learning system dubbed deep learning was developed for this software. This software thus improved itself by following the winning player's move and continued the learning process until it became better at Go. As a result, reinforcement learning method in artificial intelligence was achieved (Nart, 2019). Thus, it has become possible for artificial intelligence to learn with today's developing technology. Accordingly, it is possible to divide the history of artificial intelligence into two periods: the pre-learning period and the learning period. When explaining the topic of artificial intelligence of the learning period, the concepts of machine learning and deep learning are emphasized. Machine learning is thus defined as a discipline that deals with the processes of designing algorithms which enable machine learning based on databases (Bernard, 2016). Deep learning, on the other hand, is a branch of science exploring algorithms that are created with inspiration by the structure and function of the brain, catering machine learning (Jason, 2016).

All these developments in the science of artificial intelligence have allowed artificial intelligence to be used in a wide range of areas today, from the health sector to retail, from the public sector to agriculture, from the banking sector to the industrial sector (Bughin et al., 2017). Therefore, its impact on countries' economies is deepening day by day. For instance, a study conducted by PricewaterhouseCoopers (PwC) in 2017, entitled "Global Artificial Intelligence Study: Exploiting the AI Revolution", predicts that artificial intelligence will contribute a total of $15.7 trillion to the world economy in 2030. The main basis of this forecast is that the growth potential of artificial intelligence is rapidly spreading in different sectors. Today, many organizations have adopted the digitalization process, since it helps make decisions and speeds up the decision process, increases the accuracy and reliability of decisions, and also provides effective communication, quality improvement, reduced costs and increased efficiency. In this process, artificial intelligence technology is considered as the most important factor that significantly facilitates the undertakings of many sectors, today and in the future, and is effective in management (Önder & Saygılı, 2018: 631–632).

3. Artificial Intelligence and Management

For enterprises today, artificial intelligence technology serves at the level of contribution as a tool only in the performance of various tasks. Artificial intelligence systems are used in a wide range of areas such as selecting a suitable candidate for the job, financial analysis, customer relationship management, organizing complex logistics processes, and tracking production activities (Von Krogh, 2018). These developed artificial intelligence systems perceive the world, store data accordingly, analyze and understand the collected data. At the end of this entire process, they make informed decisions and guide managers as a result of their analyses (Bataller & Harris, 2016). In short, artificial intelligence provides decision makers with real-time, viable and active decision support (Metaxiotis et al., 2003). On the other hand, it is stated that artificial intelligence technology, which has played a role only in evaluating strategies, may play a key role in creating strategies in the near future (Thomas et al., 2016).

When we examine the research on this subject, the study conducted by Pega and Marketforce in 2018 on 845 senior managers stands out. The study determined that 72 % of participants believed that artificial intelligence would replace middle managers in business in the next ten years. The study also found that two-thirds of participants held a belief that the widespread use of artificial intelligence would create a more transparent understanding of meritocracy in the workplace (Connolly, 2018). In practice, "Bridgewater Associates", the firm with the world's largest Hedge Fund, is cited as an example of a firm that has discovered the effectiveness of artificial intelligence in management and determines strategies accordingly. The firm, which controls almost $160 billion, has recently publicly announced that it is preparing to leave management to artificial intelligence. Dalio, the founder and director of the firm, stated that he has witnessed many times that employees can make slow and wrong decisions for emotional reasons, arguing that transferring the flow of billions of dollars to artificial intelligence is the right decision. In line with this strategic decision, if artificial intelligence can manage a firm of this size more efficiently than its human employees, it will pave the way for many firms to follow the same path in the near future (Güngör, 2016). Similarly, the firm "Deep Knowledge Ventures", which provides services on medium-and long-term biotech investments in Hong Kong, announced that it has appointed artificial intelligence as a member of the board of directors and, thus, will ensure efficiency in decision-making (Sarpkaya, 2013). Moreover, Hitachi, an electronics company, has managed to implement an artificial intelligence software that can perform the tasks of production management, such as organizing task distribution and making a production plan, by developing ERP softwares (Demircan, 2017).

Therefore, as can be deduced from all these developments, companies are intensively preparing for the artificial intelligence process, where digitalization is at the forefront, and they are taking steps to redesign and implement their business models for the future. Keeping up with this process is essential for companies. Because these incredible advances in information technologies have become a structure that almost eliminates the limits of competitive forces. For artificial intelligence systems collect data from all kinds of environments, analyze collected data, and guide decision-making (Bataller & Harris, 2016). They help senior managers in critical positions within organizations to adopt a long-term perspective for the future of their companies, as well as to develop short-term goals and strategies that are compatible with this perspective (Zaccaro, 2004). Currently, artificial intelligence stands as a supporting mechanism for management. On the other hand, the question of "What happens if artificial intelligence takes over senior management"? has been answered by Dewhurst and Willmott (2014) in the following manner. They commented that the working environment will be more democratic, business units and functions will be able to make better decisions, so the organization will be able to manage itself without referring decisions to senior management. According to the authors, the probability that these developments will occur in the short haul is quite high. Also, Ünal (2019) referred to research on the subject in his study, which examined the possibility of artificial intelligence serving as chief executive officer (CEO) in the future, and stated that artificial intelligence being on the board of directors of establishments down the line is seen as an expected situation in the near future. As a result, the issue of not needing senior management in the future has taken its place in the literature as a strong prediction.

4. Conclusion

As can be observed from previous research, the argument that artificial intelligence will secure its position in management in the near future seems quite strong. The experience gained concerning today's applications of artificial intelligence technologies, which are reaching more advanced levels every day, increase efficiency and quality in production and service activities, strengthens the belief that they will contribute to increasing efficiency in management. Therefore, it is extremely important for companies to adapt to the future of artificial intelligence. The only way to achieve this is for firms to review their current policies and strategic practices and to take the right steps for the changes they need (Zarret & Malanchuk, 2005). In the first stage, businesses must understand the structure and dimensions of change. Then, they must gradually move forward with new developments for change (Glazer, 1991). In the second stage, companies should handle the process of change in the most effective way. Given the fact that each organization has its own unique structure and way of functioning, the most appropriate methods should be determined during change. In the third stage, change must be carried out together with the stakeholders of the organization. In the business models determined by artificial intelligence technologies and digitalization, its involvement in all stakeholders engaged in the stages of the value chain leads to the result that change can be realized in real terms and in all areas. In the fourth stage, information about the requirements, process and results of change should be shared transparently with employees who resist change. Providing training and consulting support to employees, especially in the process of renewal, is effective in the formation of an innovative organizational culture.

On the other hand, it is not enough for the business world alone to prepare for the artificial intelligence process. It is again a qualified human resource that can work in harmony with this technology which can implement artificial intelligence technology. If the deficit in this issue cannot be fixed, all these developments do not make much sense. Therefore, it is of great importance that states, various organizations and associations and related professional organizations establish a permanent training policy in order to provide employees with the necessary equipment in areas where the short-term effects of artificial intelligence can be predicted. It is necessary to focus more on science, technology, engineering and mathematics subjects, but also to incorporate design, art and creativity into current conditions and education. Hence, not only individual firms, but also countries should develop their own strategies. Many famous scientists and thinkers attribute future way of living to developments in the field of artificial intelligence. Not being aware of these developments and not making the necessary investments pose a serious risk to the survival of countries. In this context, creating an artificial strategy in the shortest time possible, determining and implementing policy accordingly should be among the first priorities of state administrators.

Given that with all these requirements, artificial intelligence no longer only replaces repetitive manual labor, but also repetitive cognitive labor, interested parties should once more develop various strategies for the problem of unemployment which can be created in the future. Hence, it is necessary to evaluate in the long term the various roles that only human beings can perform in the face of artificial intelligence. Therefore, jobs that focus on empathy, reasoning and creativity should be redefined, and an education policy should be defined accordingly. Consequently, discussing and evaluating all these necessary strategies will create an important guide resource for firms and policy regulators that are attempting to prepare for a future shaped by artificial intelligence. In light of all this information, conducting academic studies based on qualitative and quantitative methods related to the subject of "Artificial Intelligence in Management", the significance of which in the business world is being discerned increasingly, will make significant contributions to both the literature and the business world.

References

Aksu, H. (2019a). *Yapay zeka, oyun kurallarını yeninden yazıyor*. Available: http://www.hurriyet.com.tr/teknoloji/yapay-zeka-oyun-kurallarini-yeniden-yazi yor-41117867. Accessed on 15 February 2019.

Aksu, H. (2019b). *Yapay Zeka Etkisi: Ara kademe yönetici kalmayacak*. Available: https://turkiye.ai/yapay-zeka-etkisi-ara-kademe-yonetici-kalmaya cak/. Accessed on 20 January 2019.

Arslan, K. (2020). Eğitimde Yapay Zeka ve Uygulamaları. *Batı Anadolu Eğitim Bilimleri Dergisi,* 11(1), 71–88.

Avansas, (2018). Robot Yöneticilerle Çalışmaya Hazır mıyız?. Available: https://blog.avansas.com/robot-yoneticilerle. Accessed on 20 September 2018.

Bataller, C. & Harris, J. (2016). *Turning artificial intelligence into business value*. Today. Accenture. Available: https://pdfs.semanticscholar.org/a710/a8d529bce6bdf75ba589f42721777bf54d3b.pdf, Accessed on 17 March 2017.

Bernard, M. (2016). *What is the difference between artificial intelligence and machine learning?*. Available: https://www.forbes.com/sites/bernardmarr/2016/12/06/what-is-the-difference-between-artificial-intelligence-and-machine-learning/#7507f6742742, Accessed on 3 May 2018.

Bischof, J. (2019). *Would AI be better at governing than politicians?*. Available: https://www.weforum.org/agenda/2019/03/a-surprising-number-of-people-trust-ai-to- make-better-policy-decisions-than-politicians/ Accessed on 29 March 2019.

Boden, M. A. (2014). *Creativity and artificial intelligence: A contradiction in terms. The philosophy of creativity: New essays*, 224–246. DOI:10.1093/acprof:oso/9780199836963.003.0012.

Bughin, J., Hazan, E., Ramaswamy, S., Chui, M., Allas, T., Dahlstrom, P., ... & Trench, M. (2017). Artificial intelligence: The next digital frontier?, Available: https://apo.org.au/node/210501 Accessed on: 1 Jun 2017

Connolly, B. (2018). *Are you a middle manager? AI may take your job*. Available: https://www.cio.com.au/article/632470/middle-manager-ai-may-take-your-job/, Accessed on 23 June 2018.

Demircan, K. (2017). *"Hitachi Robot Müdür mü İşe Aldı?"*. Available: http://www.theprowess.net/index.php?option=com_content&view=article&id=465:hitachi-robot-mudur-mu-ise-aldi&catid=30&Itemid=160, Accessed on 31 July 2017.

Dewhurst, M. & Willmott, P. (2014). Manager and machine: The new leadership equation. *McKinsey Quarterly*, September. Available: https://www.mckinsey.com/featured-insights/leadership/manager-and-machine, Accessed on 20 February 2017.

Frick, W. (2015). *"Robot Patron Olursa, Harvard Business Review"*, [Online]. Available: https://hbrturkiye.com/dergi/robot-patron-olursa, Accessed on 21 July 2015.

Glazer, R. (1991). Marketing in an information intensive environment: Strategic implications of knowledge as an asset. *Journal of Marketing* 1, 6–15.

Grace, K., Salvatier, J., Dafoe, A., Zhang, B. & Evans, O. (2018). When will AI exceed human performance? Evidence from AI experts. *Journal of Artificial Intelligence Research*, 62, 729–754.

Güngör, B. (2016). *Dünyanın en büyük Hedge Fonu, yönetimi yapay zekaya bırakmaya hazırlanıyor*. Available: https://www.technopat.net/2016/12/23/160-milyar-dolari-yapay-zeka-idare-edecek/, Accessed on 23 December 2016.

Hochman, D. (2016). *Reinvent yourself: The playboy interview with Ray Kurzweil.* Available: https://www.playboy.com/articles/playboy-interview-ray-kurzweil. Accessed on 19 April 2016.

Holloway, C. (1983). Strategic management and artificial intelligence. *Long Range Planning,* 16(5), 89–93.

Jason, B. (2016). *Popular deep learning libraries.* Available: http://machinelear ningmastery.com/popular-deeplearning-libraries/, Accessed on: 01 May 2017.

Kahraman, H. (2019). *Yapay Zeka Ülke Yönetebilir mi?*. Available: https://www.endustri40.com/yapay-zeka-ulke-yonetebilir-mi/, Accessed on 17 June 2019.

Kaya, S. (2017). *İnsansı Robot, Filarmoni Orkestrası Yönetti?*. Available: https://sanatkaravani.com/insansi-robot-filarmoni-orkestrasi-yonetti/, Accessed on 13September 2017

McCarthy, J. (2007) What Is Artificial Intelligence? Available: http://jmc.stanf ord.edu/articles/whatisai/whatisai.pdf, Accessed on: 11 January 2019

McCorduck, P., Minsky, M., Selfridge, O. & Simon, H. (1977). *History of artificial intelligence.* IJCAI Proceedings. pp. 951–954. Available: https://www.ijcai.org/Proceedings/77-2/Papers/083.pdf, Accessed on 17 May 2018.

McCulloch, W. S. ve Pitts, W. (1943). A logical calculus of the ideas immanent in nervous activity. *The bulletin of mathematical biophysics,* 5(4), 115–133.

Metaxiotis, K., Ergazakis, K, Samouilidis, E. & Psarras, J. (2003). Decision support through knowledge management: The role of the artificial intelligence. *Information Management & Computer Security,* 11, 216–221.http://dx.doi.org/10.1108/09685220310500126. Accessed on 1 December 2003.

Mutlu, B. K. (2020). *İnsan Kaynakları'nda Yapay Zeka Uygulamaları.* Available: https://digitalinstitute.com.tr/blog/insan-kaynaklarinda-yapay-zeka-uygulamalari/, Accessed on 02 December 2020.

Nart, S. (2019). *The bridge between manager and artificial intelligence: Organizational change, fifth international Mediterranean social sciences congress* (MECAS V), (June 18–20, 2019), pp. 139–147.

Newell, A., & Simon, H. (1956). The logic theory machine – A complex information processing system. *IRE Transactions on information theory,* 2(3), 61–79.

Nilsson, N. J. (2010). *The quest for artificial intelligence a history of ideas and achievements.* UK: Cambridge University Press.

OECD. (2016). "Chile", in OECD Science, Technology and Innovation Outlook 2016, OECD Publishing, Paris. https://doi.org/10.1787/sti_in_outlook-2016-51-en Accessed on: 8 December 2016

Önder, M. & Saygılı, H. (2018). Yapay Zekâ ve Kamu Yönetimine Yansımaları. *Türk İdare Dergisi,* 90(487), 629–669.

PWC. (2017). Sizing the prize what's the real value of AI for your business and how can you capitalise?. Available: https://www.pwc.com/gx/en/issues/analytics/assets/pwc-ai-analysis-sizing-the-prize-report.pdf. Accessed on 28 August 2019.

Russell, S. & Norvig, P. (1995). *Artificial intelligence: A modern approach*. New Jersey: Prentice Hall.

Sarpkaya, M. (2013). *Yapay zeka yönetim kuruluna katıldı*. Available: https://www.tamindir.com/haber/yapay-zeka-yonetim-kuruluna-katildi_14461/. Accessed on 26 May 2019.

Shanks, R., Sinha, S. & Thomas, R. J. (2016). *Judgment calls: Preparing leaders to thrive in the age of intelligent machines*. Accenture Institute for High Performance Research Report. Available: https://www.accenture.com/t20170411T174032Z__w__/us-en/_acnmedia/PDF-19/Accenture-StrategyWorkforce-Judgment-Calls-V2.pdf. Accessed on 27 June 2017.

Shannon, C. E. (1948). A mathematical theory of communication. *The Bell system technical journal*, 27(3), 379–423.

Thomas, R. J., Fuchs, R. & Silverstone, Y. (2016). *A machine in the C-suite*. AIHP and Acenture Strategy Araştırma Raporu, [Online]. Available: https://www.accenture.com/t00010101T000000Z__w__/br-pt/_acnmedia/PDF13/Accenture-Strategy-WotF-Machine-CSuite.pdf. Accessed on 15 March 2017.

Turing, A. M. (1950). Computing machinery and intelligence. *Mind*, 49, 433–460.

Ünal, A. (2019). *Yapay zekâların icra kurulu başkanı olabilirliği üzerine bir araştırma*. Yayımlanmamış doktora tezi. Düzce Üniversitesi Sosyal Bilimler Enstitüsü, İşletme Anabilim Dalı, Düzce.

Ünal, A. & Kılınç, İ. (2020). Yapay Zekâ İşletme Yönetimi İlişkisi Üzerine Bir Değerlendirme. *Yönetim Bilişim Sistemleri Dergisi*, 6(1), 51–78.

Von Krogh, G. (2018). Artificial intelligence in organizations: New opportunities for phenomenon-based theorizing. *Academy of Management Discoveries*, 4(4), 404–409, https://doi.org/10.5465/amd.2018.0084. Accessed on 21 December 2018.

World Economic Forum. (2015). Deep shift: Technology tipping points and societal ımpact. Global Agenda Council on the Future of Software & Society Araştırma Raporu, Eylül, 2015. Available: http://www3.weforum.org/docs/WEF_GAC15_Technological_Tipping_Points_report 2015.pdf. Accessed on 22 June 2016.

Zaccaro, S. J. (2004). The nature of executive leadership: A conceptual and empirical analysis of success. Washington, DC, US: American Psychological Association, doi: 10.1037/10398-000.

Zarret, R. N. & Malanchuk, O. (2005). Who's computing? Gender and race differences in young adult's decisions to pursue an information technology career. *New Directions for Child and Adolescent Development*, 110, 65–84.

Tuğba ERHAN

Digital Leadership: The Competencies of Leaders (Managers) in the Digital Age

1. Introduction

Focusing on the qualifications of competent leaders of the organizations, having a long-term vision has been on the top of the list. In addition to the vision, accurate decision-making ability has also been among the skills that are expected from the leaders. However, for the vast majority of the leaders/managers of the organizations, it has been clearly understood that there are unexpected things such as this COVID-19 pandemic that has been causing tremendous and obligatory changes as well as challenges. It can be said that this unprecedented event has added a new competency for the rest of the other competencies that leaders are expected to have. From time to time, it is possible to have a rare or unique product which is only obtained from a very limited suppliers in the world. This uniqueness of the product has been perceived as the competitive advantage in the global market, however, by using highly developed technology or with the help of the devices, the unique product can be produced by several sellers and this can vanish the advantage of being the top of the market.

Definitions of leader and leadership have been shaped by the changing positive and negative developments in the twenty-first century. The current era has been forcing to adapt new leadership styles with different competencies (Petry, 2018). Leadership style affects work-related outcomes. Employees' expectations and perceptions also have been changing with the new nature of work and work environment that they experience. Among these expectations, it is considered that leaders pursue and implement the latest information to be beneficial for the individuals who follow them with great enthusiasm and passion. Being up-to-date makes all disciplines evolve and provides beneficial resources for a better living and working environment. In any kind of field from health to management, individuals have the right to take advantage of the new developments in technology. Specifically, for the treatments of the most fatal diseases such as cancer, the help needed for accuracy dosage are prepared by robots instead of manual preparation (Geersing et al., 2020). Plus, individuals with disabilities have been supported by assistive technology which has been used tremendously for the past decades (Parette et el., 1999).

Apart from the employees, even the adults with no jobs or looking for jobs have certain expectations from the people who have been interacting with medical doctors. As potential patients, individuals hope for the latest and effective medication during the period they have been experiencing an illness. As doctors and scientists are expected to manage the pandemic period with permanent solutions using the latest technology controlling the probable side effects, leaders/managers are also expected to apply organizational principles to meet the needs of the employees and the organization. Thus, it has been a prerequisite and requirement for the managers to not only lead the resources but also the rapid changes (Asri and Darma, 2020). In addition to the latest technological developments, Internet is the essential part of the digitalization (Isin and Ruppert, 2020) besides Internet provides the huge amount of data transition in the blink of an eye. This rapid process of information makes the organizational leaders alert and keep them occupied about their management duties without taking any breaks. As the online environments or platforms are the most visited and appreciated digital resources, they keep individuals busy and help them gain awareness about anything they require. Individuals obtain information by doing short- or long-term searches on the Internet to have information roughly. Both digitally skilled leaders/managers and employees help organizations gain competitive advantage.

The new era determines leaders' qualifications and adds or alters responsibilities towards the employees and organizations. Also, digitalization process is the essential step of the leaders of the organizations which provide services or products. Digitally developed leaders have the opportunities to use the latest technology as a part of their leadership style or they lead the organizations using the digitalization. Once the organizations realize and experience the advantages of digitally equipped leaders, it will be difficult to go on leading by the conventional leadership styles. However, human workforce has still been the most valuable asset in the organizations and needs to be understood well to be able to motivate and lead for greater productivity and sustainability (Uzunbacak et al., 2019). Considering the fundamental contributions primarily to the organizations and secondary to the employees who are the majority source of the business world, digital leadership has attracted the interests of scholars and practitioners. Thus, the purpose of this study is to examine the competencies of leaders (managers) in the digital age.

2. Theoretical Background

2.1. Changing Perspective of Leadership

Uncertainty is an important aspect of employee concern which often emerges between the organization and the employee. In fact, the uncertainty or an unclear future can be the result of any global crisis or phenomenon. In order to avoid the times that cause uncertainty in other words, the hardships which cannot be identified in a short period of time, employees or employers have been struggling to feel safe and be sure about their future in the organization. Specifically, management and organization fields focus on different kinds of leadership styles to be able to find the best match to meet the needs of the new digital era.

Definitions of leadership may vary, and this struggles theorist to focus on one "correct" definition (Yukl, 1994). In addition to the complex structure and disagreement on the meaning of leadership, scholars have also tried to identify some theories to reveal the leaders' roles in the organizations (Uhl-Bien and Marion, 2009). How leaders affect the organizations and fulfill the organizational goals have been related to the styles of the leaders. In the leadership literature, the leadership styles have been increasing with the newly added ones and their theories. Surrounded by the technological development in the computerized era of work and life environment, a contemporary leadership style called "digital leadership" has been included in the latest leadership literature.

Digital leadership is defined as the leaders' capacity to have a vision comprehending the digitalization process and to implement the required strategies in order to accomplish this vision (Larjovuori et al., 2016). Thus, leaders with digital skills have been considered as the experts of implementing the new technology in the organizations. When leaders realize the obligatory change in the global world in digital way, they become more aware of the effects of digitalization on the organizations and employees. Organizations should be aware of the importance of the digital era and its requirements, leaders should generate digital culture in the work environment as there may be a lack of comprehension of digitalization (Oberer and Erkollar, 2018).

Having the digitally competent leaders in the organizations provide to analyze and compare the data of the competitors. Digital leaders can differentiate what is the most beneficial part of the new technology and look for the right time to use it in the organization strategically (Kane et al., 2015).

2.1.1. Being Digital

In the world of computerization, individuals use more computer programs, automated messages, digital files, photos, communication online programs (Kim, 2001). In other words, trying to find a way to make the things easier in lives or have connections with others have become the part of the goals in humans' lives. Besides, the word "smart" has been adding in almost every product that individuals intend to buy such as smart phones, smart pans, smart applications and so on. These smart devices or tools help individually or organizationally.

Being digital refers to making more accurate and faster decisions using the data (Dörner and Edelman, 2015). The technological developments have been spreading rapidly not only through digital or social media platforms but also the users' goals to pursue a safe and comfortable life. Individuals have been exploring a newly added applications which they can use to facilitate the duties or multiple goals in their lives as it gets more challenging to manage the time and achieving the goals simultaneously.

It is clearly seen that more jobs can be replaced with robots in the near future, or it already started sounding "normal" that robots are the incontrovertible part of some current jobs. Individuals have the tendency to be adaptive to their environment, and when the adaptation process is completed, some phases of lives can be facilitated by these technologically supported devices such as robots. In addition, individuals have difficulties managing their time efficiently or productively as they long for, thus robots are thought to be the helpers of the individuals who struggle to use and manage their time.

Observing the rapid changes and developments it has been inevitable to pursue the digital world and its products or vehicles in order to manage the organizations effectively and efficiently. Especially, the term "digital" is more common to hear in everyday conversations like other technological terms.

Countries that have been developing rapidly since the twentieth century have achieved social welfare and reached their economic development goals. However, organization's future is determined by its digitality (Grünberger and Szucsich, 2021).

2.1.2. Digital Leader Perceptions of Employees

There has been a growing interest and increase in using Internet-based tools such as computers, smart phones, or digitally supported devices. The majority of the users has been considered of consisting younger adults, but the ratios of Internet users have provided evidence that older people have also been enjoying the feeling of connection. The co-existing structure of leadership which is being a traditional and a digital leader has still been questioning to be able to connect the two styles closely without putting clear and deep cuts (Malakyan, 2019).

Based on the literature review, Eberl and Drews (2021) define the digital leadership as a complex construct including customer-based organizational goals, digitally skilled leaders to be able to form working models and using these digital innovations in the management and communication/collaboration with the employees.

As being an example of the digital leadership, it has been claimed that organizations need a new kind of leadership which is called leadership 4.0 which enables the organizations adapt innovations in shorter times and result in higher customer satisfaction (Bolte et al., 2018). Besides, to fulfill the organizational goals, increase productivity, and obtain sustainable profit, leaders have been chosen according to their competencies. Twenty-first century's organizations also want to hire the leaders with digital competencies who can also apply these into the business process. Changes in the concept of leadership has affected the job descriptions and roles of the employees as well.

3. Competencies of Digital Leadership

In the leadership field, advances have always been followed closely by the leaders/managers of the organization. Along with the leaders' contemporary approaches managing the organizations, how the organization is perceived by the internal and external stakeholders has been another concern that should be led by the leaders meticulously. Organizations face with the crisis and will always continue to meet the challenges of the new era, but the style managing the crisis will make the difference.

Each leader in the organization including top management should make decisions which affect the organizational outcomes positively or negatively. During the decision-making process, rapidly changing perception of the leadership emerges. Especially in the organizational behavior field/discipline, it has been considered as significant to understand and analyze the leadership styles in the organization since the style of the leaders matters for the employees.

As any kind of leadership includes "influence" (Yulk, 1994), employees have the tendency to be convinced by their leaders/managers. Specifically, digital leadership require several competencies in addition to the conventional leadership qualifications and perspectives. While following the latest leadership style, there has been a consensus on the implementation of the traditional and contemporary leadership approaches for the longer survival and sustainability of the organizations (Kane et al., 2019). According to the study conducted by Zeike et al. (2019), digital leadership affects the employee's psychological well-being positively as the leaders with digital skills can find solutions to the challenging problems that the organization faces. This process plays a supportive role in employees' perspective of leadership style.

In today's world, it has been clearly comprehended by employees, leaders, and managers that not only intellectual but also emotional competencies are required interchangeably. In other words, the effects of globalization have been reaching quickly to each organization offering new challenges. Employees are needed to be equipped with several competencies that facilitate their intention to stay in the organization and carry on working efficiently. Having employees with intellectual and emotional capabilities help leaders/managers accomplish the organizational goals. Specifically, highlighting the emotional competencies of the leaders has been an essential part of the leadership as these kinds of competencies provide connections between the leaders and the employees. It is for sure that building emotional connections, creating meaningful work environment starts with communication. Deeper understanding or empathetic listening and observing the employees help leaders in the organizations move safely and easily.

Digital era has influenced almost all the fields from health to art. This kind of inevitable transformation has been interpreting as a result of the ongoing and unexpected pandemic. Most of the organizations have made decisions of working from home. Remote programs including learning, teaching, communicating, and meeting have been adapted and implemented in the digitally designed platforms. This transformational adaptation has taken a specific amount of time, but it can be observed that working adults and students have adapted the process.

Organizations have been starting to realize the advantages and disadvantages of the COVID-19 pandemic outcomes. This challenging and ongoing period requires leaders with innovative perspective to be able to manage the employees' psychological and physical well-being in or outside the organization. Although robots have become the part of the organizations, human workforce has still the control of the management. Thus, the leadership styles from traditional to contemporary can help find ways of understanding and adapting the new technology in the organizations. When the leaders are aware of the new technology, employees can have better approaches to the innovative products or services. Thus, openness to innovation can also satisfy the customer needs. Customer needs change rapidly, and preferences lead the organizations to produce up-to-date products.

Having and improving competencies of the leaders and employees in all types of organizations including health, education, production, or general industry have been related to work-outcomes. This ability to keep oneself up-to-date, to be able to respond and react confidently presenting creative solutions is called work-related digital competence (Bröckling et al., 2021). As the digital leadership include team effort and orientation competencies of digital leaders help them find the problems occurring while responding to innovative trends, competent digital leaders can directly spot the source of the problems that can impede the digital innovation process (Guinan et al., 2019).

To reveal the organizations' reactions to technological developments using the term *digital maturity*, Westerman et al. (2012) claim that organizations can have high digital and transformation management intensity, and low digital and transformation management intensity. According to Westerman et al. (2012), these levels include *digital beginners* who prefer to use traditional applications instead of digitalization; however, they may be unaware of the digital opportunities. The other level is called *digital fashionistas* which experience and apply many digital applications but not fully knowledgeable about the benefits or advantages. *Digital conservatives* kind of organization approaches the new digital developments carefully keeping the old and conventional ones in mind, and they may have the risk of missing the superiority obtained from the new digital developments. The last level of digital maturity is mentioned as *digirati* which is an integrated form transformative vision, attentive management, harmonious with digital investments, and by following the digital culture, these kinds of organizations can have constant competitive advantage among the global market opponents.

Imran et al. (2020) have identified five competencies of digital leaders starting from the *digital vision* of the leader which highlights the importance of strategic vision for the future of the organization. If the digital leaders want the employees' benefit and use the new technological tools, first they should show this digital ability to their employees and encourage them to use. *Digital knowledge* is another competency digital leaders are expected to have which includes the understanding the importance of using the digital tools with a remarkable knowledge rather than being a digital expert. In other words, employees should get the perception from their digital leaders that they support the new technology. *Failing fast* is the other competency mentioned. It is for sure that not all the attempts of the leaders end in achievement. Business world includes risky actions, and digital leaders are expected to take into account these potential risks that the organizations face with so there may be failures coping with the challenges. When digital leaders fail, they need to move fast to find solutions to this failure. *Empowerment* requires the digital leaders' motivation which can reflect to the employees positively, and they can also feel confident by taking a part in the decision-making process. It should not be forgotten that the number of the employees are more than the digital leaders so employees should be encouraged to take useful organizational decisions by using digitalization when necessary. *Managing diverse teams* is another competency of the digital leaders. The latest technological developments and tools can be adapted easily by a competent digital leader; however, each employee who uses these tools have different needs and sources that should be noticed by the leaders. Thus, a good digital leader is the one who can manage to communicate each team member effectively to fulfill the organizational goals.

Workplace 2025 Report has stated the five competencies of successful digital leaders. According to the report collected from 4,000 leaders, digital leaders *inspire others*, becoming an inspiration for others may not be possible by being their leaders. The employees needs and expectations should be met and considered. The second competency of digital leaders is *leverage technology* which highlights the importance of technological innovations. Employees believe and agree that the leaders should adapt the rapid changes in the digital world. Third competency of the digital leaders is identified as *encourage collaboration*. Today's competitive world forces employees spend more time at work, so they need to be supported by their leaders and feel like they are an important part of the team. They need to be engaged and connected with their colleagues, and this can be fulfilled by the leaders' efforts. The fourth competency is called *drive innovation*. Digital leaders should provide enough time and space for innovations. In order to do this, they should use the latest technology to reduce the overwork and repetitive tasks of the employees. Final competence of the digital leaders is identified as *manage risks*. Digital leaders are the ones who are willing to try the new technological tools which may include some risks for the organizations; however, taking courageous but smart steps can lead to benefit from the latest digital tools (Writer, 2021).

4. Conclusion

Competition spreads rapidly and harshly among all the fields starting from micro to macro. Change happens at every second of the global era which causes employees, organizations, and countries to be more alert about the new perspectives of these unstable changes 24/7. The new global era has also brought several requirements that need to have a clear vision and almost accurate anticipations among the unexpected events of the twenty-first century. These requirements directly or indirectly have been affecting the organizations. Employees go through and experience several stages and consequences because of the leaders or managers they have been led in the workplace. In addition to the leadership style effects on employees and organizations, the COVID-19 pandemic has made the employees experience more challenging problems that they need to be assisted to be back to normal working conditions or adapt the new working style which is working from home or hybrid. In addition, the unprecedented pandemic has changed the traditional work perception which starts in the morning and finishes in the evening. The work itself has been shaped and transformed according to the latest technological developments. This progress and speed of technology has created new challenges

It is possible to mention that as all other intangible assets for the organizations, keeping up-to-date plays a significant and distinctive role among the competitive organizations and hardships of the globalization's sudden effects. It is a fact that in order to be irreplaceable in the field of the organizational sustainability, it is a prerequisite to follow the world's leading organizations which are alert 24/7. It can be concluded that the organizations of the twenty-first century should have leaders who are digitally talented to indicate great performance using and implementing the latest high technology to be sustainable among the expected or unexpected crises by not only leading/managing the potential local and global consequences but also considering the perceptions and expectations of the stakeholders. This evolution of both leadership and organizational perspective should be considered as a priority in the organizations. Moderate approach to the digital world can provide competitive advantages and support the sustainability.

As the digital age constitutes a continuous competition pressure on organizations, it is essential to have an innovative perspective to be able to implement the knowledge into practice (Dalkir, 2013). When organizations follow the new technological developments rapidly, they can present the new products or services to their stakeholders before their opponents, thus the digitally equipped organizations have the competitive advantage which provides sustainability. The organizations which follow the latest technology can also have the chance to be an important part of this uncontrolled business world of digitalization.

References

Asri, A. A. S. M. A. N., and Darma, G. S. (2020). "Revealing the digital leadership spurs in 4.0 industrial revolution". *International Journal of Business, Economics & Management*, 3(1), 93–100.

Bolte, S., Dehmer, J., and Niemann, J. (2018). "Digital leadership 4.0". *Acta Technica Napocensis-Series: Applied Mathematics, Mechanics, And Engineering*, 61(4), 637–646.

Bröckling, G., Behr, J., and Erdmann, J. (2021). "Digital Transformation of an Educational Organization from a Media Educational Viewpoint". In Ifenthaler, D., Hofhues, S., Egloffstein, M., and Helbig, C. (Eds.), *Digital Transformation of Learning Organizations* (pp. 3–22) Springer, Cham.

Dalkir, K. (2013). *Knowledge Management in Theory and Practice*. Routledge, London, UK.

Dörner, K., and Edelman, D. (2015). *What 'digital' Really Means*. McKinsey & Company, available at http://www.mckinsey.com/industries/high-tech/our-insights/what-digital-really-means, accessed 15 May 2021.

Eberl, J. K., and Drews, P. (2021). "Digital leadership-mountain or molehill? A literature review". *Internationale Konferenz Wirtschaftsinformatik. Proceedings* 5, 1–18.

Geersing, T. H., Klous, M. G., Franssen, E. J. F., van den Heuvel, J. J. G., and Crul, M. (2020). "Robotic compounding versus manual compounding of chemotherapy: Comparing dosing accuracy and precision". *European Journal of Pharmaceutical Sciences*, 155, 105536.

Grünberger, N., and Szucsich, P. (2021). "Sustainability in a Digital Age as a Trigger for Organizational Development in Education". In *Digital Transformation of Learning Organizations* (pp. 189–202). Springer, Cham.

Guinan, P. J., Parise, S., and Langowitz, N. (2019). "Creating an innovative digital Project team: Levers to enable digital transformation". *Business Horizons*, 62(6), 717–727.

Imran, F., Shahzad, K., Butt, A., and Kantola, J. (2020). "Leadership Competencies for Digital Transformation: Evidence from Multiple Cases". In *International Conference on Applied Human Factors and Ergonomics* (pp. 81–87). Springer, Cham.

Isin, E., and Ruppert, E. (2020). *Being Digital Citizens*.London, U.K.: International/ Rowman & Littlefield Publishers.

Kane, G. C., Palmer, D., Phillips, A. N., Kiron, D., and Buckley, N. (2015). "Strategy, not technology, drives digital transformation". *MIT Sloan Management Review and Deloitte University Press*, 14, 1–25.

Kane, G. C., Phillips, A. N., Copulsky, J., and Andrus, G. (2019). "How digital leadership is (n't) different". *MIT Sloan Management Review*, 60(3), 34–39.

Kim, J. (2001). "Phenomenology of digital-being". *Human Studies*, 24(1), 87–111.

Larjovuori, R. L., Bordi, L., Mäkiniemi, J. P., and Heikkilä-Tammi, K. (2016). The role of leadership and employee well-being in organizational digitalization. *Tiziana Russo-Spenaand Cristina Mele*, 1141–1154.

Malakyan, G. P. (2019). "Digital Leader-Followership for the Digital Age: A North American Perspective". In Franco, M., (Ed.), *Digital Leadership—A New Leadership Style for the 21st Century* (pp. 59–82). IntechOpen, London, UK.

Oberer, B., and Erkollar, A. (2018). "Leadership 4.0: Digital leaders in the age of industry 4.0". *International Journal of Organizational Leadership*, 7(4), 404–412.

Parette, P., VanBiervliet, A., and Hourcade, J. J. (1999). "Family-centered decision making in assistive technology". *Journal of Special Education Technology*, 15(1), 45–55.

Petry, T. (2018). "Digital Leadership". In North, K., Maier, R., Haas, O. (Eds.), *Knowledge Management in Digital Change* (pp. 209–218), Progress in IS. Springer, Cham.

Uhl-Bien, M., and Marion, R. (2009). "Complexity leadership in bureaucratic forms of organizing: A meso model". *The Leadership Quarterly*, 20(4), 631–650.

Uzunbacak, H., Yıldız, A., and Uzun, S. (2019). Toksik liderliğin çalışanların tükenmişlik düzeylerine etkisi. *Anemon Muş Alparslan Üniversitesi Sosyal Bilimler Dergisi, 7*(1), 211–219.

Westerman, G., Tannou, M., Bonnet, D., Ferraris, P., and McAfee, A. (2012). "The digital advantage: How digital leaders outperform their peers in every industry." *MITSloan Management and Capgemini Consulting, MA*, 2, 2–23.

Writer, S. (2021, May 23). "How to Achieve Five Competencies of Effective Digital Leaders". https://www.smartsheet.com/content-center/executive-center/digital-transformation/how-achieve-five-competencies-effective-digital-leaders. Accessed 20 April 2021.

Yukl, G. A. (1994). *Leadership in Organizations*, 3rd ed., Prentice-Hall, Englewood Cliffs, NJ.

Zeike, S., Bradbury, K., Lindert, L., and Pfaff, H. (2019). "Digital leadership skills and associations with psychological well-being". *International Journal of Environmental Research and Public Health*, 16(14), 2628.

İlksun Didem ÜLBEĞİ

Digitalization and Stress: Further Validation of the Technostress Scale

1. Introduction

Information and Communication Technologies (ICTs) stands for "technologies that facilitate availability of information via telecommunications" (Christensson, 2010). This is "an umbrella term for all of the various media employed in communicating information" (oxfordreference.com). These communication technologies include all the medium for information access from the Internet to cell phones, and other communication instruments (Christensson, 2010).

ICTs have a pervasive impact on both employees and organizations. Organizations benefit ICTs from different aspects such as decreased costs, increased efficiency, and effectiveness (e.g., Melville, Kraemer, & Gurbaxani, 2004; Yunis, Tarhini, & Kassar, 2018). However, the effects of ICTs are far from being limited to only its positive effects. ICT usage can lead to work-family conflicts, cyberloafing, cyberbullying, addiction, increased pressures, unlimited connectedness among others (e.g., Lim, 2002; Walsh, White, & Young, 2008; Chen & Karahanna, 2014; Vranjes, Baillien, Vandebosch, Erreygers, & De Witte, 2017; De Wet, Koekemoer, & Nel, 2016). Another downside of ICT use is that this usage causes stress in individuals (Tarafdar, Tu, Ragu-Nathan, & Ragu-Nathan, 2007). Technostress can be defined as "a contemporary disease of adjustment developed due to inability to manage recent information technologies in a beneficial process" (Brod, 1984). And these days due to the Covid-19 outbreak, the share of ICTs in individuals' lives have evolved into more extensive and excessive than before. Accordingly, employees now have to engage increasingly with these technologies day by day which means "technology becomes the center of interest in all domains of our lives, work and non-work" (Weil & Rosen, 1997) leading to technostress.

Technostress stands for "suffering from stress due to using of ICTs" (Ragu-Nathan, Tarafdar, & Ragu-Nathan, 2008). Technostress dimensions comprise of techno-overload, techno-invasion, techno-complexity, techno-insecurity, and techno-uncertainty (Tarafdar et al., 2007). Techno-overload means ICTs pressure on individuals for working longer hours and swiftly. Techno-invasion means ICTs impact on employees uninterrupted accessibility which also intertwines work life and non-work life. Techno-complexity refers to ICTs complexity effects on employees unqualified feelings and, as a result, pressures to try harder to learn. Techno-uncertainty means the unending changes in ICTs and cause uncertainty for employees leading continuous attention and learning about the recent developments of ICTs (Tarafdar et al., 2007).

The effects of technostress on employees have been shown in various studies. Regarding performance of employees, Li & Wang (2020) showed a negative and significant effect of technostress on work performance, only techno-uncertainty displayed an insignificant effect. Brooks & Califf (2017) reported a negative relationship between social media-induced technostress and performance. Additionally, Tarafdar, Pullins, & Ragu-Nathan (2014) found a negative relationship between technostress and sales performance while Yener (2018) also showed a negative relationship between job performance.

Another important outcome of technostress has been examined as productivity. Tarafdar et al. (2007) assessed the effect of technostress on productivity and reported a negative relationship. Karr-Wisniewski & Lu (2010) examined the effect of technology overload on productivity and found a negative effect. Alam (2016) showed that techno-overload, techno-uncertainty, techno-complexity have negative relationships with productivity. Tarafdar, Ragu-Nathan, Ragu-Nathan, & Tu (2005) tested the relationships between the five dimensions of technostress and productivity and reported negative statistically significant effects.

Several studies examined the effect of technostress on employees' and customers' behaviors and attitudes. Jena (2015) showed that technostress has negative effects on organizational commitment, job satisfaction, and negative affectivity. Ragu-Nathan et al. (2008) and Fuglseth & Sørebø (2014) identified negative effect of technostress on job satisfaction. Christ-Brendemühl & Schaarschmidt (2020) reported negative relationships between technostress and customer satisfaction and customer delight.

Regarding the effect of technostress on role stress, Wang & Shu (2008) identified positive and significant correlations with technostress and role conflict as well as role overload. Tarafdar et al. (2007) showed a positive relationship between technostress as well as role stress. Tarafdar et al. (2014) also identified a positive relationship between technostress and role stress.

Physical as well as psychological health outcomes of technostress have been examined in the literature. Boonjing & Chanvarasuth (2017) reported positive and significant effects which means that technostress can effect physical and psychological health of employees. Maier, Laumer, Wirth, & Weitzel (2019) and Yener (2018) showed a positive effect on burnout.

Regarding the antecedents of technostress, personality traits, task complexity, and organizational environment have been several variables examined in literature. Wang, Shu, & Tu (2008) showed that technostress is affected by organizational environment. Additionally, Koo & Wati (2011) reported that innovation culture has a negative effect on technostress and task complexity effects technostress positively. Hsiao (2017) identified that external locus of control and materialism have positive effects on technostress. Moreover, several studies reported negative correlations between technostress and agreeableness, conscientiousness, extroversion, and openness to experience whereas others reported positive correlations with neuroticism (Hsiao, 2017; Krishnan, 2017; Maier et al., 2019).

Even though there is an increasing attention for technostress studies abroad, there seems to be little interest in Turkey. Especially these days, work and non-work domain intervened with the effect of Covid-19 pandemic, intensive technology usage goes beyond work life and consequently ICT usage have spread all over the place. Accordingly, with an increasing place in individuals' lives, technostress becomes more important in life and for a research subject. Although a translation study (Türen, Erdem & Kalkın, 2015) has been done for this scale before, that study omitted to examine the whole scale with all dimensions. In this context, this study aims to test the reliability and validity of the technostress instrument in full by using two different samples in Turkey. Thereby, the study expects to contribute to the literature by extending to use the scale in studies on technostress which has an increasing effect on organizations and several domains of individuals' lives.

2. Method

In study 1, the sample consisted of 387 private sector employees working in Adana, Turkey. 50.6 % of the participants were men and 49.4 % are women. The samples mean age was found to be 40.08 years (SD = 7.79). The samples mean job tenure was 15.05 years (SD = 7.68). This sample comprised of employees who had mostly a bachelor's degree (76.7 %).

In study 2, the sample was comprised of 453 teachers working in Adana, Turkey. 50.3 % of the participants were men and 49.7 % are women. The samples mean age was found to be 39.94 years (SD = 7.65). The samples mean job tenure was 15.22 years (SD = 12.03). This sample comprised of teachers who had mostly a bachelor's degree (87.9 %).

Technostress scale: Technostress scale consists of 5 dimensions and 25 items and was established by Tarafdar et al. (2007). In their study, they reported Cronbach's alpha for each dimension above 0.80 (0.89; 0.81; 0.84; 0.84; 0.82).

Work exhaustion scale: Work exhaustion scale was obtained from Moore (2000), this scale is from Schaufeli, Leiter, & Kalimo's (1995) the general burnout inventory and comprises of five items. Moore (2000) identified Cronbach's alpha 0.88 for this scale.

Productivity scale: Productivity scale consists of five items and adapted by Tarafdar et al. (2005) from Torkzadeh & Doll (1999). Tarafdar et al. (2000) reported Cronbach's alpha 0.92 for this scale.

Job satisfaction scale: Job satisfaction scale established by Cammann, Fichman, Jenkins, & Klesh (1983). This instrument has three items. Ülbeği, İplik, & Yalçın (2018) identified Cronbach's alpha for this scale 0.86. For all the instruments in the study, I used a 5-point Likert scale.

I conducted two separate studies in two different samples. In study1, I performed exploratory factor analysis to identify the factor structure of the technostress scale. Additionally, I examined reliability of the technostress scale by item analysis and internal consistency coefficient. In study 2, I conducted confirmatory factor analysis to verify the factor structure and examined convergent validity, discriminant validity, and nomological validity of the measure. Moreover, I run correlation analysis to determine the correlations between the variables. In order to assess the reliability of the scales, I analyzed internal consistency by Cronbach's Alpha and McDonald's Omega coefficients (Cronbach, 1951; McDonald, 1999).

3. Results

In study 1, I used exploratory factor analysis to identify the factor structure of the scale if the initial structure was consistent with the original scale. For extraction method, I used principal component analysis, and for factor rotation, varimax method with Kaiser normalization. Results showed the sample size was adequate and the dispersion of the data was also fit for exploratory factor analysis (KMO = 0.94, $\chi 2 = 5846.67$; df = 253, $p < 0.000$). Findings displayed five factor structure as in the original scale. Factor loadings were attained above 0.50 between 0.65 and 0.82 while items had no cross-loadings above 0.30. The first factor explained 16.43 % of the variance, the second factor 16.21 %, the third factor 14.57 %, the fourth factor 13.04 %, and the fifth factor explained 12.88 %, while all factors explained 73.13 % of the total variance (see Table 1).

In study 1, I also examined the reliability of the scale by using both item analysis and internal consistency coefficient. Results produced corrected item-total correlations between 0.61 and 0.80 which meets and exceeds the suggested value 0.30 (Nunnally & Bernstein, 1994: 305). This analysis also showed that deleting any items from the measure would not improve Cronbach's alpha coefficients (see Table 2). Additionally, Cronbach's alpha coefficient were obtained ranging between 0.87 and 0.92 which showed high level of reliability (see Table 2).

In study 2, I conducted confirmatory factor analysis to verify the findings of exploratory factor analysis in study 1. I used maximum likelihood method to establish the factorial validity of the scale and the analysis produced standardized factor loadings between 0.63 and 0.85 (see Figure 1). Confirmatory factor analysis showed an excellent model fit ($\chi2$ = 226.62; df = 220; $\chi2$/sd = 1.03; p = 0.37; CFI = 0.99; TLI = 0.99; RMSEA =0.008; SRMR = 0.030) (see Table 3).

In order to assess the construct validity of the scale, I also examined convergent validity, discriminant validity, and nomological validity. I used a number of criteria including factor loadings, average variance extracted (AVE), and composite reliability to assess convergent validity of the scale. According to this, factor loadings meet the condition to be above 0.50 (Hair et al., 2014: 605) ranging between 0.63 and 0.85 which confirms convergent validity of the scale. Additionally, AVE's require to be above 0.50 (Hair et al., 2014: 605), which was attained in this study by values ranging between 0.57 and 0.67. Moreover, composite reliability coefficients should be above 0.70 (Hair et al., 2014: 605) as another criterion for convergent validity. As seen in the Table 4, composite reliability coefficients were obtained between 0.84 and 0.91 for technostress scale dimensions. These findings revealed that convergent validity was provided for technostress scale.

To examine the discriminant validity of technostress scale, I considered criteria regarding AVE values. In relation to this, AVE values are required to be above MSVs and the square root of AVEs should be above the correlations between variables (Hair et al., 2014: 631). In this study, AVEs are obtained higher than MSVs, and the square root of AVEs are all above the correlations between the variables (see Tables 4 and 5). Accordingly, the discriminant validity for the technostress scale was ensured by these results.

Table 1. Factor loadings of the technostress scale

Items	Techno-overload	Techno-invasion	Techno-complexity	Techno-insecurity	Techno-uncertainty
Techno-overload					
TO1	0.82				
TO2	0.65				
TO3	0.82				
TO4	0.67				
TO5	0.78				
Techno-invasion					
TI1		0.79			
TI2		0.80			
TI3		0.78			
TI4		0.76			
Techno-complexity					
TC1			0.82		
TC2			0.82		
TC3			0.80		
TC4			0.77		
TC5			0.79		
Techno-insecurity					
TN1				0.80	
TN2				0.79	
TN3				0.78	
TN4				0.79	
TN5				0.79	
Techno-uncertainty					
TU1					0.80
TU2					0.79
TU3					0.76
TU4					0.81
% Variance explained	16.43	16.21	14.57	13.04	12.88

KMO = 0.94, Bartlett's Test of Sphericity, $\chi^2 = 5846.67$; df = 253; p < 0,000, % Variance explained = 73.13
Principal component analysis, Varimax rotation, 5 iterations

Table 2. Reliability analysis of the technostress scale

Items	Corrected Item-Total Correlation	Alpha If Item Deleted	Cronbach's Alpha
Techno-overload			0.87
TO1	0.73	0.83	
TO2	0.61	0.86	
TO3	0.74	0.83	
TO4	0.67	0.85	
TO5	0.71	0.84	
Techno-invasion			0.89
TI1	0.75	0.85	
TI2	0.77	0.85	
TI3	0.74	.055	
TI4	0.74	0.55	
Techno-complexity			0.92
TC1	0.80	0.89	
TC2	0.80	0.89	
TC3	0.78	0.90	
TC4	0.78	0.90	
TC5	0.78	0.90	
Techno-insecurity			0.92
TN1	0.78	0.89	
TN2	0.79	0.89	
TN3	0.78	0.89	
TN4	0.79	0.89	
TN5	0.76	0.90	
Techno-uncertainty			0.89
TU1	0.76	0.86	
TU2	0.76	0.86	
TU3	0.77	0.86	
TU4	0.75	0.86	

Table 3. Confirmatory factor analysis model fit results

Fit Index	Model Results	Reference Values*
χ^2	226.62	$0 \leq \chi^2 \leq 2df$
Df	220	-
χ^2 / df	1.03	$0 \leq \chi^2/df \leq 2$
p-value	0.37	$p > 0.00$
CFI	0.99	$0.90 < CFI$
TLI	0.99	$0.90 < TLI$
RMSEA	0.008	$0.00 < RMSEA < 0.05$
SRMR	0.030	$0.00 < SRMR < 0.05$

*χ^2=Chi-Square, df=Degrees of Freedom, CFI=Comparative Fit Index, TLI=Tucker-Lewis Index, RMSEA=Root Mean Square Error of Approximation, SRMR=Standardized Root Mean Square Residual, *Reference Values adapted from* Bayram, 2010; Meydan & Şeşen, 2011; Hair et al., 2014.

To establish the nomological validity in this study, I analyzed the correlations between variables. The correlations between technostress dimensions displayed positive and significant while the correlations between these dimensions and work exhaustion also obtained positive and significant. Moreover, correlations between technostress dimensions with productivity and job satisfaction acquired negative and statistically significant (see Table 5).

In study 2, I also checked reliability coefficient Cronbach's alpha and McDonald's omega. As shown in Table 4, they displayed values between 0.84 and 0.92 for technostress dimension which refers to high reliability. Regarding the construct validity and reliability of the scale, these results showed that techno-stress is a valid and reliable measure.

Table 4. Means, standard deviations, Cronbach's alphas, McDonald's omegas, composite reliabilities, AVEs, and MSVs of the scales used

Variables	A	CR-ω	AVE	MSV	Mean	SD
TO	0.87	0.90	0.63	0.32	3.58	0.81
TI	0.89	0.89	0.67	0.32	2.79	0.87
TC	0.92	0.91	0.66	0.35	3.05	0.87
TN	0.92	0.91	0.66	0.35	2.86	0.86
TU	0.89	0.84	0.57	0.31	3.67	0.84
EX	0.90	0.88	0.60	0.20	4.02	077
PR	0.87	0.87	0.62	0.18	4.25	0.71
JS	0.84	0.82	0.61	0.16	4.35	0.70

TO = Techno-overload, TI = Techno-invasion, TC = Techno-complexity, TU = Techno-uncertainty, EX = Work exhaustion, P = Productivity, JS = Job satisfaction, α = Cronbach's Alpha Coefficient, CR- ω = Composite Reliability, McDonald's Omega Coefficient, AVE = Average Variance Extracted, MSV = Maximum Shared Variance, SD = Standard Deviation.

Table 5. Correlations of the scales used

Variables	TO	TI	TC	TN	TU	EX	PR	JS
TO	0.80							
TI	0.55**	0.82						
TC	0.57**	0.56**	0.81					
TN	0.56**	0.57**	0.59**	0.82				
TU	0.55**	0.54**	0.55**	0.56**	0.75			
EX	0.42**	0.44**	0.45**	0.44**	0.41**	0.78		
PR	-0.37**	-0.42**	-0.41**	-0.40**	-0.38**	-0.37**	0.79	
JS	-0.38**	-0.40**	-0.39**	-0.40**	-0.36**	-0.35**	-0.37**	0.78

*TO=Techno-overload, TI=Techno-invasion, TC=Techno-complexity, TU=Techno-uncertainty, EX= Work exhaustion, P=Productivity, JS=Job satisfaction, Diagonal values are the square root of AVEs, **p<0.01.*

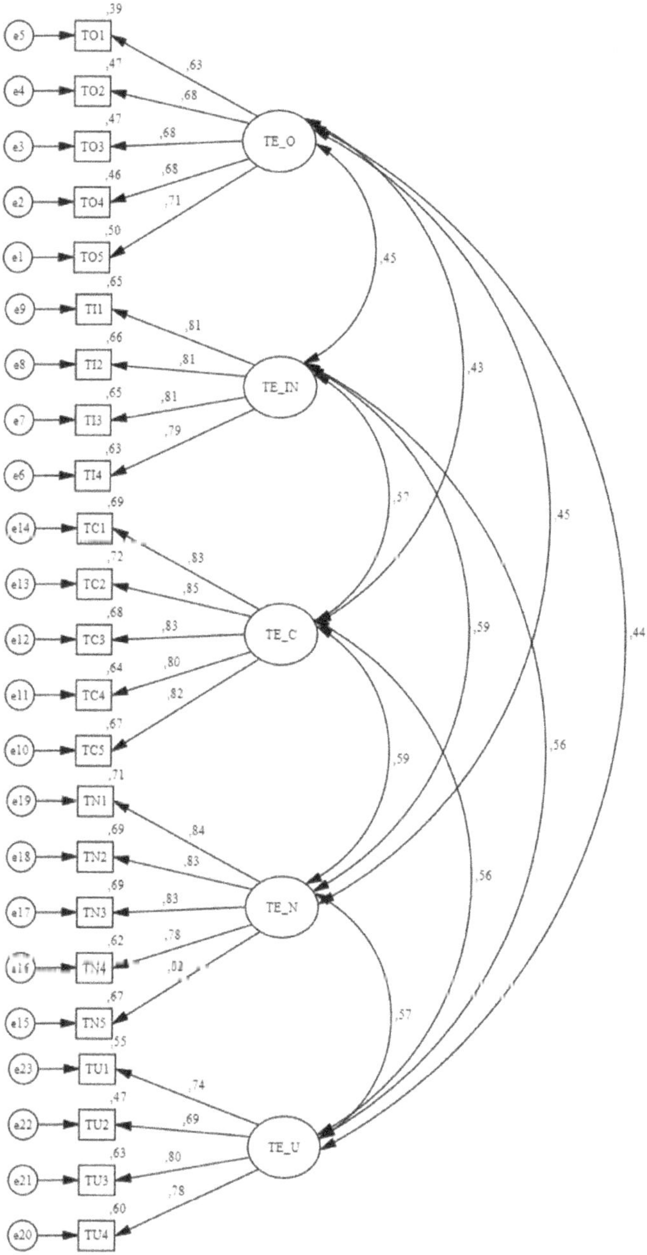

Figure 1. Technostress scale confirmatory factor analysis results

4. Discussion

In this study, the main purpose was to assess the validity and reliability of the technostress instrument by Tarafdar et al. (2007) in two different samples in Turkey. Exploratory factor analysis results provided five factors of technostress which are techno-overload, techno-invasion, techno-complexity, techno-insecurity, and techno-uncertainty. Factor loadings attained between 0.65 and 0.82, and these five factors explained 73.13 % of the total variance.

Confirmatory factor analysis revealed findings showing the five-factor structure and excellent model fit ($\chi 2 = 226.62$; df = 220; $\chi 2/sd = 1.03$; $p = 0.37$; CFI = 0.99; TLI = 0.99; RMSEA =0.008; SRMR = 0.030). Factor loadings were obtained between 0.63 and 0.85. These results are consistent with previous studies on technostress (e.g., Tarafdar et al., 2007; Tarafdar, Tu, & Ragu-Nathan, 2010). Moreover, this study also examined convergent validity, discriminant validity, and nomological validity. Validity findings also revealed the construct validity of the scale as in former studies (e.g., Tarafdar et al., 2007; Ragu-Nathan et al., 2008).

Additionally, in this study, reliability of the technostress has also been revealed by examining both item analysis and internal consistency coefficients. Corrected item-total correlations produced between 0.61 and 0.80. Moreover, internal consistency coefficients, Cronbach's alpha and McDonald's omega showed satisfactory results ranging between 0.84 and 0.92 for all five dimensions of technostress scale. Reliability findings showed consistent results with former studies on technostress (e.g., Tarafdar et al., 2007, 2010).

There are several limitations in this study. The samples were only private sector employees and teachers. Additionally, three variables were used for nomological validity testing. Future studies should conduct studies with different occupational samples. Moreover, studies should design research with different antecedents and outcomes of technostress.

The main purpose of this study was to examine technostress scale in Turkish samples. Study results displayed that the technostress scale consisted of five-factor structure with satisfactory reliabilities in two different samples. The findings showed that technostress instrument is valid as well as reliable to utilize in Turkish studies. Technostress literature is a growing field, in this regard this study is expected to contribute for future studies in Turkish literature.

References

Alam, M. A. (2016). Techno-stress and productivity: Survey evidence from the aviation industry. *Journal of Air Transport Management, 50,* 62–70.

Bayram, N. (2010). *Yapısal eşitlik modellemesine giriş.* İstanbul: Ezgi Kitabevi.

Boonjing, V., & Chanvarasuth, P. (2017). Risk of overusing mobile phones: Technostress effect. *Procedia Computer Science, 111,* 196–202.

Brod, C. (1984). *Technostress: The human cost of the computer revolution.* Boston, MA: Addison-Wesley.

Brooks, S., & Califf, C. (2017). Social media-induced technostress: Its impact on the job performance of it professionals and the moderating role of job characteristics. *Computer Networks, 114,* 143–153.

Cammann, C., Fichman, M., Jenkins, G. D., & Klesh, J. (1983). Michigan organizational assessment questionnaire. In S.E. Seashore, E. E. Lawler, P. H. Mirvis, & C. Cammann (Eds.), Assessing organizational change: A guide to methods, measures, and practices (pp. 71–138). New York: Wiley-Interscience.

Chen, A., & Karahanna, E. (2014). Boundaryless technology: Understanding the effects of technology-mediated interruptions across the boundaries between work and personal life. *AIS Transactions on Human-Computer Interaction, 6*(2), 16–36.

Christ-Brendemühl, S., & Schaarschmidt, M. (2020). The impact of service employees' technostress on customer satisfaction and delight: A dyadic analysis. *Journal of Business Research, 117,* 378–388.

Christensson, P. (2010). ICT Definition. https://techterms.com. Accessed 2 May 2021.

Cronbach, L. J. (1951). Coefficient alpha and the internal structure of tests. *Psychometrika, 16,* 297–334.

De Wet, W., Koekemoer, E., & Nel, J. A. (2016). Exploring the impact of information and communication technology on employees' work and personal lives. *SA Journal of Industrial Psychology, 42*(1), 1–11.

Fuglseth, A. M., & Sørebø, Ø. (2014). The effects of technostress within the context of employee use of ICT. *Computers in Human Behavior, 40,* 161–170.

Hair, J. F., Black, W. C., Babin, B. J., & Anderson, R. E. (2014). *Multivariate data analysis.* Pearson International Edition, 7th Edition. US: Pearson Education Limited.

Hsiao, K.-L. (2017). Compulsive mobile application usage and technostress: The role of personality traits. *Online Information Review, 41*(2), 272–295.

Jena, R. K. (2015). Technostress in ICT enabled collaborative learning environment: An empirical study among Indian academician. *Computers in Human Behavior, 51,* 1116–1123.

Karr-Wisniewski, P., & Lu, Y. (2010). When more is too much: Operationalizing technology overload and exploring its impact on knowledge worker productivity. *Computers in Human Behavior, 26*(5), 1061–1072.

Koo, C., & Wati, Y. (2011). What Factors Do Really Influence the Level of Technostress in Organizations?: An Empirical Study. In N. T. Nguyen, B. Trawinski, & J. J Jung (Eds.), *New Challenges for Intelligent Information, Studies in Computational Intelligence 351,* (pp. 339–348). Berlin, Heidelberg: Springer-Verlag.

Krishnan, S. (2017). Personality and espoused cultural differences in technostress creators. *Computers in Human Behavior, 66,* 154–167.

Li, L., & Wang, X. (2020). Technostress inhibitors and creators and their impacts on university teachers' work performance in higher education. *Cognition, Technology & Work, 23,* 315–330.

Lim, V. K. G. (2002). The IT way of loafing on the job: Cyberloafing, neutralizing and organizational justice. *Journal of Organizational Behavior, 23*(5), 675–694.

Maier, C., Laumer, S., Wirth, J., & Weitzel, T. (2019). Technostress and the hierarchical levels of personality: A two-wave study with multiple data samples. *European Journal of Information Systems, 28*(5), 496–522.

McDonald, R. P. (1999). *Test theory: A unified treatment.* Mahwah, NJ: Erlbaum.

Melville, N., Kraemer, K., & Gurbaxani, V. (2004). Information technology and organizational performance: An integrative model of IT business value. *MIS Quarterly, 28*(2), 283–322.

Meydan, C. H., & Şeşen, H. (2011). *Yapısal Eşitlik Modellemesi AMOS Uygulamaları.* Ankara: Detay Yayıncılık.

Moore, J. E. (2000). One road to turnover: An examination of work exhaustion in technology professionals. *MIS Quarterly, 24*(1), 141–168.

Nunnally, J. C., & Bernstein, I. H. (1994). *Psychometric theory.* 3rd Edition. New York, NY: McGraw-Hill, Inc.oxfordreference.com (2021). In oxfordreference.com. https://www.oxfordreference.com/view/10.1093/oi/authority.20110803100002983. Accessed 2 May 2021.

Ragu-Nathan, T. S., Tarafdar, M., Ragu-Nathan, B. S., & Tu, Q. (2008). The consequences of technostress for end users in organizations: Conceptual development and empirical validation. *Information Systems Research, 19*(4), 417–433.

Schaufeli, W. B., Leiter, M. P., & Kalimo, R. (1995). "*The General Burnout Inventory: A Self-report Questionnaire to Assess Burnout at the Workplace*," paper presented at Work, Stress and Health '95: Creating Healthier Workplaces, Washington, D.C.

Tarafdar, M., Pullins, E. B., & Ragu-Nathan, T. S. (2014). Technostress: Negative effect on performance and possible mitigations. *Information Systems Journal, 25*(2), 103–132.

Tarafdar, M., Ragu-Nathan, B.S., Ragu-Nathan, T.S., & Tu, Q. (2005). *Exploring the impact of technostress on productivity.* Paperpresented at the 2005 Decision Sciences Institute Annual Meeting, San Francisco, CA, 19–22 November (pp. 13771–13776).

Tarafdar, M., Tu, Q., Ragu-Nathan, B. S., & Ragu-Nathan, T. S. (2007). The impact of technostress on role stress and productivity. *Journal of Management Information Systems, 24*(1), 301–328.

Tarafdar, M., Tu, Q., & Ragu-Nathan, T. S. (2010). Impact of technostress on end-user satisfaction and performance. *Journal of Management Information Systems, 27*(3), 303–334.

Torkzadeh, G., & Doll, W. J. (1999). The development of a tool for measuring the perceived impact of information technology on work. *OMEGA: The International Journal of Management Science, 27*(3), 327–339.

Türen, U., Erdem, H., & Kalkın, G. (2015). İşyerinde Tekno-Stres Ölçeği: Havacılık ve Bankacılık Sektöründe Bir Araştırma. *Çalışma İlişkileri Dergisi, 6*(1), 1–19.

Ülbeği, İ. D., İplik, E., & Yalçın, A. (2018). Etik Liderliğin İş Tatmini ve İşten Ayrılma Niyetine Etkisinde İşe Adanmanın Rolü. *Sayıştay Dergisi, 111*, 173–196.

Vranjes, I., Baillien, E., Vandebosch, H., Erreygers, S., & De Witte, H. (2017). The dark side of working online: Towards a definition and an Emotion Reaction model of workplace cyberbullying. *Computers in Human Behavior, 69*, 324–334.

Walsh, S., White, K., & Young, R. (2008). Over-connected? A qualitative exploration of the relationship between Australian youth and their mobile phones. *Journal of Adolescence, 31*(1), 77–92.

Wang, K., & Shu, Q. (2008). The Moderating Impact of Perceived Organizational Support on the Relaitonship between Technostress and Role Stress. In Bhowmick, S. S., Küng, J., Wagner, R. (Eds.), *DEXA 2008. LNCS, vol. 5181.* Heidelberg: Springer.

Wang, K., Shu, Q., & Tu, Q. (2008). Technostress under different organizational environment: An empirical investigation. *Computer in Human Behavior, 24*, 3002–3013.

Weil, M. M., & Rosen, L. D. (1997). *TechnoStress: Coping with Technology @work @home @play*. New York: John Wiley.

Yener, S. (2018). Teknostresin İş Performansı Üzerindeki Etkisi; Tükenmişliğin Aracı Rolü. *Afyon Kocatepe Üniversitesi Sosyal Bilimler Dergisi, 20*(2), 85–101.

Yunis, M., Tarhini, A., & Kassar, A. (2018). The role of ICT and innovation in enhancing organizational performance: The catalysing effect of corporate entrepreneurship. *Journal of Business Research, 88*, 344–356.

Fatma ZEYBEK & Hatice BATMANTAŞ

The Impact of Digitalization on Human Resource Management

1. Introduction

After the industrial revolution, there have been radical changes in both social and daily life. Studies on international trade, industrial relations and legal structure have increased and reforms have emerged in engineering, social and health sciences. The developments that emerged with the industrial revolution caused some changes and developments in personnel management. Deficiencies in personnel management were noticed and those deficiencies were tried to be eliminated. Thus, the meaning of "personnel management" has changed and employees have begun to be considered as the most important element for competition with the continuous renewal of technology and knowledge, knowledge and skills have taken place in the quality of human resources. The need for storing human resources data in electronic media also shows an increasing trend. In our time, human resources management information is transferred to electronic environments and as a result, digitalization practices take place in businesses.

In this chapter, the history of human resource management will be expounded upon and the effects of digitalizations on human resources will be exemplified.

2. Human Resource Management

Human resource management, defined as "activities designed to provide human resources to an institution or organization and to coordinate this process" (Osibanjo and Adeniji, 2012), is a concept that has changed shape, function and name over time in line with developments in economics, politics and the business world. It is impossible not to mention the orientation and management of a person in an environment in which they exist and work. Thus, human resource management can be said to be as aged a concept as human history. Indeed, the first recorded historical sources are the *wage rates* used by King Hammurabi of Babylon in the 1800s B.C.E and again the applications of *division of labor* that had emerged in China in the 1600s B.C.E. (Akgemici and Demirsel, 2004: 279). Moreover, it has been established that the first *shift* system was employed during the construction of the pyramids in Egypt, whereas the first *talent management* applications were carried out in the Ottoman Empire (Ceylan, 2007).

Due to the Industrial Revolution, emerged in the second half of the eighteenth century in England and spread all over the world, migration from villages to cities increased, which led to an increase in the number of workers, and radical changes in the structure of production, economic and commercial rights that people had. As a result of industrialization, the approach to the human element has changed, it has been understood that man is not an input element for production, but an important resource. Thus, the concept of human resources has gained importance. Thanks to the expansion of factory-type production, it has become possible for managers to manage a large, specialized audience rather than a small group (Mucuk, 2003: 14). Another factor that played a role in the development of the concept of staff management was the contribution of Taylorism and labor welfare movements to industry and human psychology (Altundal, 2020). Taylor's scientific management approach aimed at increasing production. With this goal in mind, Taylor conducted the 'time study' and implemented the 'incentive plan' to measure how soon an employee can do a job the best (Köroğlu and Koç, 2017: 4). Although putting tasks into a systematic framework instead of haphazard work and the scientific treatment of management have led to radical changes in the field of management, the concepts of effectiveness and efficiency have been brought to the fore in Taylorism, which treats enterprises as a closed system and addresses the human element after efficiency.

Mobility and labor division practices, which appeared as a result of industrialization at the beginning of the nineteenth century, have allowed two different terms to be introduced into the literature of business: "employees" and "workers". Around the same time, some measures were taken by the socialist Robert Owen to improve working conditions in order to increase productivity. Working hours were reduced and the tradition of employing child workers, preferred because of low wages, was also abolished. On the other hand, a systematic approach was introduced to staff selection (Koçak, 2006: 62). In the 1900s, human resource management began to be called "staff management", which was defined as "a system established to ensure that employees achieve both individual and group goals" (Yoder, 1972: 4). During this period, a person was perceived as a robot charged with performing the tasks assigned, the staff management department in enterprises was only interested in basic practices such as recruitment processes, overtime inputs and outputs, while people's feelings and thoughts were ignored.

In the last quarter of the nineteenth century, changes to the labor structure were implemented because of the expansion of heavy industry, the establishment of large enterprises, and, by extension, the rapid increase in the number of workers. Specialization in the labor force gained importance, a shift from unskilled labor to skilled occurred, and qualified labor became a sought-after asset in enterprises. In order to have a qualified labor force, the training of workers was also given weight during this period. The demand for qualified employees gifted the term 'professional manager', or 'white-collar employee', to the literature (Koçak, 2006: 62–63). In this period, trade unions, which are workers' organizations, were established, concepts such as contracts, strikes, quitting emerged, and the concept of industrial relations became one of the functions of staff management.

It can be said that the 1980s constituted a zenith and a turning point for human resource management. For businesses that want to achieve success in the face of rapid changes, employees ceased to be a factor or expense in production and became a value of production (Bayraktaroğlu, 2003:4). During this period, staff management evolved and entered the process of turning into "human resource management" and gained overall improvement (Dulebohn, Ferris, & Stodd, 1995: 18–40). While staff management is occupied with daily, routine tasks with an operational outlook, human resource management, which aims to develop a human-oriented culture in the organization, offers a conceptual framework on how human resources can be mined together with other resources and how human resources can be employed and managed.

Since the 1990s, a multifaceted economic and social transformation has started in the world, and knowledge is understood to be the main catalyst for changes observed in various areas. This period witnessed the realization that intellectual knowledge is the most important property that will help companies stand out among others and gain sustainable competitive edge, as well as the emergence of *intellectual capital* which compasses the knowledge, experience, skills, and behaviors of employees, in other words, all intangible assets that have the potential to create value for companies. Along with the arrival of this new notion, human resource management evolved into "intellectual capital management". During the global economic crisis of 2009, the value of the human element was better understood which led to a reassessment of how employees are perceived in the business world. Discussions on this issue birthed the concept of "talent management", which is a new understanding in the process of human resource management. Concerning a talent management that is desired today, it is essential to create an attractive organizational structure and culture and encourage, develop, and retain talent for those with outstanding talent (Benligiray, 2016).

In short, HR-related applications are implemented on "manpower management" which treat people as muscle power only, "personnel management" which encompasses both knowledge and skills, "human resources" which prioritizes brain power over the aforementioned qualities, then, "intellectual capital management" as the result of the acknowledgement of the importance of skills and competencies, and "talent management" which has been adopted today along with innovation and creativity coming to the fore. In the next chapter, the impact of digitalization in human resource management is discussed and the changes and innovations shown in human resources by big data technology, the effects of artificial intelligence and social media tools that are increasingly important today are expressed with examples.

3. Human Resource Management under the Influence of Digitalization

The widespread use of the Internet and the involvement of technology in all areas of life have affected the functioning of both the public and private sectors. Human resource management, which is one of the basic building blocks of management, has started to adapt to the digital world in addition to traditional methods. As human resources employees quickly adapted to technology, they began to use it intensively, and thus the digital transformation gained further momentum.

Before digital transformation awareness begins to be spread in companies, the firm needs to determine its potential functions and positions well. In this context, companies should:

- Save time by automating routine tasks or using external resources,
- Resort to applications that will enable effective and strong communication between employees by increasing teamwork,
- Predict and develop human resources processes,
- Make its operations faster with the impact of digitalization,
- Organize online trainings and implement effective time management so that employees can access the information they need instantly,
- Provide a flexible working environment,
- Augment the employee experience by applying the customer experience to internal customers,
- Widely use digital applications and business solutions to increase employee loyalty and operational efficiency (Emcan, 2015).

With the effect of digitalization, communication between human resources companies and employees has accelerated and the opportunity to access various information easily and quickly has been born. In human resources, personal affairs, recruitment processes, performance evaluations can be managed more effectively and quickly, flexible working from the office environment can be offered with cloud infrastructure systems and various mobile technologies, and the opportunity to easily access the desired information is created (Taşkıran, 2017: 103–104; Göktaş ve Baysal, 2018: 1416).

In order to adopt digital transformation awareness throughout the company, in-service training programs, inter-agency information and feedback from employees should be ensured and this flow should be maintained. The creation of a technical and financial structure for digital transformation should be ensured. However, employees should experience new technologies, follow new technologies and adapt. In addition, with the implementation of training simulations in human resources, the training costs of employees can be reduced and some mishaps that may occur in the work environment can be determined in advance and managed. It can be said that training simulation applications are applied especially in the flight training processes of aircraft companies (Taşkıran, 2017: 106; Daly, 2012: 124).

Digital transformation needs to be clearly expressed to its employees by management to cover all visions and strategies of the company. In addition, digital transformation should not only shape the internal structure and employees of the company, but also be designed taking into account the needs of its customers outside the company, thus a holistic perspective should dominate (The 2018 Digital University, 2016). To adapt to this digital transformation, employees need to be flexible, be motivated for learning, communicate effectively with colleagues and exchange information, act with the ability to be a team, have analytical thinking skills that are open to innovations and changes, and closely follow workflow processes and technology (Sural Özer et al., 2018: 807).

When examining the impact of digitalization in human resources, the effects of big data technology, artificial intelligence and social media will be mentioned, respectively.

3.1. Big Data Technology

Big data typically includes Internet click-through figures, conversations and messages via mobile phones, content generated on social media, and purchases made from online shopping or physical stores (Weng and Lin, 2014; George et al., 2014).

Thanks to big data, data from numerous computers can be collected together, the data obtained in customer relationship management (CRM) and human resource management (HRM) can be analyzed by analyzing the profiles of employees and customer profiles and characteristics of employees can be determined in detail according to this data. At the same time, thanks to CRM, the behavior of consumers can be examined, and current trends can be followed, and possible trends can be predicted (Sözer, 2017). Therefore, big data offers the opportunity to access performance evaluations of potential future candidates in their previous jobs, the results of the exams they are responsible for in the processes and the information of managers about the candidates, so that human resources managers can manage their recruitment, selection and placement processes based on this data. Google, one of the companies that uses big data most efficiently in the selection of candidates and managers, can be given as an example in this regard (Göçoğlu and Kurt, 2018: 364; Barman and Ahmed, 2015:13).

According to the Mckinsey Global Institute, it has been determined that big data plays an important role in performance improvements, the formation of detailed customer data, the availability of new business models, the development of existing products and services, the launch of new products and services, providing faster circulation and playing an effective role in making decisions easier for management. However, it can be said that big data continues to dominate not only in the field of human resources, but nearly in many areas. For companies to achieve a sustainable competitive advantage, data scientists responsible for analyzing big data should create employment opportunities and these data scientists should extract data that does not comply with the policies of the companies and harmonize the values expressed by the data with the company's basic objectives and policies (Kubinaa et al., 2015).

3.2. Artificial Intelligence

In addition to traditional methods, digital methods have started to be employed in job interviews. Digital transformation and artificial intelligence applications, which continue their impact in many sectors, have started to be implemented in recruitment processes. Thanks to digitization, potential candidates can participate in interviews, participate in online exams and answer questions over Zoom and other applications online. In addition, thanks to artificial intelligence, the word choices, facial features, speaking style and gestures of the potential candidate in the job interview video that lasts for a few minutes are analyzed and processed; according to the data obtained afterwards, which positions the candidate is suitable for are determined. In addition, with the help of simple formulations and filtering features in the data, candidates with the desired characteristics can be instantly identified in the system, candidates can be contacted, and thus companies can save costs and time (Malhotra, 2017: 539; Can, 2018). Moreover, artificial intelligence applications in human resources reduce the workload of administrative staff in the company, ensure the selection of the right candidates for the job, and allow employees in the workplace to evaluate their loyalty to the organization (Yawalkar, 2019: 22–23).

Companies use programs such as Microsoft 365 for employee productivity, Engazify for feedback, Obie and Niles for information transfer, Wade and Wendy for career development, and Duolingo for learning structure (Jain, 2017: 221). In addition, many companies are turning to artificial intelligence technology applications, including chatbots, machine learning and robot process automation, which offer opportunities such as job adaptation programs and interviews. Chatbot is a social platform that communicates with its users by talking or texting, and thanks to Chatbot, candidates can be contacted 24/7 and can receive quick replies. In this way, the workload of human resources personnel can be eased, allowing human resources personnel to devote more time to their other work (Eubanks, 2019: 103–105; Kıvrak, 2018: 193).

The process of selecting and placing potential candidates of companies under the influence of digitalization in human resources is shown in the following Figure 1.

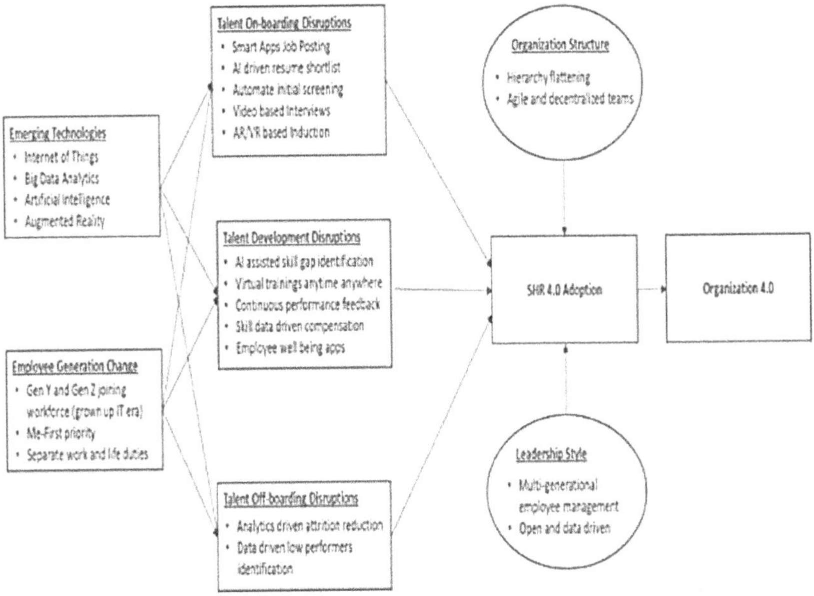

Figure 1. HR 4.0 conceptual framework in the impact of digitalization (Sivathanu and Pillai, 2018: 2)

After selecting and placing potential candidates of companies under the influence of digitalization in human resources, the topic of robot trainers, which is one of the new technological developments in the training and management of candidates, will be discussed.

With the development of robotic technologies, robot instructors who are involved in our lives behave exactly like humans, recognize sound and images, and discuss and create solutions on various issues (Ford, 2018: 158–168). These robot instructors contribute to training in employee process management and can analyze each employee and detect employee learning speeds. A robot teacher can train groups of employees with an average of four to seven people, talk about the same topic again when there is an incomprehensible topic, can offer motivational phrases that encourage training during training, ensuring that the training achieved participation and efficiency (Stone et al., 2018: 13–20).

3.3. Social Media

The influence of social media in the human resources department has been increasing day by day. The use of social media channels through mobile devices, the fact that potential candidates constantly follow various channels, the existence of web-based sites, and the ability to communicate and interact with employees through channels have enabled the widespread use and public adoption of social media (Boyd and Ellison, 2007).

In recruitment processes, companies use social media channels to reach potential candidates, communicate and view and examine their CVs. As a result of Accu-Screen's work in the United States, it was determined that 53 % of CVs sent to companies lacked accurate information, 78 % of CVs had misdirection and 21 % did not provide accurate information about education. Therefore, companies examine the social media profiles of the candidates in detail in addition to the references of the candidates during recruitment, obtain various information about the candidates and decide on the selection and placement of the candidates (Cülcüloğlu, 2013:14; Arthur, 2012).

Social media platforms provide areas of active communication, information and experience sharing between departments and persons, and contribute to the ability to track people in the desired sector according to their areas of expertise, therefore, help people keep up-to-date with current information and new developments in the sector. Furthermore, with the creation of a large pool of candidates in the recruitment process, candidates with the desired characteristics can be found in a short time, national and international communication can be easily established and, therefore, time savings can be achieved in human resources processes and costs can be eased (Vardarlıer, 2014: 89–90; idenfit.com, 2021). In an American study, it was determined that 90 % of recruitment specialists evaluated the candidate's social media accounts in detail before or after the interview (Sağır, 2018).

According to a study conducted, LinkedIn usage among social media channels during the recruitment process was 68 % and Facebook usage, which contributes to human resources with various career pages, was 52 % (kariyer.net, 2016).

Through the case of LinkedIn, one of the leading professional social sharing platforms, the impact of social media on human resource management will be expressed. Through LinkedIn, one of the social networking platforms, potential candidates can share their experience on this platform and the information they want companies to which they apply to know, apply for positions, and establish a business network with employees or human resources managers in the companies they are interested in. The LinkedIn platform is also an open platform for new job opportunities and offers opportunities to reach candidates who have not submitted any applications for existing ads (Baykal and Bayarçelik, 2020: 3378).

In education and development management, LinkedIn creates educational organizations that can be attended by anyone with learning content and provides participants with intra-group sharing opportunities, paving the way for individuals in the group to exchange information with each other. Companies can share posts on their corporate pages on LinkedIn about the topics their employees want them to improve, and employees can give mutual and more efficient feedback viewing this content in a more comfortable environment without pressure (Taş, 2020: 94). One of the most important factors behind the activation of social media in almost every sector is the ability to reach out to unreachable persons or institutions and to establish healthy communication. Employees can communicate with people or institutions they see as the target they need to reach in business life via LinkedIn and easily ask these people or institutions the questions they are curious about and often get quick feedback. Thus, employees or candidates who want to advance in the field of their liking can perform career management for the field they want by clarifying the question marks in their minds (Taş, 2020: 98).

With the effect of digitalization, the approach of pushing candidates through social media platforms has come to the forefront, rather than the approach of attracting candidates to companies in the selection and placement processes during recruitment. Companies develop new recruitment techniques by enabling candidates with the desired talent and skills to find them and interact with their social media channels (Baykal, 2020: 52).

Various studies also support the fact that the use of social media in human resources is increasing. A few examples of these studies can be given. According to the study of Baykal and Bayarçelik (2020), it was determined that the activation of social media in human resources provides rapid interaction in the selection and placement of potential candidates. Yılmaz (2016) examined the effects of social networking sites in recruitment processes in his work in the retail sector and found that each of the companies in the study had corporate accounts to reach a large pool of candidates on social networking sites. It has been determined that firms often use LinkedIn and Facebook accounts effectively, and in particular, LinkedIn has a widespread network of uses in recruitment processes. According to another study, Bozkurt and Triki (2016) evaluated recruitment decisions and the effects of processes on social media. According to the research, social media has a significant decisive effect on human resources managers and HR managers make inferences about the personality and psychological characteristics of candidates during the recruitment decision and the accuracy of these inferences is examined.

According to PwC, Turkey's research carried out in the first quarter of 2021 with human resources managers of national and international companies of different sizes from sectors such as retail, automotive, technology and health, human resources managers in Turkey emphasized that they are "moving towards future business models, employee experience and development of transformational leadership, digital HR and data analytics studies, and the construction of critical skills and competencies" (PwC, 2021). Transformational leadership refers to the orientation of employees in the direction of the vision of the business and the motivation of employees to perform high (Bass, 1999). On the other hand, data analytics briefly refers to the analysis of raw data and its conversion to meaningful information and reports (Le Roux, 2012).

4. Conclusion

Today, the idea of human resources has turned into talent management and has become applicable. In addition to traditional human resources practices, the widespread use of the Internet and the inclusion of technology in every aspect of life have influenced human resource management as well. With the effect of digital transformation, human resources employees should have flexible structure and analytical thinking skills in order to adopt quickly to the digital world. In addition, personnel affairs recruitment processes, performance evaluations in human resources can be managed more effectively and quikly.

The effects of big data technology, artificial intelligence, and social media seem to be increasingly crucial in examining the effect of digitalization in human resources. While examining the effect of digitalization in human resources, the effects of big data technology, artificial intelligence and social media are mentioned. With the employment of big data, the profiles of the employees in human resources management can be analyzed and the characteristics of the employees can be determined with artificial intelligence, the word choices, facial features, speaking style and facial expressions of the potential candidate in a few minutes of job interview video can be analyzed. Then, according to the data obtained, it can be determined in which positions the candidate is suitable. Companies can obtain various information about candidates by using social media channels in their recruitment processes and can decide on the recruitment of candidates.

References

Adem, Ö. Ğ. Ü. T., Akgemci, T., Tahir Demirsel, M. (2004). Stratejik İnsan Kaynakları Yönetimi bağlamında Örgütlerde İşgören Motivasyonu Süreci. *Selçuk Üniversitesi Sosyal Bilimler Enstitüsü Dergisi*, (12), 277–290.

Adeniji, A. A. ve Osibanjo, A. O. (2012). *Human Resource Management: Theory and Practice*. Pumark Lagos: Nigeria Limited.

Altundal, Y. (2020). *Personel Yönetiminden İnsan Kaynaklarına, İnsan Kaynaklarındanİnsan Kıymetlerine Dönüşüm: İnsan Kıymetleri Savunucuları Üzerine Bir İnceleme*. Bandırma, Türkiye: Bandırma Onyedi Eylül Üniversitesi.

Arthur, D. (2012). *Recruiting, Interviewing, Selecting & Orienting New Employees*. USA: Amacom.

Barman, A., Ahmed, H. (2015). *Big Data in Human Resource Management-Developing Research Context*, doi: http://dx.doi.org/10.13140/RG.2.1.3113.6166. Accessed 5 July 2021.

Bass, B. M. (1999). Two decades of research and development in transformational leadership. *European Journal of Work and Organizational Psycholog*, 8(1), 9–32, doi: 10.1080/135943299398410.

Baykal, İ. E. (2020). *Sosyal Medya Kullanımının İnsan Kaynakları Fonksiyonlarına Etkisinin Araştırılması*, Yüksek Lisans Tezi, Bahçeşehir Üniversitesi, İstanbul.

Baykal, İ. E., Bayarçelik, E. B. (2020). Sosyal Medya Kullanımının İnsan Kaynakları Fonksiyonları Üzerindeki Etkisi Üzerine Bir Araştırma, *Business & Management Studies: An International Journal*, 8(3), 3359–3392.

Bayraktaroğlu, S. (2003). *İnsan kaynakları yönetimi*. İstanbul: Sakarya Kitabevi.

Benligiray, S. (2016). *İnsan Kaynakları Yönetimi*. Eskişehir: Nisan Kitabevi.

Boyd, D., Ellison, N. (2007). Social network sites: Definition, history, and scholarship, *Journal of Computer-Mediated Communication*, 13(1), 210–230. doi: https://doi.org/10.1111/j.1083-6101.2007.00393.x. Accessed 5 July 2021.

Bozkurt, F. G., Trıkı, M. (2016). Bir Kurum Olarak Sosyal Medyanın İnsan Kaynakları Yöneticilerinin İş Gören Tedarik-Seçim ve İşe Alma Kararları Üzerindeki Etkisi: Tunus Örneği, *Çukurova Üniversitesi İktisadi ve İdari Bilimler Fakültesi Dergisi*, 20(1), 89–107.

Can, A. (2018). *Önce yapay zekayı geçmeniz gerekiyor*. Retrieved March 22, 2019 Erişim adresi: http://www.hurriyet.com.tr/ik-yeni-ekonomi-41007016. Accessed 15 June 2021.

Ceylan, N. (2007). İnsan Kaynakları Yönetiminde Yetenek Yönetimi ve Bir Uygulama. *Basılmamış Yüksek Lisans Tezi, İstanbul: İÜ Sosyal Bilimler Enstitüsü İşletme Anabilim Dalı, İnsan Kaynakları Yönetimi Bilim Dalı*, 84–93.

Cülcüloğlu, E. (2013). *Socıal Medıa in Recruıtment*, Humanities Faculty of Utrecht University at Utrecht, Yüksek Lisans Tezi, Utrecht, Netherlands. Erişim adresi: https://dspace.library.uu.nl/handle/1874/285247. Accessed 22 June 2021.

Daly, J. L. (2012). *Human Resource Management in the Public Sector.* New York: Routledge.

Dulebohn, J. H., Ferris, G., Stodd, J. T. (1995). *The History and Evulation of Human Resource Management*. Cambridge: Blackwell Publisher.

Emcan, M. (2015). *İnsan Kaynaklarının Dijitalleşme Yolculuğu*, Pwc.

Eubanks, B. (2019). *Artificial Intelligence For Hr Use Aı To Support And Develop A Successful Workforce*. The USA: Kogan Press.

Ford, M. (2018). *Robotların Yükselişi*, 5. Bs., İstanbul: Kronik Yayıncılık.

George, G., Haas, M. R., Pentland, A. (2014). Big Data and Management, *Academy of Management Journal*, 57(2), 321–326. doi: https://doi.org/10.5465/amj.2014.4002. Accessed 5 July 2021.

Göçoğlu, V., Kurt, İ. D. (2018). Kamu Kurumlarında İnsan Kaynakları Yönetimi ve Teknolojı: Gelecek Odaklı Bır Degerlendırme, *Uluslararası Yönetım Akademisi Dergisi*, 1(3), 357–367.

Göktaş, P., Baysal, H. (2018). Türkiye'de Dijital İnsan Kaynakları Yönetiminde Bulut Bilişim. *Süleyman Demirel Üniversitesi İktisadi ve İdari Bilimler Fakültesi Dergisi*, 23(4), 1409–1424.

idenfit.com (2021). *Dijital İK, İnsan Kaynaklarında Sosyal Medya Kullanımı* (22 Şubat 2021), Erişim adresi: https://idenfit.com/blog/insan-kaynaklarinda-sosyal-medya-kullanimi/. Accessed 5 July 2021.

Jain, S. (2017). *Is Artıfıcıal Intellıgence –The Next Bıg Thıng In Hr?*, International Conference on Innovative Research in Science Technology and Management Modi Institute of Management & Technolohy, Dadabari, Kota, Rajasthan.

Kıvrak, O. (2018). *The Effect of Chatbots and Augmented Reality on Marketing*, Icopec, 9. International Conference on Political Economy, Greece, 6–9 Eylül, 191–196.

Koç, M., Köroğlu, V. (2017). Stratejik Yönetim Açısından Taylorizm Prensiplerinin Zamanımıza Yansımaları.

Koçak, A. T. (2006). *Globalleşme Sürecinde İnsan Kaynakları Yönetiminde Değişimler*. İstanbul, Türkiye: İstanbul Üniversitesi.

Kubinaa, M., Varmusa, M., Kubinova, I. (2015). *Use of Big Data for Competitive Advantage of Company,* 4th World Conference on Business, Economics and Management, WCBEM, Procedia Economics and Finance. doi: http://dx.doi.org/10.1016/S2212-5671(15)00955-7. Accessed 22 June 2021.

Le Roux, Y. (2012). Privacy and Data Analytics, CA Technology Exchange: Insights from CA Technologies.

Malhotra, M. (2017). Digital transformation in HR. *International Journal of Interdisciplinary and Multidisciplinary Studies,* 4(3), 536–544.

Mucuk, İ. (2003). *Modern İşletmecililik.* İstanbul: Türkmen Kitabevi.

PwC *İnsan Kaynakları Liderlerinin Gündemi* (2021). pwc.com.tr/tr/Hizmetlerimiz/insan-yonetimi-ve-organizasyon-danismanligi/yayinlar/insan-kaynaklari-liderlerinin-gundemi-3.pdf

Sağır, G. (2018). *İşe Alım Süreçlerinde Yeni Bir Trend Sosyal Medya Hesapları.* Erişim tarihi: 15 Mart, 2018, http://blog.youthall.com/ise-alim-sureclerinde-yeni-bir-trend-sosyal- medya-hesaplari/. Accessed 22 June 2021.

Sivathanu, B., Pillai, R. (2018). *Smart HR 4.0 – how industry 4.0 is disrupting HR.* Human Resource Management International Digest.

Sözer, B. Ö. (2017). *İK'nın Geleceği Büyük Veride*, E-Haber, http://www.hurriyet.com.tr/ik-yeni-ekonomi/iknin-gelecegi-buyuk-veride-40423034 Erişim tarihi: 28.05.201.

Süral Özer, P., Eriş, E. D., Timurcanday Özmen, Ö. N. (2018). *Endüstri 4.0: İnsan ve insan kaynakları yönetimi neresinde?* 26. Ulusal Yönetim ve Organizasyon Kongresi, Karadeniz Teknik Üniversitesi-Trabzon: 765–770.

Stone, C. B., Neely, A. R. Lengnıck-Hall, M. L. (2018). *Human Resource Management İn The Digital Age: Big Data*, Hr Analytics and Artificial Intelligence, in Management and Technological Challenges in the Digital Age, 1. Bs., The USA: CRC Press.

Taş, H. (2020). *Sosyal Medyada İnsan Kaynakları Uygulamalarının Genel Görünümü: İnsan Kaynakları Profesyonelleri Üzerine Bir Araştırma*, Yüksek Lisans Tezi, Çanakkale Onsekiz Mart Üniversitesi Lisansüstü Eğitim Enstitüsü İşletme Anabilim Dalı, Çanakkale.

Taşkıran, A. (2017). Dijital çağda yükseköğretim. Yüksek Lisans Tezi, *Açıköğretim Uygulamaları ve Araştırmaları Dergisi* 3, 96–109.

The 2018 *Digital University: Staying relevant in the digital age* (2016). http://www.pwc.co.uk/assets/pdf/the-2018-digital-university-staying-relevant-in-thedigital-age.pdf Erişim Tarihi: 26.12.2016.

Vardarlıer, P. (2014). *İnsan Kaynakları Yönetiminde Sosyal Medyanın Rolü.* Beykent Üniversitesi Sosyal Bilimler Enstitüsü, Doktora Tezi, İstanbul.

Weng, W. H., Lin, W. T. (2014). Development trends and strategy planning in big data industry. *Contemporary Management Research*, 10(3), 203–214. doi: https://doi.org/10.7903/cmr.12288. Accessed 19 June 2021.

Yawalkar, V. V. (2019). Study of artificial intelligence and its role in human resource management. *International Journal of Research and Analytical Reviews* (IJRAR): 20 24.

Yılmaz, P. (2016). Sosyal Medyanın İnsan Kaynakları Yönetiminde İşe Alım Süreci Üzerindeki Etkisi. *ABMYO Dergisi*, 41, 35–50.

Yoder, D. (1972). *Personnel Management and Industrial Relations.* India: Prentice-Hall.

Zümrüt Hatun DEMİREL

Artificial Intelligence Applications in Human Resource Management

1. Introduction

Artificial intelligence is a technology that aims to augment human intelligence's methods of learning, reasoning, sensing, and critical thinking by using computer programs that are guided through the logic of algorithm (Stone, Neely and Lengnick, 2018: 37). New generation technologies, such as artificial intelligence, are creating a new wave of transformation in the business world. These technologies are transforming the face of applications in nearly every industry and business (Merlin and Jayam, 2018: 1894). Artificial intelligence (AI) is a technology that allows codes consisting of numbers 0 and 1 to analyze, solve problems, and make decisions like the human brain (Dilsizian and Siegel, 2014: 441). Artificial intelligence includes technologies such as robots, virtual reality, autonomous appliances, machine learning and data processing. Large enterprises, especially, are making significant investments in the use of these technologies (Tiftik, 2021: 376).

The business function most affected by these technological developments is human resource management. Human resource management is widely regarded as one of the most important assets of any organization. Managing this asset successfully is considered a very crucial management task (Devanna, Fombrun and Tichy, 1984: 34). Human resource management covers a wide range of and diverse tasks, such as employee procurement, evaluation of employee performance, managing and developing the employee's career, and paying for the employee's labor and effort (Strohmeier and Piazza, 2015: 150).

Artificial intelligence has been applied gradually in corporate decision-making processes in human resource management. It allowed human resource managers to accelerate their manually repetitive daily work, and therefore save time and costs (Kırılmaz, 2020: 189). Artificial intelligence has traditionally had a major impact in transforming the forms of recruitment, training, and development in human resource management. Moreover, by targeting employees who are considering leaving the organization with predictive methods, it has reduced the costs and difficulties associated with the turnover rate of workers (Iqbal, 2018: 103). It has been determined that artificial intelligence can be applied in six basic functions of human resource management (Jia, Guo, Li, Li, and Chen, 2018). In this chapter, how enterprises use artificial intelligence technology in their functions in human resource management, such as finding candidates, hiring, training and development, performance evaluation, career, and wage management, was investigated.

2. Artificial Intelligence Applications

When most people hear the concept of "artificial intelligence," the first thing that comes to mind is robots. This is due to the fact that big-budget Hollywood movies and novels feature stories about human-like machines that ravage the world (Bora and Borah, 2020: 435). However, artificial intelligence is the development of computers that will be included in human-specific thinking processes such as reasoning, learning, and self-correction (Smith et al., 1998: 28). Artificial intelligence refers to the simulation of human intelligence in machines programmed to think like humans and mimic their actions. In other words, it is defined as a machine that exhibits characteristics associated with the human mind, such as learning and problem solving (Frankenfield, 2021).

Alan Turing is considered a pioneer of machine intelligence as the scholar who made the first study on artificial intelligence. Turing described how human intelligence can be distinguished from machine intelligence using the "Turing Test" at the Dartmouth Conference in 1950. Turing not only laid the foundations for computer science, but also explored the philosophical aspects of artificial intelligence developments (Muggleton, 2014: 6). The first consideration of the concept of "artificial intelligence" in a full-scale project was in 1955 at Dartmouth Summer School with the research project of John McCarthy and his friends titled "A Proposal for the Dartmouth Summer Research Project on Artificial Intelligence". This study was based on the assumption that any form of learning or other intelligence characteristic might, in principle, be achieved by a machine that would simulate it (McCarthy, Minsky, Rochester, and Shannon, 2006: 12). In 1956, Newell, Simon, and Shaw, the engineers of IBM, developed the "General Problem Solver" program to prove that there were improvements in the resolution of a problem with intelligence other than human intelligence (James et al., 2017: 51)

The studies by Turing, McCarthy and other artificial intelligence pioneers laid the foundations for studies to be made on artificial intelligence in the middle of the twentieth century (Haton, 2006: 10). Researchers were looking for ways to model the functioning of the human brain and apply it to machines. With the development of semiconductor microprocessors and microchips and the spread of mass production of personal computers, the first artificial neural networks began to be created (McCarthy and Feigenbaum, 1990: 10).

In 1979, Jack Myers and Harry Pople, academics at the University of Pittsburg, developed the first knowledge-based software "Internist", based on their clinical experience. In 1980, the American Artificial Intelligence Association organized its first Artificial Intelligence Conference. In 1981, the innovations of the Japanese in fifth generation computers became one of the important developments in the field of artificial intelligence (Yücebalkan, 2019: 87). In 1997, an artificial intelligence robot called Deep Blue defeated Kasparov, the world chess champion (Rahimov, 2019: 6).

The most important development in the chronology of artificial intelligence is the development of the self-learning AlphaGo Assistant, developed in 2015 by DeepMind, a London-based AI company owned by Google (Makridakis, 2017: 51). Today, whether they are noticed by humans or not, artificial intelligence applications are used in many areas of life such as law, agriculture, military banking, automotive, music, communication, finance, journalism and health (Tiftik, 2021: 376; Göksungur, 2008: 104).

3. Artificial Intelligence Applications in Human Resource Management

Thanks to technological developments, industrial advances have brought along a new world order called the "Digital Revolution" or even the "Digital Age" (Yalçın, Yalçın and Adıgüzel, 2018: 7). Rapid changes in the new world order require faster decision-making. Situations such as forecasting supply and demand for labor force, employee qualifications and their development necessitate more data entry, hence, the storage of this data. Artificial intelligence further strengthens the analytical capabilities of the human resources system to provide more reference output in the decision-making process (Arora, 2020: 595). Artificial intelligence is used in all functions of human resource management, such as recruitment, employment, training and development, performance evaluation, career, and wage management.

3.1. Applications of Artificial Intelligence in Candidate Search Process

In the candidate search process, one of the important functions of human resources management, it is necessary to scan and examine the CVs transmitted to the organization by the candidates and to determine the suitable candidate for the job. Basic AI programs that can help employers in their human resource discovery and screening processes include filtering programs, automated social media scraping tools, and chatbots.

In the process of finding candidates, required criteria for the job, for example, experience, age, school and foreign language, are uploaded to the relevant program by human resources specialists. Then, the CVs from the candidates are scanned with filtering algorithms in accordance with predetermined criteria and lists are created (Chang, 2009: 253). Filtering programs are already being employed by global companies such as British Airways, Unilever, BBC, Ford Automotive (Tandon, Joshi, and Rastogi, 2017: 64).

In the next stage, the social media accounts of the candidates in the lists are checked with social media scraping tools. Social media scraping tools are able to collect large amounts of data through an applicant's social media profiles and use these data to predict certain behaviors, such as future participation levels (Ahmed, 2018: 972). Chatbots are used to pre-evaluate candidates who have passed both stages. Chatbots are a social platform that can communicate with the candidate 24/7 via chat, text message, Skype, or email (Kıvrak, 2018: 193). Chatbots communicate via text and help make the decision-making process of human resources more impartial (Eubanks, 2019: 104).

3.2. Artificial Intelligence Applications in Recruitment Process

Hiring people is one of the main functions of human resource management. Because the characteristics, competencies, values, and motivations of the candidates that should be compatible with the goals of the organization are determined at this stage. Through these elected persons, the organization achieves success (Jatoba et al., 2019: 98). By giving up manpower to recruit promising candidates, the use of machinery is a groundbreaking innovation in increasing the competition among organizations in the age of technology (Geetha and Reddy, 2018: 65).

Every recruitment process involves costs that are sometimes difficult to measure. It is quite a challenging task to compare the characteristics of a candidate from a large pool of applicants with the characteristics of existing successful employees in order to find the right candidate in a limited amount of time (McFadden, 2019). Artificial intelligence software rejects 75 % of inappropriate resumes after scanning and evaluating them (Bucland, 2014). Intelligent scanning software powered by artificial intelligence lists the strongest candidate or candidates by viewing the resume and analyzing the candidate's performance and turnover after determining his/her experience and skills. After that, the candidate or candidates in this list are taken to a digital interview. In the digital interview, the AI app evaluates the candidate's speech, word choice, body language via video and voice and analyzes the personality trait suitable for the job (Folick, 2016). Artificial intelligence helps human resource professionals find the perfect match for recruitment by using skills, knowledge, experience, and performance values and comparing them with intra-organization standards (Merlin and Jayam, 2018: 1893).

3.3. Artificial Intelligence Applications in Training and Development Process

In order for organizations to exist in a highly competitive environment driven by digitalization, their employees need to have the most up-to-date information (Premnath and Chully, 2019: 1195). In the training of employees in organizations, two methods are applied: on-the-job and off-the-job training (Şimşek and Öge, 2012: 262). Today, organizations have to structure both training methods based on technology, whether they use training on the job or off the job in instructing their employees (Demirkaya and Sarpel, 2018: 234).

E-learning platforms and robotic technologies are used in the training of employees. E-learning is defined as synchronous or asynchronous education published on the Internet, containing sound, images, and interactions (Baki et al., 2009: 86). Through using e-learning platforms, organizations provide personalized training to their employees by obtaining certain flexibilities in subjects such as time and space depending on the profiles of employees and the skills they want to have or develop, starting with the motto "learn wherever, whenever, whatever you want to learn" (Wright and Atkinson, 2019).

In addition to e-learning platforms, robot teachers are also used in trainings. Robot teachers are instructors who can behave like humans, recognize images and sounds. A robot teacher can train an average of four to seven employees (Kambur, 2020: 59). During the training process, the robot teacher uses the visual scanning system to observe each student's daily learning status and to provide education at different levels of stimulation through data analysis by accurately calculating the average values of the attention of all students. Robot teachers can adjust relaxation levels and learning rhythms according to student feedback (Oshima, Oshima and Miyake, 2012: 260). In addition, the big data analysis method is used in human resource management applications during the training process. Through big data analysis, a personalized training curriculum is created from the database containing extensive information which can comprehensively test and position the level of the employee with technical tools and encourage the employee with personalized courses (Merlin and Jayam, 2018: 1893).

3.4. Artificial Intelligence Applications in Performance Evaluation Process

The performance evaluation process is one of the most difficult and problematic processes of human resource management. For, when evaluating the performance of employees in the workplace, managers can make mistakes such as evaluating everyone the same, mixing performance with the potential to favor employees whom they love and who think the same as themselves (Merlin and Jayam, 2018: 1893).

The AI application provides a detailed assessment of the employee using data such as the pre-measured performance values of the employee, the trainings he has received before and the results of the exams carried out during these trainings, the projects involving the employee, the way he does business and his experiences (Otley, 1999: 365). As a result of this evaluation, a performance value for each employee is assigned. In addition, if desired, the system also evaluates individual performance targets, department manager score, personal score, precedent score, and customer score for each employee separately (Jia et al., 2018: 111).

With the help of artificial intelligence, decision makers can recommend that training programs be organized for the deficiencies observed in performance indicators (Malik, Ikram, Batool and Aslam, 2018: 746). Human resource experts can use artificial intelligence assistants to determine the level of loyalty of employees to the organization and the employees who tend to quit their jobs in the organization. However, they can also find the reasons why organizations have high turnover rates (He, 2019).

3.5. Artificial Intelligence Applications in Career Management Process

In the career management process, the application of artificial intelligence uses big data to perform activities such as improving the skills of employees and determining the promotions of employees. Accordingly, it makes predictions for the future using past data of the employee (Wang and Lin, 2018: 516). The AI application analyzes real-time photos, videos, and audio recordings of employees in the talent development process, helping human resource management both in identifying the skills missing from existing employees and in creating the employee profile with the qualifications that will be needed in the future (McGovern et al., 2018: 4).

The first company to use artificial intelligence in the talent development process is the technology company IBM. They identify the skills needed in their industry with an application called Talent Framework that they have developed (Eubanks, 2019: 88). Employees are then sorted according to their skills. In the latest stage, recommendations are presented to ensure that employees acquire those skills by comparing the current skills of the employees with the skills that the organization will need in the future (Sumser, 2019: 56).

The application of artificial intelligence guides human resource management in making promotion decisions in the organization. Artificial Intelligence controls the performance evaluation results of employees and performs data verification. In data verification, the skills which are not included in the CV sent to the organization in the job application process, but which the employee has acquired in the organization and the skills he/she has gained on the job, are discovered. With the revelation of these skills, the most suitable candidate or candidates for promotion are determined. These candidate(s) are notified to human resource managers and the final decision in determining the candidate to be promoted is left to the human resource manager (Kolah, 2015: 17).

3.6. Artificial Intelligence Applications in Wage Management Process

Wage management is a dynamic system that determines, assigns, and adjusts employee remuneration principles, strategies, levels, structures and factors under organizational development guidance (Henderson, 2003: 76). In wage management, it is necessary to coordinate data including all information contained in the resumes of employees, results of tests applied to the employee during the recruitment process, training received by the employee during the training process and their impact on the performance of these trainings, talents, and skills of the employee (Tomar, 2015: 49). All these data are evaluated as a whole by using the algorithmic and automated artificial intelligence in wage management. Apart from these data, the employee's salary is calculated after the employee's performance evaluation feedback is added to the artificial intelligence database (Goldfarb Taska and Teodoridis 2020: 402).

Artificial intelligence is used to analyze the individual differences of employees, the environment in which the organization is located and external factors to create indicators of different angles and different levels, and to create individualized, targeted, and fair wage prices according to the actual performance of employees (Wang and Lin, 2018: 516).

4. Conclusion

Technological advances have revealed changes in parallel with artificial intelligence applications in human resource management. Job descriptions that are valid by traditional and manual methods have been replaced by a completely new operation. AI is used in human resource management functions such as the use of AI robots in recruitment and the hiring process, regulation of routine work in digital environments including leave, payroll, reports, pursuing trainings on e-learning platforms, and conducting of salary and career management through the analysis of big data by robots. These applications speed up the operation, saving time and cost. It also positively affects the loyalty of employees, as it allows them to manage processes more impartially and fairly. Moreover, since operational work in human resource management is done faster and in a shorter amount of time in digital environments, artificial intelligence allows human resource workers to focus on issues such as improvement, problem determination, prediction and diagnostic processes, trend, and environmental analysis, which are more strategic for the organization.

References

Ahmed, O. (2018). Artificial Intelligence in HR. *International Journal of Research and Analytical Reviews*, 5(4), 971–978.

Arora, S. (2020). Revamping Human Resources with Artificial Intelligence. *IJRAR*, 7(1), 595–600.

Baki, A., Karal, H., Çebi, A., Şılbır, L. ve Pekşen, M. (2009). Uzaktan Eğitimde Öğretim Yönetim Sistemi ve Senkron Eğitim Platformu Tasarım Süreci: KTÜ Örneği. *Turkish Journal Of Computer and Mathematics Education.* Cilt:1 Sayı:1. 85–101.

Bora, K. ve Borah, U. (2020). A Study on the Application of Artificial Intelligence in Human Resource Management. *Journal of Interdisciplinary Cycle Research,* 12(7), 434–450.

Buckland, M. (2014 August 14). *Fun Facts About Resumes, Interviews & Social Recruitment.* https://www.business2community.com/human-resources/25-fun-facts-resumes-interviews-socialrecruitment-0975676 (Erişim tarihi 07.02.2021).

Chang, H. Y. (2009). Employee Turnover: A Novel Prediction Solution with Effective Feature Selection. *WSEAS Transactions on Information Science and Applications*, 6(3), 252–256.

Demirkaya, H. ve Sarpel, E. (2018). Eğitim ve Geliştirme Uygulamalarında Yeni Nesil Bilişim Teknolojilerinden Sanal Gerçeklik, Bulut Bilişim Ve Yapay Zekâ. *Karadeniz Uluslararası Bilimsel Dergi*, 40, Winter-2018, 231–245.

Devanna, M. A., Fombrun, C. J., and Tichy, N. (1984). A Framework for Strategic Human Resource Management. In: Fombrun, C. J., Tichy, N., Devanna, M. A. (eds.), *Strategic Human Resource Management* (pp. 33–51). New York: Wiley.

Dilsizian, S. E. ve Siegel, E. L. (2014). Artificial Intelligence in Medicine and Cardiac İmaging: Harnessing Big Data and Advanced Computing to Provide Personalized Medical Diagnosis and Treatment. *Current Cardiology Reports*, 16(1), 441.

Eubanks, B. (2019). *Artificial Intelligence for HR Use AI to Support and Develop a Successful Workforce*. The USA: Kogan Press.

Frankenfield, J. (2021 March 8). What Is Artificial Intelligence (AI)? https:/www.investopedia.com/terms/a/artificial-intelligence ai.asp#:~:text=Artificial%20intelligence%20(AI)%20refers%20to,as%20learning%20and%20problem-solving. (Erişim Tarihi 12.03.2021).

Folick, O. (2016, October 17). *AI for Recruiting: A Definitive Guide for HR Professionals*. https://ideal.com/ai-recruiting/ (Erişim Tarihi 02.03.2021).

Geetha, R., and Reddy, B. S. D. (2018). Recruıtment Through Artıfıcıal Intellıgence: A Conceptual Study. *International Journal of Mechanical Engineering and Technology (IJMET)*, 9(7), 63–70.

Göksungur, A. E. (2008). *Stok Kontrolünde Yapay Zekâ Kavramı ve Bir Uygulama*, Yayınlanmamış Doktora Tezi, Marmara Üniversitesi, Sosyal Bilimler Enstitüsü, İstanbul.

Goldfarb, A., Taska, B. ve Teodorıdıs, F. (2020). Artificial Intelligence in Health Care? Evidence from Online Job Postings. *In AEA Papers and Proceedings*, 110(11), 400–404.

Haton, J. P. (2006). A Brief İntroduction to Artificial İntelligence. *IFAC Proceedings Volumes*, 39(4), 8–16.

He, E. (2019, April 3). *The Advantages of Re-Humanizing HR with Artificial Intelligence*. https://www.hrtechnologist.com/articles/digital-transformation/the-advantages-of-rehumanizing-hrwith-artificial-intelligence/ (Erişim tarihi 02.02.2021).

Henderson, R. I. (2003). *Compensation Management in a Knowledge-Based World* (10th ed.). New Jersey, MA: Prentice Hall.

Iqbal, F. (2018). Can Artificial Intelligence Change the Way in Which Companies Recruit, Train, Develop and Manage Human Resources in Workplace? *Asian Journal of Social Sciences and Management Studies,* 5(3), 102–104.

James, C., James, B., Miner, N., Vineyard, C., Rothganger, F., Carlson, K., Mulder, S., Draelos, T., Faust, A., Marinella, M., Naegle, J., and Plimpton, S. (2017). A Historical Survey of Algorithms and Hardware Architectures for Neural-İnspired and Neuromorphic Computing Applications. *Biologically Inspired Cognitive Architectures,* 19, 49–64.

Jatoba, M.,Santos, J., Gutierriz, I., Moscon, D., Fernandes, P. O. ve Teixeeira, P. (2019). Evolution of Artificial Intelligence Research in Human Resources. *Procedia Computer Science,* 164(2019), 137–142.

Jıa, Q., Guo, Y., Lı, R., Lı, Y. ve Chen, Y. (2018). A Conceptual Artificial Intelligence Application Framework in Human Resource Management. *International Conference on Electronic Business (ICEB) Proceedings,* New Castle, 8–12 Aralık, 106–114.

Kambur, E. (2020). *Yapay Zekânın İnsan Kaynakları Süreçlerinde Yaratabileceği Değişiklikler ve Algılanma Düzeyleri.* Doktora Tezi, Bandırma Onyedi Eylül Üniversitesi, Sosyal Bilimler Enstitüsü, İşletme Anabilim Dalı, Balıkesir.

Kırılmaz, S. K. (2020). Dıgıtal Transformatıon in Human Resources Management: Investıgatıon of Dıgıtal HRM Practıces of Busınesses. *Research Journal of Business and Management (RJBM),* V.7(3), 188–200.

Kıvrak, O. (2018). "The Effect of Chatbots and Augmented Reality on Marketing", *ICOPEC, 9. International Conference on Political Economy, Greece*, 6–9 Eylül, ss. 191–196.

Kolah, A. (2015). *Improving the Performance of Sponsorship,* 1st ed. England: Taylor&Francis Group and Information Business Press.

Makridakis, S. (2017). The forthcoming Artificial Intelligence (AI) Revolution: Its Impact on Society and Firms. *Futures,* 90, 46–60.

Malık, M., Ikram, A., Batool, S. N. ve Aslam, W. (2018). "A Performance Assessment of Rose Plant Classification Using Machine Learning". In *International Conference on Intelligent Technologies and Applications,* Singapore, 5–9 Ekim, ss. 745–756.

McCarthy, J. ve Feigenbaum, E. (1990). Arthur Samuel: Pioneer in Machine Learning. *AI Magazine,* 11(3), 10–11.

McCarthy, J., Minsky, M. L., Rochester, N., and Shannon, C. E. (2006). A Proposal for the Dartmouth Summer Research Project on Artificial Intelligence. *AI Magazine,* 27(4), 12–14.

McFadden, C. (2019, August 20). *7 Ways AI Is Helping Revolutionize the Recruitment Industry.* https://interestingengineering.com/7-amazing-ways-companies-use-ai-to-recruit-employees (Erişim Tarihi 12.02.2021).

McGovern, S. L., Pandey, V., Gill, S., Aldrich, T., Myers, C., Desai, C. ve Balasubramanian, V. (2018). *The New Age: Artificial Intelligence for Human Resource Opportunities and Functions*. London: Ernst&Young Press.

Merlin, R. P. and Jayam, R. (2018). Artificial Intelligence in Human Resource Management. *International Journal of Pure and Applied Mathematics,* 119(17), 1891–1895.

Muggleton, S. (2014). Alan Turing and the Development of Artificial Intelligence. *AI Communications,* 27(1), 3–10.

Oshima, J, Oshima, R, ve Miyake, N. (2012). *Collaborative Reading Comprehension with Communication Robots as Learning Partners.* In Proceedings of International Conference of the Learning Sciences (pp.). ICLS, Sydney, Australia, July 2–6, 256–267.

Otley, D. (1999). Performance Management: A Framework for Management Control Systems Research. *Management Accounting Research*, 10(4), 363–382.

Premnath, S. N. and Chully, A. A. (2019). A Qualitative Study of Artificial Intelligence Application Framework in Human Resource Management. *Journal of Xi'an University of Architecture & Technology,* XI(XII), 1193–1209.

Rahimov, F. (2019). *Artıfıcıal Intellıgence (AI) Integratıon in Busıness Envıronment and Processes: Perceptıon Among Managers in Turkey*. Master's Thesis. Dokuz Eylül Unıversıty, Graduate School of Socıal Scıences, Department of Busıness Admınıstratıon (Englısh), Busıness Admınıstratıon (Englısh) Program, İzmir.

Smith, S.S., Morris, W.and Voorheis, R.W. (1988), *The New International Webster's Comprehensive Dictionary of the English Language: Encyclopedic Edition*, Naples, Trident Press International.

Şimşek, M. Ş. ve Öge, H. S. (2012). *İnsan Kaynakları Yönetimi.* Konya: Eğitim Akademi Yayınları.

Stone, C. B., Neely, A. R. ve Lengnıck-Hall, M. L. (2018). *Human Resource Management in the Digital Age: Big Data, HR Analytics and Artificial Intelligence, in Management and Technological Challenges in the Digital Age,* 1. bs. The USA: CRC Press.

Strohmeier, S.ve Piazza, F. (2015). Artificial Intelligence Techniques in Human Resource Management—A Conceptual Exploration. In C. Kahraman and S. Çevik Onar (eds.), *Intelligent Techniques in Engineering Management,* Intelligent Systems Reference Library Volume 87, pp. 149–172. DOI 10.1007/978-3-319-17906-3_7.

Sumser, J. (2019). *Into the Maze: An Introduction to Intelligent Tools in HRTechnology.* The USA: Hrexamıner Press.

Tandon, L. S., Joshı, P. ve Rastogı, R. K. (2017). Understanding the Scope of Artificial Intelligence in Human Resource Management Process: A Theoretical Perspective. *IJBARR*, 1(19), 62–66.

Tiftik, C. (2021). İnsan Kaynakları Yönetiminde Yapay Zekâ Uygulamaları. *IBAD Sosyal Bilimler Dergisi*, 9, 374–390.

Tomar, J. S. (2015). Business Intelligence: Achieving Fineness through Data, Text and Web Mining. *International Journal of Computer Applications*, 128(12), 46–52.

Wang, T. ve Lin, J. (2018). Research on the Influence of Artificial Intelligence on Human Resource Management Teaching and Work. *2018 International Conference on Humanities and Advanced Education Technology* (ICHAET 2018), pp. 512–517.

Wright, J. ve Atkinson, D. (2019). *The impact of artificial intelligence within the recruitment industry: Defining a new way of recruiting.* https://www.cfsearch.com/wpcontent/uploads/2019/10/ Erişim Tarihi 02.02.2021.

Yalçın, N., Yalçın, A. M. ve Adıgüzel, B. F. (2018). Developıng a Software for Increasıng Readıng Rate and Effectıve Readıng Comprehensıon: Read Fast Enhancememory. *International Women Online Journal of Distance Education*, 7(4), 1–43.

Yücebalkan, B. (2019). *The Hıstory of the Artıfıcıal Intellıgenceas an Alternatıve Workforce and the Possıble Opportunıtıes/Threats for Its Future* (Business and Management, Editör Sefer YILMAZ, pp. 83–99), Ankara: Akademisyen Kitabevi.

Volkan TEMİZKAN & Abdülkadir ÖZTÜRK

Digital Public Relations as a Marketing Communication Tool: Examining Five Brands with High Interaction on Facebook

1. Introduction

The development of PR is closely related to technological advances. Along with the Internet, it has changed how PR practitioners distribute information, interact with target audiences, deal with crises and manage problems. Especially the creation of YouTube and Facebook between 2004 and 2006, Twitter in 2007, and Instagram in 2010 accelerated the digitalisation of PR (Huang et al., 2017). Digital communication tools have increased interaction and mutual dialogue relations by overcoming the limitations of time and space. Thus, the Internet has revealed the concepts of digital public relations, new public relations, P.R. 2.0, and E-PR (Kent, 2013). Today, an increasing number of PR practitioners see websites and social networks as practical tools to communicate with stakeholders (Guillory & Sundar, 2014). According to a survey study with 283 PR practitioners, Eyrich et al. (2008) reported that an average participant uses 5.98 different social media blogs such as social networks. The results of similar empirical studies have also revealed that PR activities carried out through the website and social networks are essential in maintaining direct interaction and positive relations with the target audience (Guillory & Sundar, 2014; Rybalko & Seltzer, 2010). Digital public relations, which has become a necessity for businesses, allow businesses to express themselves to more people and instantly perceive the target audience's wishes.

Businesses can reach audiences that are very difficult to reach through different platforms on the Internet. In this context, digital public relations is carried out through the following tools (Gifford, 2010: 63):

- corporate blogs
- online press releases
- search engine optimisation
- corporate website
- social media management (Facebook, Twitter, Instagram, LinkedIn, YouTube)
- relationships with online communities
- forums
- other areas (wikis, podcasting, email, mobile phones, fax)

Digital public relations involves disseminating information via the Internet to inform stakeholders about an organisation's services or updates to those services (Huang et al., 2017: 1366). It is crucial to announce corporate identity and build trust with more audiences on the Internet. Thus, the business will emphasise certain aspects or achievements to its target audience. In addition, while marketing public relations activities establish strong ties with customers, a positive contribution is made to customer attitudes and business reputation (Khang et al., 2012). Public relations for marketing purposes plays an essential role in the integrated marketing communication efforts of organisations. This situation is associated with the support of brands or product sales (De Pelsmacker et al., 2001).

2. Conceptual Framework

2.1. Public Relations in Marketing Communications

Communication refers to the message intended to be conveyed to the target audience in different communication media and tools. The message is for persuading the target audience by obtaining information regarding the message subject, in other words, the audience's perception is tried to be controlled (İlter, 2017: 65).

The marketing communication process includes all 4Ps (product, price, promotion, and place), which are marketing components. Consumer expectations are the determinants of the product to be produced in this process and the medium that will mediate the communication. Therefore, all product elements such as design, packaging, price, promotion efforts, distribution, and brand are communicated with the consumer (Odabaşı & Oyman 2005: 36). According to Elden et al. (2005: 33), it is precious for businesses to create a loyal customer group who is always willing to buy the product, communicates with the brand, and trusts the brand.

Public relations is the interpretation and communication of information and ideas provided to an organisation's target audience. In other words, it can be considered as an effort to interpret ideas, opinions, and information of the target audience towards the organisation and develop mutual communication. As can be seen in this definition, the emphasis is on constantly considering the target audience's views and establishing a two-way communication to ensure harmony (Grunig & Hunt, 1984: 42). Today, communication is mainly made through websites, blogs, or social media together with the Internet. When businesses launch a new product or experience a crisis, they implement digital PR campaigns. In this respect, businesses use digital PR to reach a large number of people in order to protect themselves from the effects of malicious channels that want to spoil the brand image or damage the brand's reputation with a smear campaign.

There should be credibility, clarity, continuity, and consistency in public relations communication. Thus, businesses will reach their desired goals through public relations activities such as increasing recognition, improving relations, informing, creating preferences, creating an image, increasing reliability, educating consumers, and creating sympathy (Guillory & Sundar, 2014).

2.2. Digital Public Relations

As an applied management and communication discipline, public relations has been heavily influenced by information and communication technologies (ICTS), especially in recent years. The Internet makes it possible for people who cannot communicate (Brown, 2009).

According to statistics, people spend most of their time in front of the screen (such as TV, mobile phone, computer) (Lin et al., 2020: 583). In particular, people's use of various social media platforms and spending time have made social media a vital communication channel for businesses in reaching them. Businesses that have discovered the power of social media use the power of these platforms to communicate with their target audience (Huang et al., 2017).

One-way communication channels such as television or newspaper have been replaced by social media platforms, where there are instant and mutual communication. In these platforms, people can express their feelings and thoughts in the face of events and situations, and a familiar voice of the majority can be formed (Brown, 2009). While the ratings of TV channels or the circulation of newspapers were determinative in the past, today, the number of followers is decisive. However, social media platforms are also open to manipulations. Only events and situations that have a place in the public conscience can find their actual value (Duhé, 2007). Especially during the pandemic period, opportunistic businesses that watch for people's hard times were disclosed via social media, and many people were informed of the situation. People punish businesses very quickly over social media, and they also make their judgments with the public conscience by rewarding them very quickly. Companies that produce or donate respirators during the pandemic period have become imprinted on people's minds, making them popular.

Institutions or businesses can be remembered with a photo frame or 140 characters shared on social media. For this reason, businesses should design their digital marketing strategies with a well-thought-out setup. Businesses must analyse both social media and consumer behaviour dynamics well (Wright and Hinson, 2017).

Digital PR, which includes all the processes of traditional PR, is much more effective in meeting changing consumer expectations, needs, and purchasing habits. Today's market conditions use the necessary platforms to reach the current and potential target audience. It is thought that the most effective digital PR methods are social networks (Grunig, 2009). The unique rules of social networks require brands to make their presence visible and influential in this area. It has been determined that the target audience exposed to online information has high interaction. For this reason, public relations efforts carried out through social networks affect the target audience more (Painter, 2015: 802).

The Internet providing a suitable environment for interactive communication has made digital platforms of great importance. Digital PR management has become mandatory during the increasing competition. Research shows that many people use social media to access information or follow the news (Wright & Hinson, 2017: 1). Now everyone shares their positive/negative experiences with others, primarily through social media platforms. A positive/negative news about businesses can also reach millions very quickly and low cost with social media posts.

Social media and the corporate website of the enterprise are very effective in sending messages to the target audience. Since public relations means reputation management, businesses should design the content on their web pages for this purpose (Brown, 2009: 149). In this respect, most public relations areas such as social responsibility, crisis management, sponsorship, reputation management, marketing communication can be carried out in digital environments.

3. Method

3.1. Purpose and Scope of the Research

Social networks, which are an essential element of digital public relations, announcing the news about the business to the target audience and the public, expressing opinions on various issues, establishing communication and relations, creating a perception and image, gaining new customers, creating attitude and awareness towards the brand, building goodwill, supporting campaigns, crisis and corporate reputation management can be used for many different purposes, such as realising corporate social responsibility communication (Ezeah, 2005: 138). This study examines the strategies that increase the interaction of brands that apply social media interaction intensively in their social network (Facebook) shares and the main goals behind these shares.

Interaction enables the client's secret wishes, interests, and concerns to be revealed and understood (Doğan & Öze, 2018). Statistics such as comments, likes, shares, and the number of followers on the shares made by the brand for digital marketing, marketing communication, and PR purposes are seen as some of the success indicators of interaction (Quesenberry and Coolsen, 2019). For this purpose, the data were evaluated based on public relations for marketing purposes, taking into account the interaction between the business and the target audience.

3.2. Sample of the Study and Data Collection Process

The research universe consists of the 100 most successful brands on Facebook, which is included in the SocialBrands top 100 list, followed by consumers in Turkey, covering the period 1–31 May 2021 of the social media brand index SocialBrands. Based on the scores prepared by SocialBrands, five brands determined to have successful Facebook accounts constitute the research sample. The Facebook accounts of these brands were examined, and the shares they made were analysed by the content analysis method between 1 and 31 May 2021.

Content analysis, which is a qualitative analysis method, is a systematic, unbiased and numerical analysis to measure the variables in a text (Wimmer and Dominick, 2000, pp. 135–136). In this study, content analysis was carried out according to the criteria Wilcox and Cameron (2006) call public relations objectives. These criteria are raising awareness, informing, educating, providing understanding, building trust, establishing friendships, giving people reasons to buy.

3.3. Data Collection Tools

Focusing on the performance of brands for the period between 1 and 31 May 2021, SocialBrands statistically analysed 603,309 messages on 18,961 pages on Facebook, 1,093,715 Tweets shared by 14,161 accounts on Twitter, and 494.956 messages shared by 24,620 accounts on Instagram, which accounts for 2 million 191,980 content by 57,742 different social media accounts. SocialBrands has compiled dozens of different publicly available performance data such as followers on all accounts and pages, increase in followers, page structure, page information, all messages shared throughout the month, message types, likes, comments, shares, retweets, interaction rate per message, hashtags, mentions, and comparative status in the sector (SocialBrands, 2021). According to the data, five brands determined to have successful interaction on Facebook are listed in Table 1, and they were subjected to content analysis according to the criteria. As an ethical concern, brand names were not specified, and codes were given in alphabetical order.

Table 1. Brands with successful Facebook accounts

Channel	Brand	Main Sector	Sub Sector	Follower	Interaction	Social Score
Facebook	A	Durable Consumption	Home and Decoration	1.621.777	304.477	88
Facebook	B	Automotive	Producers	4.397.578	395.976	88
Facebook	C	Durable Consumption	Furniture	270.371	198.139	85
Facebook	D	Durable Consumption	Furniture	420.761	129.584	82
Facebook	E	Fast Moving Consumer Goods	Pet	183.391	83.096	82

Source: https://www.boomsocial.com/Social-Brands/2021/June/Facebook

4. Analysis of Data

Table 2 shows the data of the draw organized by five successful businesses with Facebook accounts between 1 and 31 May.

Table 2. Information on the gift draw organized by brands on Facebook between 1 and 31 May

Actions	A	B	C	D	E
Last Gift	Cup set	No	Floor lamp	Single seat	Dog food
Request likes and comments	Yes	No	Yes	Yes	Yes
Condition to follow the page	Yes	No	Yes	Yes	Yes
Request hashtags	Yes	No	Yes	Yes	yok
Product image	Yes	No	Yes	Yes	Yes
Tagging friends	No	No	No	Yes	Yes
Request sharing	No	No	No	No	No
Number of comments	7.600	No	15.000	2.000	36
Number of shares	181	No	44	85	19
Number of likes	5.000	No	5.000	4.300	2.500
Number of draws	2	No	3	1	1
Customer question answer rate	100 %	No	100 %	100 %	100 %

** Brand A announced its draws on Facebook but directed its users to their Instagram and Twitter accounts for participation.*

According to these data, it is seen that brand B did not organise a gift draw in May. It was observed that brand C organised three gift draws in May. With these gift draws, when compared to brand A, which has six times more followers than brand C, it is seen that it is successful in terms of the number of comments. According to the number of followers, the number of likes received by brand E shows high interaction with its followers.

Table 3. Information on shares of brands on Facebook between 1 and 31 May

Actions	A	B	C	D	E
Redirect to corporate site	Yes	Yes	Yes	Yes	Yes
Product promotion	33	18	37	34	9
Campaign announcement	19	0	25	30	0
Likes	317.215	15.756	135.474	125.008	79.200
Comments	11.535	619	54.729	4.273	1.497
Sharing	3.960	208	1.530	910	1.679
Number of shares per day	1,2	0,6	1,66	1,53	0,7
Number of videos	5	3	16	8	0
New product promotion	Yes	Yes	Yes	Yes	Yes
Special day and holiday celebration	Yes	No	Yes	Yes	Yes

From the data in Table 3, it is understood that brand E has the highest rate of sharing brand posts according to the number of followers. This situation can be interpreted as the fact that brand E sells pet food, sharing pets in its images, and making exciting campaigns, which is considered worthy of being shared by animal lover followers.

The shares of the companies that make up the sample on Facebook are analysed in Table 4 with content analysis in line with Wilcox and Cameron's (2006) public relations goals.

Table 4. Content analysis of the sample according to Wilcox and Cameron public relations goals variables

Variables	A	B	C	D	E
Increase awareness	ok	ok	ok	ok	ok
Informing the consumer	ok	ok	ok	ok	ok
Educating the consumer	ok	ok	ok	ok	ok
Providing understanding	ok	ok	ok	ok	ok
Building trust	ok	ok	ok	ok	ok
Making friends	ok	ok	ok	ok	ok
Giving people reasons to buy	ok	ok	ok	ok	ok

Businesses' award practices emphasise their style, adopting a particular slogan, having values that they attach importance to, sharing product and price information transparently, and acting with a sense of us creating trust between people and businesses. Information and awareness can be provided through product promotions. Sometimes, messages written in a friendly and sincere language from daily life instead of corporate concepts are thought to strengthen the relationship with the consumer. Sharing in this direction offer people a reason to buy the products of the business.

The activities of the brands making up the sample on Instagram and Twitter are also examined in Table 5.

Table 5. Information on shares of brands on Instagram and Twitter between 1 and 31 May

Actions	A		B		C		D		E	
	Instag.	Twit.	Instag.	Twit.	Instag.	Twit.	Instag.	Twit.	Instag.	Twit.
Corporate website link	Yes	Yes	Yes	Yes	Yes	Yes	Yes	Yes	Yes	Yes
Product promotion	33	33	20	18	31	31	34	34	14	13
Campaign announcement	19	16	0	0	26	29	30	27	0	0
Likes	716.252	5813	43.232	331	300.789	9494	260.425	3463	11.016	638
Comments	85.542	6464	981	47	3583	4562	21.804	2201	11.112	737
Retweet	-	1382	-	20	-	3227	-	1626	-	265
Number of shares per day	1,29	1,25	0.64	0.61	1,48	1.87	1,48	1,58	0,77	1,1
Number of videos	5	6	3	3	12	13	8	9	Yok	0

Table 5. Continued

Actions	A		B		C		D		E	
New product promotion	Yes	Yes	Yes	Yes	Yes	Yes	Yes	Yes	Yes	Yes
Special day and holiday celebration	Yes	Yes	No	No	Yes	Yes	Yes	Yes	Yes	Yes
Number of draws	3	2	0	0	0	2	1	1	1	1
Number of followers	2.908.897	79.965	202.353	50.241	308.426	20.199	187.499	42.833	27.834	4.874

Tables 3 and 5 show that all businesses provide links to their corporate sites on their Facebook, Instagram, and Twitter accounts, promote products, do not exceed two posts per day, and promote new products. Brands B and E do not announce their campaigns on any of their social media accounts. In addition to these, brand B does not organize the draw and does not share about special days and holidays. Brand E does not share videos. Regarding the number of followers, most comments were made on the Instagram account of Brand E. As draws require followers to like and comment on the brand's campaign and tag their friends, this results in high interactions between social media users.

5. Conclusion and Recommendations

Contests, giveaways, and games organised on social networks ensure that followers stay in touch. As seen in the research results, even the small gifts given in the draws cause significant interactions while increasing the number of followers. More importantly, it is essential in terms of interaction that brands respond to consumer questions through social networks appropriately and practically. It is imperative to create the "feeling that I can communicate with this brand" to the follower by providing instant and fast feedback to incoming questions or comments. In addition, it is thought that sharing effective, short, and remarkable video content at certain intervals will increase the interaction.

Today, almost every business has a corporate website. It is recommended that corporate websites have high interaction and user-friendly content that will reflect business images. Along with corporate websites, digital marketing and public relations studies should be carried out with social networks. Thus, social networks can contribute to brand images with instant communication and interaction. Ensuring awareness, recognition and loyalty of people to a brand can be achieved using social media effectively.

Digital public relations is more interactive, fast, flexible, low-cost, strategic, and result-oriented than traditional public relations activities. Consumers who can access social networks from any screen connected to the Internet (e.g., YouTube is watched heavily on smart TVs) spend much time in these channels. Realising that consumers were gathered and spending time in these networks, brands have started to perform their public relations management through these platforms. Social media plays a vital role for businesses that want to increase or renew their brand and corporate image. In addition, it plays a vital role in protecting businesses against those who want to spoil the brand image or damage the brand's reputation.

Consumers can easily access much information about products and businesses. Just as people are now looking for information in the digital environment, businesses also need to express themselves by taking part in digital environments.

Regarding digital public relations, it is thought that it has become an important management strategy that yields profit from its impact on customer loyalty, awareness, recognition, corporate image, and online corporate reputation management.

In future studies, the shares and interactions of brands on social responsibility and sponsorship activities from their social media accounts can be examined. Finally, the social media shares of some brands, whose reputation has been shaken, about crisis and reputation management can be analysed.

References

BoomSocial. (2021). *Social Media Brand Index, Brands Top 100 List*. Retrieved from https://www.boomsocial.com/SocialBrands/2021/Haziran/Facebook (accessed June 9, 2021).

Brown, R. (2009). *Public Relations and the Social Web: How to Use Social Media and Web 2.0 in Communications*. London: Kogan Page.

De Pelsmacker, P., Geuens, M., Van Den Bergh, J., & Van Winkel, K. (2001). *Marketing Communications: Teacher's Manual*. New York: Financial Times/ Prentice Hall.

Doğan, E., & Öze, N. (2018). *Issues in Communication Media & Public Relations*. London: IJOPEC Publication.

Duhé, S. C. (2007). *New Media and Public Relations*. New York: Peter Lang.

Elden, M., Ulukök, Ö., & Yeygel, S. (2005). *Şimdi Reklamlar*, İletişim Yayınları, İstanbul. (Now Ads, İletişim Publications, Istanbul).

Eyrich, N., Padman, M. L., & Sweetser, K. D. (2008). PR practitioners' use of social media tools and communication technology. *Public Relations Review*, *34*(4), 412–414.

Ezeah, G. H. (2005). Digital public relations: A new strategy in corporate management. *Nsukka Journal of the Humanities*, *15*, 135–143.

Gifford, J. (2010). Digital public relations: E-marketing's big secret. *Continuing Higher Ed*ucation Review, *74*, 62–72.

Grunig, J., & Hunt, T. (1984). *Managing Public Relations*. New York: Holt, Rinehart & Winston.

Grunig, J. E. (2009). Paradigms of global public relations in an age of digitalisation. *PRism*, *6*(2), 1–19.

Guillory, J. E., & Sundar, S. S. (2014). How does web site interactivity affect our perceptions of an organization?. *Journal of Public Relations Research*, *26*(1), 44–61.

Huang, Y. H. C., Wu, F., & Huang, Q. (2017). Does research on digital public relations indicate a paradigm shift? An analysis and critique of recent trends. *Telematics and informatics*, *34*(7), 1364–1376.

İlter, B. (2017). Girişimcilik faaliyetlerinde pazarlama iletişim çabalarının etkisi. *Girişimcilik ve Kalkınma Dergisi, 12*(2), 65–74 (The effect of marketing communication efforts on entrepreneurial activities. *Journal of Entrepreneurship and Development*, *12*(2), 65–74).

Kent, M. L. (2013). Using social media dialogically: Public relations role in reviving democracy. *Public Relations Review*, *39*(4), 337–345.

Khang, H., Ki, E. J., & Ye, L. (2012). Social media research in advertising, communication, marketing, and public relations, 1997–2010. *Journalism & Mass Communication Quarterly*, *89*(2), 279–298.

Lin, T. T., Kononova, A., & Chiang, Y. H. (2020). Screen addiction and media multitasking among American and Taiwanese users. *Journal of Computer Information Systems*, *60*(6), 583–592.

Odabaşı, Y., & Oyman, M. (2005). *Pazarlama İletişimi Yönetimi*, Mediacat Yayınları, Eskişehir. (Marketing Communication Management, Mediacat Publications, Eskisehir.)

Painter, D. L. (2015). Online political public relations and trust: Source and interactivity effects in the 2012 US presidential campaign. *Public Relations Review*, *41*(5), 801–808.

Quesenberry, K. A., & Coolsen, M. K. (2019). What makes Facebook brand posts engaging? A content analysis of Facebook brand post text that increases shares, likes, and comments to influence organic viral reach. *Journal of Current Issues & Research in Advertising, 40*(3), 229–244.

Rybalko, S., & Seltzer, T. (2010). Dialogic communication in 140 characters or less: How Fortune 500 companies engage stakeholders using Twitter. *Public relations review, 36*(4), 336–341.

SocialBrands. (2021). *How did we measure?*. Retrieved from https://www.boomsocial.com/Social-Brands (accessed June 11, 2021).

Wilcox, L. D. ve Cameron, G. T. (2006). *Public Relations Strategies and Tactics.* 8th Edition. Boston: Pearson Education.

Wimmer, R. D., ve Dominick, J. R. (2000). *Mass Media Research: An Indroduction.* Belmont: Wadsworth Publishing Company.

Wright, D., & Hinson, M. (2017). Tracking how social and other digital media are being used in public relations practice: A twelve-year study. *Public Relations Journal, 11*(1), 1–30.

Elif KOÇ

Digital Marketing

1. Introduction

Technological developments throughout the history of mankind have significantly affected the field of marketing and radically changed the relations between marketers and customers. With digital technologies, people can be connected both with networks and each other whenever and wherever they want. This has resulted in technologies causing devastating changes in the field of marketing. Today, the understanding of marketing is under extensive developments with the effects of digitalization (Ryan, 2021: 5).

Digital marketing, which was initially expressed with concepts such as e-marketing and Internet marketing, is the essential part of digital business models. Firms make an effort to establish closer relations with customers, add value to products and services, develop distribution channels and ultimately increase sales through digital marketing channels (e.g., social media, influencer marketing, affiliate marketing) (Chaffey and Smith, 2017: 13). The Digital Marketing Institute (DMI) defines digital marketing as *"the use of digital technologies to create an integrated, targeted and measurable communication which helps to acquire and retain customers while building deeper relationships with them"*. In another study, Kannan (2017: 23) states that digital marketing is *"an adaptive, technology-enabled process by which firms collaborate with customers and partners to jointly create, communicate, deliver, and sustain value for all stakeholders"*. Joshi (2013) also refers to digital marketing as *"the method in which products and services are promoted through digital distribution channels"*.

Along with digital marketing, concepts such as social media, mobile marketing have entered our lives. With accelerating number of digital marketing tools, the main goal is the continuation of traditional marketing and digital marketing together. One should not replace the other, but should coexist with varying roles. Traditional marketing tools play a crucial role in initiating the first interaction between brands and customers. It is the focal point in creating interest and awareness of the customer. Digital marketing gains significance as interaction progresses (Kotler, Kartajaya and Setiawan, 2016: 53). Enterprises engage in digital marketing by using digital channels in all or part of their marketing activities. These channels make it easy for marketers to communicate with the customer in a continuous, two-way, and customized manner. This established dialogue is like a neural network, and customers interact with each other through digital means (Wertime and Fenwick, 2008: 30).

Besides technology, one of the critical points of digital marketing is the concept of people. In this context, it overlaps with traditional marketing (Ryan, 2014: 16). Today, customers become more participatory, and they engage in several digital interactions. Consumers actively express their opinions through the web, podcasts, blogs, etc. The aim of the firms is the engagement of customers which includes their emotional interests and positive feelings towards the brand (Wertime and Fenwick, 2008: 32). With digital marketing, customers can find a business environment where they can participate in product/service production or delivery processes with a variety of methods and convey their needs, demands and various feedbacks (Royle and Laing, 2014: 68; Chaffey and Smith, 2017: 14). In this way, both marketers and customers can be interacted more and also more specialized services can be offered to customers. Digitized systems offer customized communication platforms that increase customer engagement (Joshi, 2013).

In digital marketing, companies can reach large audiences through digital environment. On the other hand, it can be also effective to identify and communicate with the specific audience, rather than addressing large audiences. For example, a company that sells baby clothes can only show its advertisements to women who are pregnant or have a baby by means of digital marketing, while on television the ads are broadcasted to a general audience like old, young, female, male without a specific target (Royle and Laing, 2014: 68; Bala and Verma, 2018: 335; Gedik, 2020). Digital marketing is more measurable than traditional marketing, and the aim is guiding and managing results (Kotler, Kartajaya and Setiawan, 2016: 53). Digital environments provide access to a wide variety of data, such as click data, customer ratings, labels, customer responses to marketing actions, information about collaborators and competitors. These data allow you to identify customer behavior, develop marketing strategies and measure the effectiveness of these strategies (Kannan, 2017: 38).

2. From Traditional to Digital Marketing

Along with digitalization, there have been large-scale developments in the traditional marketing approach. The birth of digitalization has occurred along with the development of technology. Looking at the historical process, developments in marketing have paralleled to technological developments and digitalization. Technological inventions such as printing, radio, television, and the Internet have also radically influenced the field of marketing. Digitalization took place, especially following the developments in Internet technology.

As seen in Figure 1, the starting point of the development of the Internet is called Web 1.0. The Web 1.0 era began with the use of the Internet in daily life. Web 1.0 Internet technologies have a fairly simple structure. In Web 1.0 applications, user intervention or inclusion of users in the system is not possible. Personal sites are quite few, rather corporate sites are accessed (Friedman, 2009: 87). The web is like a source of information and sales. The website owner publishes information on the web pages. Marketers also advertise, and these ads are published on sites. These applications are like an electronic catalog of information, goods or services. Interaction with the user is at the minimum level. User actions are about simple matters, such as clicking on links, entering credit card or delivery data (Wertime and Fenwick, 2008: 59).

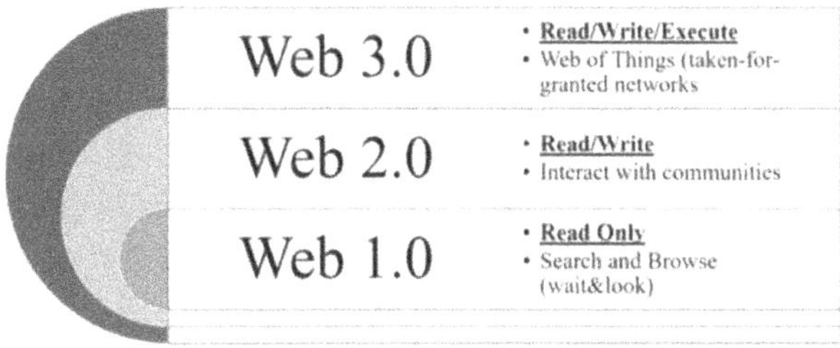

Figure 1. Stages of web development
Source: Wertime and Fenwick (2008: 60)

In time, the web has become more than just a source of information and sales but a platform that asks what the user want and allows the system to change accordingly. The Web 2.0 era was groundbreaking in technology because it included many essential features. During the Web 2.0 era, users created their own content and began to share this content with other users. Web 2.0 does not have a centralized and hierarchical structure like Web 1.0. It aims to deliver what the user wants (Wertime and Fenwick, 2008: 61). Content created by various communities and consumers is added with Web 2.0 to the centrally managed content of Web 1.0. Thus, content is developed jointly by marketers and consumers. During the period of Web 2.0, users became active, communicating and interacting with each other both individually and institutionally (Dilmen and Ogut, 2010: 260).

Recently, these technologies have become a social field. Along with Web 3.0, these platforms have become environments where a wide range of participants interact, rather than just a store of information. The Web 3.0 is still in development and has a lot of promise for the future (Wertime and Fenwick, 2008: 57). Web 3.0 is also called "Semantic Web". It is expressed as the next phase of Web 2.0. Its main difference from Web 2.0 is that control function has passed from people to software systems. The goal is to maximize the experience of users. According to the consensus of many Internet scientists, we are at the dawn of the Web 3.0 age. In Web 3.0, software and especially artificial intelligence are included in the processes. Artificial intelligence evolves itself like a human being and constantly update itself based on the changing demands of users (Civelek, 2009: 3). These developments, which have led to digitalization over the years, have been integrated into the mainstream of marketing and adapted to marketing practices. Marketers who follow innovations largely benefit from technological applications when connecting with their target audiences (Ryan, 2021: 4).

Traditional marketing is the most well-known form of marketing and non-digital methods are utilized to promote products/services. In digital marketing, digital methods are used in marketing activities (Kotler, Kartajaya and Setiawan, 2016: 84). Digital marketing employ relatively cheaper tools compared to traditional practices (Yasmin et al., 2015: 71). In traditional marketing, there is one way communication, but in digital marketing, there is two-way communication. Traditional marketers divide consumers into segments based on common traits. They deliver messages concerning products/services in one way to the target audience based on marketing strategies. In digital marketing, users meet on a common platform (in various online platforms) according to their shared characteristics. Customers and firms are often in two-way communication on these platforms. In digital marketing, marketers constantly interact with customers.

Furthermore, any consumer may exchange ideas by communicating with other consumers. In traditional marketing, local customers can be more easily reached, while in digital marketing, it is possible to connect with a group of customers from anywhere in the world. While marketing activities can be done at any time of the day in digital marketing, parties can reach each other whenever they want from anywhere in the world, there are place and time constraints in traditional marketing (Yasmin et al., 2015; Gedik, 2020). In many traditional marketing methods, the message to be conveyed has to be summarized and kept short due to various constraints (e.g., cost) while digital channels make it possible to use more comprehensive content. In most traditional marketing tools, marketing activities require a fairly long process. Digital practices, on the other hand, can be prepared and presented in a much shorter period of time. In addition, when there is a need for contextual changes in digital marketing, updates can be done easily and quickly. This gives brands a wide range of movement and flexibility (Royle and Laing, 2014: 68; Bala and Verma, 2018: 335; Gedik, 2020).

In traditional marketing, it is quite challenging to set goals and measure results related to marketing strategies; while digital marketing tools provide the opportunity to measure and report results in a practical way (Kannan, 2017: 38). Digital marketing is more effective in reaching the target audience, and there is a certain measurability in how many people see and watch the posts. In this way, how many people see a share in a digital medium, how many people click, how many people download and subscribe (if it is a mobile application), or even demographic and locational data can be accessed and measured (Cakir 2004: 174). In traditional marketing, it takes a long time to gather information about consumer characteristics and to analyze the results. In digital marketing, on the other hand, instant information about user characteristics can be obtained by examining the content of Internet users' shares, comments and likes. Brands can view the reactions of consumers to messages transmitted in digital marketing and how effective these messages are in a short amount of time (Inanoglu, 2009: 114).

The traditional marketing strategy involved customers, collaborators, competitors, context, and companies. As can be seen from Figure 2, competitors, collaborators, and company form the circle of a business together with the customer as the focus in digital marketing. Stakeholders in this environment communicate and interact with each other on various digital media platforms (social media, search engines, etc.) and certain customer behaviors are affected in this process.

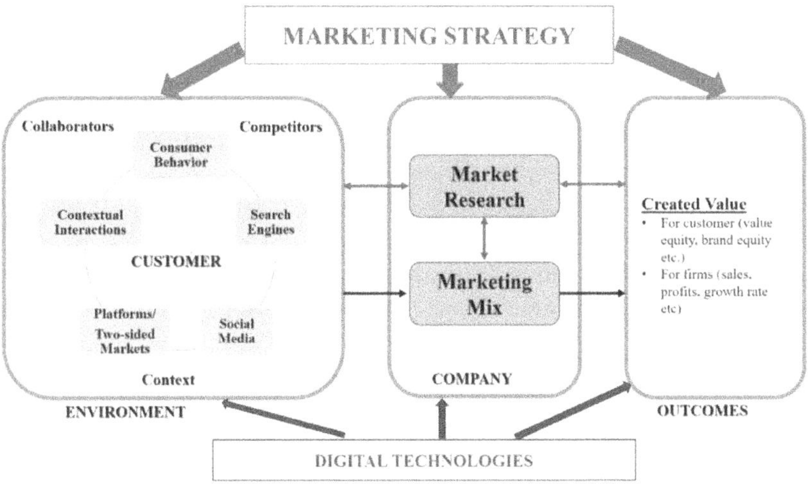

Figure 2. The framework of digital marketing
Source: Kannan (2017: 24)

Interactions in this environment and numerous analyses create input for the market research and marketing mix processes that are carried out when determining a marketing strategy of a company. In this created framework, digital technologies have a significant impact on key touch points. As a result, all these marketing activities in the digital framework have ultimately created value for both customers and enterprises.

2.1. Digital Marketing Strategy

Digital marketing strategy draws on traditional marketing principles while leveraging technology and digital media (Strokes, 2011: 22). Interactions and integrations between traditional methods of the digital world (online) and traditional methods (offline) are the sine qua non of successful digital marketing strategies (Chaffey and Ellis-Chadwick, 2016: 16). Today, it is inevitable that companies will act within the framework of a digital approach integrated with offline methods to strategically manage their brand and customers in an ever-changing world. Additionally, the adoption of new marketing channels, new shopping devices and new customer interactions require an updated marketing strategy (Kannan, 2017: 38).

Traditional marketing starts with segmentation based on the practice of dividing the market into homogenous groups according to geographic, demographic and behavioral characteristics. Each segment has different needs and ways to respond to market changes. Segmentation is followed by targeting, which involves the practice of selecting one or more segments (Smith and Zook, 2011: 229). These practices are one-sided decisions of marketers. Customer engagement is often limited to their input in market research, which performs before segmentation and targeting exercises. There is a vertical relationship between customer and brand. Customers who are "targeted" are often exposed to irrelevant messages directed to them without their permission. As effects of digitalization, customers are horizontally connected to each other in online networks called "communities". Communities are formed within the limits set by customers. These communities are the new segments. To effectively interact with a community of customers, brands must request permission. Similar to the mechanism used by various social media apps, customers decide to "approve" or "ignore" their friends' requests. This is also a proof of the horizontal relationship between brands and customers. Online customers of businesses in digital marketing have different features and behaviors than offline customers. Particular approaches to segmentation may be required compared to traditional marketing, and a micro-sized targeting may be more effective (Chaffey and Bosomworth, 2013: 12; Kotler, Kartajaya and Setiawan, 2016: 48).

After the targeting practice, "positioning" is performed. Positioning confirms the accuracy of the message to be transmitted (Smith and Zook, 2011: 386). The brand concept is closely related to positioning. In positioning, an attractive promise is conveyed to win the minds and hearts of customers. In order for positioning to be proper, the brand should have a unique differentiation tool. In addition, the promises made through marketing mix are embodied and differentiation is based on strong foundations (Kotler, Kartajaya and Setiawan, 2016: 49). In digital marketing, it is necessary to be positioned in customer's mind in the online environment. Here, online value proportions are of great importance. With positioning, when a customer interacts with the firm, the first thing they perceive immediately should be the messages the firm aims to transmit (Chaffey and Bosomworth, 2013: 12). As in traditional marketing strategies, digital marketing strategies do not have a single business method. The company needs to develop its own unique strategy based on the company characteristics, field of activities, resources and so on. Although the contents of the strategies created will be similar, they will be unique and company-specific.

2.2. Digital Market Research

Market research involves the process of collecting and analyzing data about customers and competitors to understand the market and make decisions about it. In digital marketing, research can be based on primary or secondary data. Secondary data is already existing, published data, while primary data is the data collected in accordance with a specific research problem. As can be seen in Figure 3, blogs, published articles, white papers are secondary data, while web analytics, surveys, listening labs belong to data types in the primary group. The Internet platform is a decisive tool in carrying out studies based on these two types of data. On this platform both data groups interact with each other (Strokes, 2011: 42).

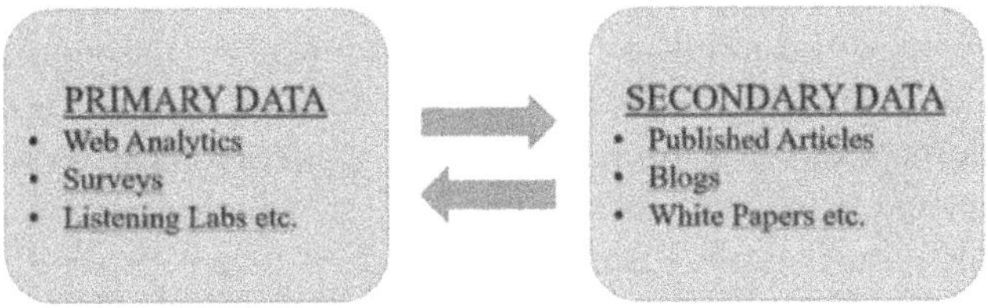

Figure 3. Sources of primary and secondary data
Source: Strokes (2011: 45)

Market research in digital marketing focuses on the information produced as a result of the use of digital technologies and the processing of this information to understand the interactions in the business environment and the consequences of the marketing activities. At this point, social interactions and online reviews of these interactions are of great importance. For instance, the firm can investigate the customers' browsing behavior on websites and mobile sites with comparing the online search and mobile search behavior. Thus, market research makes it possible to understand how a firm is perceived in the market (Kannan, 2017: 25).

2.3. Digital Marketing Mix

The marketing mix is a conceptual framework that guides companies to plan for each market segment. They allocate their resources within this marketing mix (Chaffey and Smith, 2017: 52). In traditional marketing, 4P's of the marketing mix consists of product/service, price, place, and promotion (Kotler, Kartajaya and Setiawan, 2016: 50). The 4P approach was updated to 7P in the new generation marketing approaches, and people, physical evidence and process were added to it. In creating digital marketing strategies, it is necessary to take these seven elements into account.

Product: Firms can sell three types of products in digital environments. These are physical products (e.g., books, clothing, electronics), non-material products and services (e.g., accommodation services, insurance services, consulting), digitized products (e.g., computer games, software, music, film). Products or services are often developed according to the needs and demands of customers identified through market research. With digitalization, companies are making efforts to create products or services together with customers. Customers are getting involved more and more in product/service development stages. In this way, customers can get more personalized service (Kotler, Kartajaya and Setiawan, 2016: 51; Chaffey and Smith, 2017: 67).

Price: Pricing in digital environments is regulated by the product range (Chaffey and Ellis-Chadwick, 2016: 278). The prevalence of search engines and price-comparison websites gives customers the convenience to compare product/service prices. Thus, companies should expand their product range and offer these products on digital platforms at discounted prices compared to competing firms (Ryan and Jones, 2009: 30; Strokes, 2011: 25). To determine a sales price for a product, companies use a combination of one or more methods of pricing that is traditionally based on cost, competition, or customer value. But with digitalization, pricing has been evolving from traditional methods to more flexible and dynamic ways. With the benefits of the digital tools, companies are developing different pricing strategies based on large data analysis, supply-demand or differing customer profiles. Thus, firms further optimize their profits (Kotler, Kartajaya and Setiawan, 2016: 51; Pistol, 2017: 761). In the digital environment, it is not necessary to be the cheapest product/service provider. However, in order to compete, the price must be convincing to the customers with the value offered (Ryan and Jones, 2009: 30).

Place: The customer wants to be able to procure their products reliably and as soon as possible. In parallel with technological developments, the concept of place is also changing. With digitization, a customer anywhere in the world can instantly have an access to products or services at any time. Brands that cannot compete under normal circumstances can also compete against each other (Kotler, Kartajaya and Setiawan, 2016: 51). Thanks to the opportunities digitalization offers, customers can perform their shopping on digital platforms and they can categorize products, add products to their cart, securely make payment and identify shipping company (Pistol, 2017: 762; Kingsnorth, 2019: 10).

Promotion: Companies convey information concerning products or services to the target audience with a variety of promotion methods such as advertising, public relations and sales campaigns (Kotler, Kartaj and Setiawan, 2016: 50). Online promotion activities in digital environments are an extension of the offline environment. However, they have certain differences as online promotion is more complex but more measurable in terms of targeting and tracking. Traditional promotion methods, such as advertising, personal sales, promotion-based marketing, and public relations, can also be implemented online. Methods such as search engines, social media channels, mobile marketing, email channels, influencers can also be utilized. The most essential aspect is that the people who contact their customers should be selected from professional experts because these people are the faces of the company (Strokes, 2011: 27). In addition, with the spread of social media today, promotional activities have shifted to a platform of mutual communication between customers and brands. Customers can write messages to product and service servers in online environments and respond to messages from them. In addition, customers interact with each other on systems where they can leave ratings such as Trip Advisor and Yelp. Brand assessments are presented on these common platforms (Kotler, Kartajaya and Setiawan, 2016: 51).

People: This later added element emphasizes the study of humans, a powerful element in the digitally connected world. Here, the importance of personalization, peer-to-peer sharing, communities, customer-centric organizations are emphasized. Especially on digital sharing platforms, it is possible for people to participate in brand stories (Strokes, 2011: 27). With the transition from traditional marketing to digital marketing, consumers can have a direct impact on the products and marketing activities of the firms before production, during production, and after production. Consumers contribute to the development of products or services with digital marketing (Pistol, 2017: 763: Chaffey and Smith 2017: 90).

Physical evidence: Another concept added to the traditional marketing mix is physical proofs. This concept refers to the concrete expression of a product or service, how it is purchased and used. In traditional marketing, this concept consists of production areas and stores. In the online context, this concept refers to the customer's experience of the company through its website. The experience includes the subjects such as navigating the website, ease of use and website performance (Chaffey and Ellis-Chadwick, 2016: 288). As part of physical evidence, companies can include a large number of products and services on their web pages and offer their customers the opportunity to purchase without time limit. In addition, various payment options, promotional codes, product delivery options are considered as physical evidences (Chaffey and Smith, 2017: 92).

Process: The process is expressed as companies producing a product/service and offering it to customers, and customers buying and using this product or service. It is of great importance that the purchasing processes on digital platforms are designed to be smooth and fast, and that precautions are taken against potential problems. The smooth progress of the system is an essential factor that emphasizes the service quality of enterprises (Chaffey, 2019: 156). Proper and successful processes can create a competitive advantage. But processes that damage the brand and negatively affect sales can also occur. For this reason, efficient and effective implementation of processes is vital (Chaffey and Smith, 2017: 97).

3. Digital Marketing Tools

There are a wide range of tools used in digital marketing. These tools are utilized in running promotional activities by marketers through digital networks, and shared value is created with customers (Key, 2017: 28). Features of the main tools used and the advantages as well as disadvantages of these tools are summarized below.

3.1. Social Media Marketing

Social media marketing comprises marketing activities conducted through social web tools such as social networks, blogs, forums, online chat rooms, video/photo sharing platforms, podcasts, social marketing, and content sharing, which allow for the promotion of a product/service, increasing awareness and brand recognition, and taking action for the company or product/service (Gunelius 2011: 10; Zahay, 2015: 77). Facebook, Instagram, YouTube, and Snapchat are among these platforms and their content is found in various formats such as videos and photos (Key, 2017: 31). The benefits of social media marketing can be listed as below (Ryan, 2014: 205; Chaffey and Ellis-Chadwick, 2016: 532; Ajina, 2019: 1514):

Advantages

- It offers great opportunities for businesses to achieve their marketing goals at considerably low costs.
- Social media channels allow businesses to have constant access to information, whereby they can learn their customers' true thoughts about them.
- By establishing positive relationships on these platforms with people who have positive thoughts about the brand, businesses have the possibility to turn them into brand advocates.
- Due to the interactivity of social media, the ideas and comments of consumers can be evaluated directly, and the necessary improvements can be implemented quickly.

Disadvantages

- A negative viral news piece about the brand can spread quickly and damage the brand's reputation.
- It is very difficult for the firms to participate in customer-owned social media chat platforms and positively influence conversations there.
- It is difficult for brands to find content on these platforms that will engage and attract audiences.

3.2. Email Marketing

Email marketing is one of the most effective ways to connect directly with the target audience and is a form of direct marketing that is largely used in digital marketing today. It is also an effective addressing technique for identifying potential or existing customers. With this method, companies reach their customers quickly, economically, and easily. It provides firms access, flexibility, and control over forwarding messages (Monaghan, 2015: 188). The main advantages and disadvantages of email marketing can be listed as follows (Monaghan, 2015: 188; Chaffey and Ellis-Chadwick, 2016: 525; Hudak et al., 2017: 342):

Advantages

- Email marketing usually encourages impulsively clicking on a website where the offer can be reviewed immediately. This, in turn, allows companies to attract customers to the website.
- Customization is easy and inexpensive, tailored to the target people or audiences. This allows for more interesting and targeted messages.
- It can be integrated with methods such as direct mail, mobile messaging, and web personalization, which in turn supports the advantages.

Disadvantages

- It may be difficult to view an advertisement element caused by different email viewing systems.
- Messages may not reach their intended destination due to various Internet service providers and firewalls.
- Messages can end up in the spam folder before they reach the user because of the increased volume of emails nowadays fail to filter past various rules, or the consumer not wanting them.

3.3. Mobile Marketing

Mobile marketing is the marketing of products and services through mobile communication channels. With the increased usage of smart phones and tablets, that is, mobile platforms, mobile marketing has become crucial. This has led to both the need for enterprises to adapt their content to mobile platforms and the production of mobile-specific content (Hofacker et al., 2016: 27; Kumar, 2020: 1367). Mobile marketing is a revolutionary tool for companies to connect with each and every one of their customers through their mobile devices in the right place at the right time and with the appropriate direct message (Gedik, 2020: 72). The main advantages and disadvantages of mobile marketing can be listed as follows (Hopkins and Turner 2013: 124; Coelhoso, 2019: 31):

Advantages

- Individuals can carry their mobile devices with them anytime and anywhere.
- Consumers can be directed to the right brand and promotions through messages or instant notifications sent via mobile applications, and the benefits can be instantly presented to the user via their mobile device.

- Instant location-based communication can be established with application users. For example, when a customer passes in front of the store, it is possible to instantly offer a promotion to the user, thus introducing them to the store.
- More detailed information about the customer can be collected through mobile applications.

Disadvantages

- Mobile applications of brands that do not offer ease of use can distance users from the sales process and damage the brand image.
- If the new version of an app does not meet expectations after an update, this can redirect the user to another application.
- Tired of heavy communication and notification traffic, users can turn off communication permissions and notifications in the app, thus resisting the message that the brand aims to deliver to them.

3.4. Search Engine Marketing (SEM)

Search engine marketing (SEM) is a type of online marketing strategy that promotes the brand by increasing the ranking and visibility of websites in various search engines such as Google and Yahoo (Gedik, 2020: 71). Today, search engines are considered the main source of information acquisition. These are the most important tools that allow users to access websites (Yuksel and Tolon, 2019: 237). There are two different types of searches. These are paid research (called pay-per click, PPC) and unpaid research (called search engine optimization). PPC is defined as a text advertisement that contains a link to a web page, which appears when a search engine user types on the search bar. Thus, in pay-per click, payment is made for advertisements that appear around the search engine page (top, bottom, side of the page). The purpose of PPC is to attract a user's attention, to have them click on a link and direct it to the marketer's website (Wertime and Fenwick, 2008: 96; Cant and Van Rooyen, 2017: 284). Search engine optimization (SEO) refers to the optimization of a website in order for it to be found by search engines and appear at the top in search engine results (Dixit and Agarwal, 2016; Zahay, 2015: 44; Chaffey and Ellis-Chadwick 2016: 484). Companies implement search engine optimization (SEO) strategies to put their websites on the first page (Wertime and Fenwick, 2008: 96). The primary advantages and disadvantages of SEM are as follows (Moreno and Martinez, 2013: 1; Shih, Chen and Chen, 2013: 529; Kritzinger and Weideman, 2017: 5):

Advantages

- SEMs are very useful for effectively increasing the traffic volume from search engines to individual sites and the visibility of websites.
- Through its use of attractive and informative content, it becomes an effective tool for gaining consumer value and directing the consumer to make purchases.

Disadvantages

- Compared to other marketing tools, it is difficult to predict results for investment, and the environment is highly competitive.
- It has complex and dynamic structures. Search engines reckon a considerable number of factors, and ranking factors can vary over time.
- Continuous effort is required for development and improvement.

3.5. Content Marketing

Content marketing is the marketing process that creates and distributes relevant and valuable content to attract, interact with, and promote to a specific target audience (Baltes, 2015: 112). In content marketing, activities take place to ensure the formation of meaningful content around the brand in order to promote brand loyalty and engagement. Content marketing is about deciding on the brand story and publishing consistent content across all digital marketing channels. The qualities of the products or services are marketed with the enhanced effect of text, image, or video. The main advantages and disadvantages of content marketing can be listed as follows (Zahay, 2015: 76; Lieb, 2012: 3; Baltes, 2015: 114; Chaffey and Ellis-Chadwick, 2016: 43):

Advantages

- It creates a trust-based communication process with customers.
- It formulates a new form of need in the customers' minds.
- It can produce news for a product or service that will reverberate through a large audience.
- It supports the development of search terms on digital platforms that empower the brand story.

Disadvantages

- It is a far-reaching and difficult process.
- Both the static content that creates web pages and the dynamic media content that encourages interaction must act in harmony.

3.6. Affiliate Marketing

Affiliate marketing is a win-win strategy utilized in digital media. In this marketing strategy, sales partners generate revenue from products or services that do not belong to them while brands have the potential to reach more users at a lower cost (Penpece, 2013: 119; Smith & Zook, 2011: 128). In this system, organizations to advertise products and services free of charge and pay a fee when the system users turn into potential customers (e.g., by visiting, registering, or making purchases on the website) (Wertime and Fenwick, 2008: 104). Main advantages and disadvantages of affiliate marketing can be listed as follows (Smith and Zook, 2011: 276; Chaffey and Ellis-Chadwick, 2016; Ryan, 2021: 364):

Advantages

- It provides an advantage in terms of budget spending, as it requires a promise of budget commitment only after successful advertisement.
- It helps raise awareness about a new brand or a new product.
- Businesses have the opportunity to experiment with innovations they implement on a low budget. This guarantees the return on marketing investments more easily.

Disadvantages

- Calculating the cost of such marketing activities is more difficult than calculating the cost of individual consumer interaction.
- Achieving success requires providers to have expertise.
- Affiliates may abuse the brand name. This also damages brand reputation.

3.7. Impact Marketing (Influencer Marketing)

"Influencer Marketing" is marketing and communication activities conducted through people who have a high-following rates on social media, have the ability to influence audiences and create trends, are specialized in a specific field and/or are perceived as "popular" across society (IAB Turkey, 2020: 2). Influencers are third parties that meaningfully shape the purchasing decisions of consumers (Brown and Hayes, 2008: 50). As traditional advertising places become less and less popular, influencer marketing has a significant influence on consumers' purchasing decisions (Fortune Turkey, 2017). Within influencer marketing, brands conduct several joint activities with people who are followed on various social networks and whose follower count is above average, including celebrities, bloggers, vloggers, social media influencers (e.g., Instagram, Twitter, YouTube celebrities), and so on (Canoz, Gulmez and Eroglu, 2020). Many national and international institutions that aim to gain a competitive advantage engage in sponsorship work with influencers who have a high follower count on social media and will represent the brand well (Kircova and Enginkaya, 2015: 95). The main advantages and disadvantages of influencer marketing can be listed as follows (Draganova, 2018: 22; Gaytan, 2018: 19; IAB Turkey, 2020: 3):

Advantages

- It is a new marketing technique that serves as a bridge between consumers and brands.
- It is an effective marketing tool especially when aimed at Generation Z.
- Communication may quickly lead to actions such as product sales.

Disadvantages

- Selecting an inappropriate platform and an inappropriate influencer may result in failure.
- If the way influencers present their marketing agreement and the content they share is not appropriate with the brand message, the brand image can be damaged.

4. Measurement in Digital Marketing

One of the biggest advantages of digital marketing is that its effects can be measured. Measurement denotes the use of certain metrics that provide a range of analytical information to measure whether a digital marketing activity achieves strategic objectives and targets. These measurements provide real-time information (Key, 2017: 30). Technological advances have automated data collection and distribution considerably. Visible and traceable digital communication has also improved measurability (Hennig-Thurau et al., 2010)

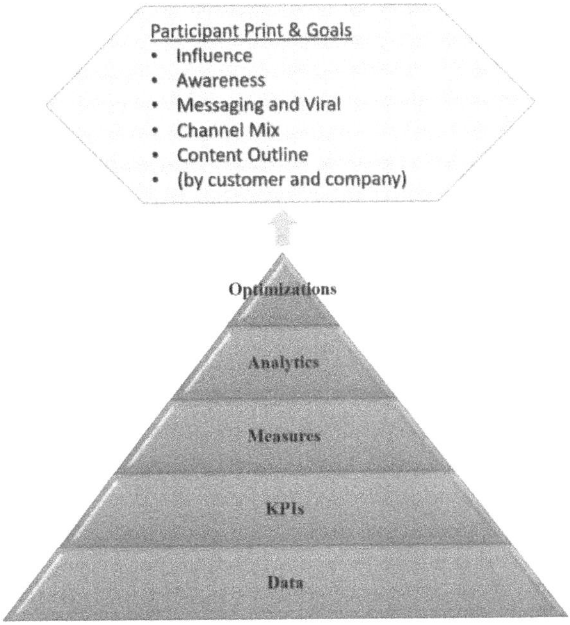

Figure 4. Digital marketing planning framework
Source: Wertime and Fenwick (2008: 385)

Metrics related to marketing performance are created through digitally generated data (Kannan, 2017: 37). There are a breadth of platforms and data in digital marketing. Measuring these data according to their own goals and values provides more robust outcomes. Therefore, each enterprise should determine the measurement criteria according to its targets. Efficiency can also be measured using free tools, such as Google Analytics and Boom Social, which have been developed for tracking and data analysis. These tools allow the user to learn how people react, whereby the user can develop promotions and apps accordingly (Barutcu and Tomas, 2013: 20). Identified strategies will evolve as we obtain more and better information on digital marketing participants. As Figure 4 shows, this is an iterative process. As the data provided becomes richer, measurement and subsequent optimization processes based on these data become more effective. The more engagement increases, the better the strategies can be developed. If the system is implemented well, customers will be keen about staying connected more with the firms, and provide more data for measurements (Wertime and Fenwick, 2008: 386).

5. Conclusion

This book section details fundamental issues related to digital marketing and is intended to provide guidance for academics, students, and practitioners in understanding the digital marketing process. Technology continues to evolve rapidly, and these advances provide a broad range of opportunities for marketing. With digitalization, marketing has a lot of potential and digital marketing methods are on their way to becoming the mainstream in marketing. Furthermore, these methods are expected to shape the largest revolution in marketing history. Today, the widespread adoption of digital marketing techniques contributes to the individualization of marketing services offered by both goods and services providers. In this environment, marketers can interact one-on-one with individual consumers and provide personalized products or services based on their feedback (Simmons, 2008; Royle and Laing, 2014).

When implementing digital marketing practices, businesses encounter various obstacles and overcoming them is critical for achieving success in the long term. The main hindrance is the lack of human and expert resources (Jarvinen et al., 2012). Companies should recruit employees with strategic competencies that will carry out the aforementioned activities. Here, firms might have difficulties in employing individuals with digital marketing skills. The need for marketers who have the necessary technical skills and competencies, especially in digital marketing, and who can apply this knowledge with a sound communication foundation, is expected to increase in the near future. Enterprises wishing to take advantage of digital marketing need to overcome this shortcoming in human resources. In addition, the continued uncertain benefits of various social media tools for some B2B companies, particularly the difficulty in identifying return on investments (ROI), can hamper digital marketing investments. In addition to uncertain benefits, there may be various perceived risks. The difficulty in controlling digital media and the need for specialized message distribution and control while using digital tools appear to be a major risk (Jarvien et al., 2012; Royle and Laing, 2014). To improve technical capabilities whose absence is detected, employers should make the skill management system effective. It is also crucial that firms develop long-term strategies for developing and managing existing capabilities. Finding and employing the talent needed will thus give brands a crucial competitive advantage.

In summary, when companies define digital marketing strategies in line with their mission, vision and targets, the starting point should be the information obtained from data related to customers, markets and competitors. The storage and analysis of this data is one of the basic principles of digital marketing. Diversifying digital marketing tools and ensuring customer engagement is an essential consideration on the road to success. Enterprises that can benefit from customers and interact with them can gain competitive advantage. Focusing on mobile and responsive designs while communicating with them is important for the widespread use of digital applications. Whether digital marketing management succeeds is also determined by developing metrics and key performance indicators (KPI). While these are implemented, it is of great importance for managers to have a command of the field and the necessary technical equipment, to be able to respond timely in moments of crisis, and to have all employees adopt new marketing approaches.

References

Ajina, A. (2019). The Perceived Value of Social Media Marketing: An Empirical Study of Online Word-of-Mouth in Saudi Arabian Context. *Entrepreneurship and Sustainability Issues*, 6(3), 1512–1527.

Bala, M. and Verma, D. (2018). A Critical Review of Digital Marketing. *International Journal of Management, IT & Engineering*, 8(10), 321–339.

Baltes, L. P. (2015). Content Marketing-the Fundamental Tool of Digital Marketing. *Bulletin of the Transilvania University of Brasov. Economic Sciences*, Series V, 8(2), 111.

Barutcu, S. and Tomas, M. (2013). Sürdürülebilir Sosyal Medya Pazarlaması ve Sosyal Medya Pazarlaması Etkinliğinin Ölçümü. *Journal of Internet Applications and Management*, 4(1), 5–24.

Brown, D. and Hayes, N. (2008). *Influencer Marketing: Who Really Influences Your Customers?* UK: Routledge.

Cakir, V. (2004). Yeni İletişim Teknolojilerinin Reklam Üzerine Etkileri. *Selçuk Üniversitesi İletişim Fakültesi Akademik Dergisi*, 3(2), 168–181.

Canoz, K., Gulmez, O. and Eroglu, G. (2020). Pazarlamanın Yükselen Yıldızı Influencer Marketing: Influencer Takipçilerinin Satın Alma Davranışını Belirlemeye Yönelik Bir Araştırma. *Selçuk Üniversitesi Sosyal Bilimler Meslek Yüksekokulu Dergisi*, 23(1), 73–91.

Cant, M. C. and Van Rooyen, N. (2017). The Use of Search Engines in the Marketing of Accommodation Establishments: Adopt or Reject the Use of

Google AdWords?. *International Review of Management and Marketing*, *7*(3), 281–287.

Chaffey, D. (2019). *Digital Marketing*. UK: Pearson.

Chaffey, D. and Bosomworth, D. (2013). *Digital Marketing Strategy. Planning Template*. UK: Smart Insights Limited.

Chaffey, D. and Ellis-Chadwick, F. (2016). *Digital Marketing: Strategy, Implementation and Practice*. Six Edition. UK: Pearson Education.

Chaffey, D. and Smith, P. R. (2017). *Digital Marketing Excellence: Planning, Optimizing and Integrating Online Marketing*. NY: Taylor & Francis.

Civelek, M. E. (2009). *İnternet Çağı Dinamikleri*. Istanbul: Beta Yayıncılık.

Coelhoso, J. P. E. (2019). *Factors Influencing Mobile Marketing Acceptance in Higher Education Students in the United Arab Emirates (Doctoral Dissertation)*. Portugal: Universidade Fernando Pessoa.

Dilmen, N. E. and Ogut, S. (2010). Sosyalleşmenin Yeni Yüzü: Sosyal Paylaşım Ağları. *Marmara Üniversitesi Yeni Medya ve Etkileşim Konferansı Bildiri Kitapçığı*, 237–242.

Dixit, A. and Agarwal, M. (2016). Hybrid Approach to Search Engine Optimization (SEO) Techniques. *Suresh Gyan Vihar University Journal of Engineering & Technology*, 1(4), 1–5.

Draganova, I. (2018). *Influencer Marketing: Consumer Perception on Influencers and Its Role in Digital Communication Management*. Vienna: Webster University.

Fortune Turkey. (2017). *Influencer'lar ve markaları bir araya getiren pazar yeri*. https://www.fortuneturkey.com/influencerlar-ve-markalari-bir-araya-getiren-pazar-yeri-43379, (18.06.2021).

Friedman, T. L. (2009). *Yirmi Birinci Yüzyılın Kısa Tarihi/ Dünya Düzdür*. Çev. L. Cinemre. Istanbul: Boyner Yayınları.

Gaytan, A. C. (2018). *The Use of Social Media among First-Year Students in the College Search Process: A Phenomenological Study*. Beaumont, TX: Lamar University-Beaumont.

Gedik, Y. (2020). Pazarlamada Yeni Bir Pencere: Dijital Pazarlama. *Journal of Business in the Digital Age*, *3*(1), 63–75.

Gunelius, S. (2011). *30-Minute Social Media Marketing: Step-By-Step Techniques to Spread the Word about Your Business*. New York: McGraw-Hill.

Hennig-Thurau, T., Malthouse, E. C., Friege, C., Gensler, S., Lobschat, L., Rangaswamy, A., and Skiera, B. (2010). The Impact of New Media on Customer Relationships. *Journal of Service Research*, 13(3), 311–330.

Hofacker, C. F., De Ruyter, K., Lurie, N. H., Manchanda, P. and Donaldson, J. (2016). Gamification and Mobile Marketing Effectiveness. *Journal of Interactive Marketing*, 34, 25–36.

Hopkins, J. and Turner, J. (2013). *Mobil Pazarlama Hakkında Her Şey*. B. Gündüz (Çev.), Istanbul: Optimist Kitap.

Hudak, M., Kianickova, E. and Madlenak, R. (2017). The Importance of E-mail Marketing in E-commerce. *Procedia Engineering*, 192, 342–347.

IAB Turkey. (2020). Influencer Pazarlaması Nedir? IAB Turkey Influencer Pazarlaması *Çalışma Grubu Raporu*. https://iabtr.org/UploadFiles/Reports/Influencer-marketing-nedir26122019142300.pdf, (15.05.2021).

Inanoglu, T. (2009). *Pazarlamada Modern Yöntemler*. Bursa: Elit Yayınları.

Jarvinen, J., Tollinen, A., Karjaluoto, H. and Jayawardhena, C. (2012). Digital and Social Media Marketing Usage in B2B Industrial Section. *Marketing Management Journal*, 22(2), 102–117.

Joshi, S. (2013). A Study on Digital Marketing Preferences of Generation Y with Specific Reference to the Purchase of Laptops. In *PRIMA*, 4(1). New Delhi: Publishing India Group.

Kannan, P. K. (2017). Digital Marketing: A Framework, Review and Research Agenda. *International Journal of Research in Marketing*, 34(1), 22–45.

Key, T. M. (2017). Domains of Digital Marketing Channels in the Sharing Economy. *Journal of Marketing Channels*, 24(1–2), 27–38.

Kingsnorth, S. (2019). *Digital Marketing Strategy: An Integrated Approach to Online Marketing*. UK: Kogan Page Publishers.

Kircova, I. and Enginkaya, E. (2015). *Sosyal Medya Pazarlama*. Istanbul: Beta Yayıncılık.

Kotler, P., Kartajaya, H. and Setiawan, I. (2016). *Marketing 4.0: Moving from Traditional to Digital*. New Jersey: John Wiley & Sons.

Kritzinger, W. T. and Weideman, M. (2017). Parallel Search Engine Optimisation and Pay-per-click Campaigns: A Comparison of Cost per Acquisition. *South African Journal of Information Management*, 19, 1–13.

Kumar, S. (2020). Impact of Digital Marketing–Strategies and Challenges. *Studies in Indian Place Names*, 40(18), 1362–1371.

Lieb, R. (2012). *Content Marketıng: Think Like a Publisher – How to Use Content to Market Online and in Social Media*. Indianapolis: Que Publishing.

Monaghan, D. (2015). *Digital Minds: 12 Things Every Business Needs to Know About Digital Marketing*. Canada: Friesen Press.

Moreno, L. and Martinez, P. (2013). Overlapping Factors in Search Engine Optimization and Web Accessibility. *Online Information Review*, 37(4), 564–580.

Penpece, D. (2013). *Digital Content Marketing*. Adana: Karahan Kitabevi.

Pistol, L. (2017). The 7P and 1G That Rule in the Digital World the Marketing Mix. *De Gruyter*, 11(1), 760–769.

Royle, J. and Laing, A. (2014). The Digital Marketing Skills Gap: Developing a Digital Marketer Model for the Communication Industries. *International Journal of Information Management*, 34(2), 65–73.

Ryan, D. (2014). *Understanding Digital Marketing: Marketing Strategies for Engaging the Digital Generation*. UK: Kogan Page Publishers.

Ryan, D. (2021). *Understanding Digital Marketing. A Complete Guide to Engaging Customers and Implementing Successful Digital Campaigns*. UK: Kogan Page Publishers.

Ryan, D. and Jones, C. (2009). *Digital Marketing: Marketing Strategies for Engaging the Digital Generation*. UK: Kogan Page Publishers.

Shih, B. Y., Chen, C. Y. and Chen, Z. S. (2013). An Empirical Study of an Internet Marketing Strategy for Search Engine Optimization. *Human Factors and Ergonomics in Manufacturing & Service Industries*, 23(6), 528–540.

Simmons, G. (2008). Marketing to Postmodern Consumers: Introducing the Internetchameleon. *European Journal of Marketing*, 42(3/4), 299–310.

Smith, P. R. and Zook, Z. (2011). *Marketing Communications. Integrating Offline and Online with Social Media*. UK: Kogan Page Publishers.

Wertime, K. and Fenwick, I. (2008). *DigiMarketing*. ExecuGo Media.

Yasmin, A., Tasneem, S. and Fatema, K. (2015). Effectiveness of Digital Marketing in the Challenging Age: An Empirical Study. *International Journal of Management Science and Business Administration*, 1(5), 69–80.

Yuksel, D. and Tolon, M. (2019). Dijital Pazarlama Stratejisi Olarak Arama Motoru Optimizasyonu (SEO). *International Journal of 3D Printing Technologies and Digital Industry*, 3(3), 236–243.

Zahay, D. (2015). *Digital Marketing Management: A Handbook for the Current (or Future) CEO*. USA:5 Business Expert Press.

İbrahim Tolga ÇOŞKUN

Finance Management and Digitalization

1. Introduction

The main reason for the establishment of businesses is to provide profitability and increase their profit margins. For this purpose, management, marketing, finance, accounting, human resources and public relations functions should be successfully organized and carry out their business activities in coordination. Apart from these functions, especially in the last 20 years, the concepts of supply chain, entrepreneurship, strategy, crisis and innovation management have become more prominent. Through these functions, businesses have started to focus more on planning, strategic development, shaping their mission and vision, and increased their efforts towards medium- and long-term goals.

In order for businesses to become more effective, the establishment of the business, the start of activities and the ability of the business are necessary to operate its activities. In all these stages, the fundamental condition is to provide the necessary capital. Management of financial resources and assets of businesses whose main purpose is to grow by generating profit should be handled within the framework of financial management. Funding and finance management are required for the creation of physical areas, the acquisition of necessary equipment, specialized machinery, and the purchase of production tools, briefly, for the fulfillment of business functions.

One of the concepts that has become more and more important in recent years is digital transformation. Instead of the concept of digital transformation, the expression of digitalization is widely used. In reality, the common expression used for the digital transformation of the economy and society is digitalization. Alam et al. (2019: 1) defines digitalization as the use of digital technologies to change a business model and provide new revenue and value (in terms of generating opportunities) in the transition to a digital business.

Digital transformation, which affects and changes every field in the present world, has also led to a rapid change in the management and structuring of business environments. In order for business managers/owners to continue their business activities, it has become imperative to stay up-to-date in the digital transformation race, and to follow innovations, to know and use the rapidly developing and changing technologies and to adapt them to their businesses. The point of view that "those who do not make progress are destined to decline and disappear" imposes great and important responsibilities on businesses. In this context, one of the business functions that should be implemented is the financial management approach.

In this study, the importance and functions of financial management are elaborated on and the effects of new financial instruments and technologies on financial management are examined. The present and future of the innovations brought about by digitalization and financial management in the transition to digital businesses are also investigated.

2. Financial Management

After the industrial revolution, particularly in Europe, new inventions affected production, and thanks to the rapidly increasing mechanization, large quantities and low-cost products started to be produced in a short time. With the increase in production volume, parallel with the population growth, capital accumulation accelerated and the interest in financial assets such as bonds and stocks increased. With innovations and technological developments not only in production technologies but also in fields such as communication and transportation, the world has become a global market and the required capital volume has begun to increase. The development process of financial institutions, which have a bridge function in meeting capital supply and demand, has begun.

Thanks to the innovations brought about by the third industrial revolution, radical changes have occurred in the financial management approach. Finance managers have started to determine financial policies and strategies and to control and analyze the results by using effective methods to make plans and implement these plans.

Finance is a field that deals with the allocation (investment) of assets and liabilities over time and place, often under conditions of risk or uncertainty. Finance can also be defined as the science of money management. Finance can be divided into three subcategories: public finance, corporate finance, and personal finance. The word "finance" was originally a French word and was adapted by English-speaking communities to mean "management of money" in the eighteenth century. Today finance is not just a word, it has become a major academic discipline. Finance has become an organic function by being organized as a branch of Economics and has become an indispensable part of our daily life (Kumar, 2018: 3).

The word "financing" means finding money, providing means of payment, and supplying funds. In the most general terms, the financing function is defined as "providing the funds needed by enterprises at the most appropriate time, with the most appropriate conditions and using them in the most efficient way". Financial management is the process of determining the amount, duration and quality of the necessary funds, providing these funds at the appropriate time and conditions, allocating them to efficient and profitable areas (use-investment) in accordance with the goals (planning) set by financial managers taking into account the operating conditions (İpekten, 2019: 3–4).

2.1 Importance of Financial Management

Financial planning, which is one of the basic business functions, is one of the most important activities for all businesses, regardless of the size of the businesses. In the process of growth after the establishment of enterprises, the issue that needs to be constantly addressed and emphasized is in what position the enterprise will be in the future. Financial planning should be carried out with a systematic approach and targets, alternative investments, all financial business and transactions should be evaluated in accordance with macro and micro conditions.

Issues such as determining business policies, economic factors concerning its activities, sources of funds or credits, sectoral competition status, changing customer requests or needs, and proper management of capital increase the responsibilities of financial management. In addition, changes in foreign exchange or interest rate system, decrease in profit rates as a result of increased competition, product diversification and increase in market shares of rival companies, emergence of larger enterprises through mergers, developments in transportation and communication, innovations brought about by technology, increase in production scales, global economic risk factors, political uncertainties, conditions brought about by global epidemics, oblige businesses to take various precautions. Factors such as the need to be prepared for risks and uncertainties and the ability to adapt quickly to technological developments have also made financial management and the process of developing financial policies important.

2.2 Responsibilities and Objectives of Financial Management

The main functions in the organizational structure of many enterprises are production, marketing and finance. Business sizes also significantly affect the structure of these functions. In adverse economic conditions, the financing function has a critical importance in the protection and expansion of business assets, making financing decisions and determining policies. The fulfillment of this function or managing financial factors is performed by financial managers. The position of the finance manager within the organization is at the level of deputy general manager or manager and varies depending on the size of the business. The fact that the finance manager holds senior positions in large enterprises is due to the importance of his/her position. Although there is a transfer of authority to levels in various functions in many companies, the transfer of authority in the finance department is limited. Because decisions are about the existence and future of businesses, it is believed that it will be right for the decisions to be made by the center (Ertürk, 2017: 366–367).

In the past, the main tasks of financial managers were to prepare financial reports, provide the funds needed by the business, and maintain accounting records, while today they have become increasingly more important. Apart from tasks such as determining financing policies and strategies, preparing and controlling appropriate programs, the incumbencies of financial management are as follows (Özgen et al., 2001: 289):

- financial analysis and control
- financial planning
- investment decisions
- providing funds (resources)
- solution of financial problems faced by the business

The main objectives of businesses are to provide profitability and increase it. Maximizing business value is also the goal accepted by the market. The position of the business in the market compared with similar or rival businesses is expressed in terms of the market value of the business (stock market value in joint stock companies). Planning the funds needed by the business and providing these resources at the lowest cost, ensuring the appropriate allocation of business resources to various units, keeping the financial structure strong and managing it in accordance with changing conditions, developing financial plans and programs by considering the current situation and growth potential of the business are the objectives of finance management.

3. Digitalization and Finance

Digitalization is one of the most important concepts that have an impact on the technological changes that businesses have undergone. Digitalization is starting to use digital technologies for purposes such as changing/transforming a business model and creating opportunities that can generate new earnings and value (Bilgiç et al., 2020: 57). According to Geisberger and Broy (2012), digitalization has led to significant changes in the business models and processes of enterprises, and for businesses, digitalization is the rapid transformation of the company's internal processes, product/service components, communication channels and other key elements in the supply chain.

The best examples of digitalization are observed in businesses operating in the retail sector, with billion-dollar sales of Amazon and Alibaba companies being carried out through conventional stores on the Internet. Likewise, many transactions in the hospitality and tourism industries are planned via the Internet, in many subfields of activity, meetings are held in online virtual environments among stakeholders and financial transactions are carried out on mobile (Bilgiç et al., 2020: 58).

Digitization has also revolutionized money and payment systems. Digital currencies now facilitate instant cross-party money transfers that were previously impossible. The emergence of new coins could reshape the nature of money competition, the architecture of the International Monetary System, and the role of government-issued public money. Digital money has already appeared in various contexts. WeChat and Alipay's digital wallets have begun to dominate the payment system in China. In Africa, mobile providers have launched successful money transfer services, such as Safaricom's M-Pesa. Facebook has spearheaded the creation of digital currencies for social media networks and announced plans to issue its own currency, Libra, a type of "stable coin" that will be pegged to a basket of official currencies (Brunnermeier et al., 2019: 2).

Digitalization has accelerated especially in the process of the widespread use of the Internet and it has started to experience its golden ages with the start of the Industry 4.0 revolution (Parida, 2018: 23–36). In this context, in order to understand digitalization, especially in terms of financial management and digitalization of finance, the Industry 4.0 revolution should be addressed first. In this section, the effects of the Industry 4.0 revolution on financial services and the concepts of digital finance are discussed.

3.1 The Impact of Industry 4.0 on Finance

The first Industrial Revolution started in the late eighteenth century, with the effect of new inventions on production factors in Europe, along with the industrial revolution, and operating of mechanical production facilities of machines working with water and steam power. At the beginning of the twentieth century, mass production with electrical energy was introduced and assembly lines began to be established. These developments after the first industrial revolution caused the second industrial revolution. In the first years of the 1970s, the third industrial revolution began with the inclusion of electronics and information technologies in production systems. The era of cyber-physical production systems is the fourth industrial revolution.

The concept of Industry 4.0 was first used in 2011 at the Hannover Fair in Germany. This concept is part of the high-tech strategy as an initiative of industry representatives, politicians and academics aimed at increasing the competitiveness of the German manufacturing industry. Industry 4.0 is a set of values consisting of the Internet of things, services of the Internet and cyber-physical systems. The Industry 4.0 approach is the technology-based intelligent integration of cyber-physical production systems triggered by information and communication technologies, providing flexibility in accordance with the customized product demand of industrial production systems (Kagermann, et al, 2013: 12–25). Machine learning algorithms, real-time data processing, analysis of mass data, programmable machines, network-capable awareness created by smart sensors, optimized production and logistics processes, three-dimensional modeling, wireless networks, machine-to-machine communication (M2M), and virtual identities of physical elements in production stored in cloud applications form the components of smart factories, which are autonomous systems that make their own decisions. The concept of Industry 4.0 is not limited to production, as it includes all services and functions related to the business. Industry 4.0 is a value chain management and an approach with six dimensions (Karavardar, 2019: 6–8);

1. Strategy and organization (investments, innovation management, organizational transformation management),
2. Smart factories (information systems, data collection and use, digital modelling),
3. Intelligent operations (cloud storage, value chain integration),
4. Smart products (physical components and virtual identity),
5. Data-driven services (prediction and optimization of business results),
6. Human resources (enhancing the skills of employees, continuing education activities).

The fourth industrial revolution has spread across all sectors with a fairly positive effect. The financial services sector is also one of the sectors that has benefited significantly from the impact of Industry 4.0. Banking, insurance, mortgages, forex, equities and many other financial sectors are booming due to the positive momentum of digital innovation and financial process automation. The new crypto finance system based on blockchain technology will transform the financial industry in the near future. Taking these into account, the impact of industry 4.0 on financial services can be summarized as follows (Vida et al., 2020: 37):

- Much faster and cheaper global financial transactions,
- Significant decrease in operational costs of financial institutions,
- Easy access to financial services at any time,
- Simplification of financial systems and interfaces,
- Expanded use of robotics and artificial intelligence,
- A new era in marketing: more effective, more efficient, more targeted and personalized,
- Reduced risks thanks to advanced business intelligence and data-driven assessments,
- More transparency and increased trust,
- Minimizing human error in financial activities,
- The rise of new business areas, for example, FinTech, payment gateways,
- More efficient use of existing assets and money,
- Reduction in the number of fraud and theft,
- Increased customer satisfaction,
- Smart contracts powered by blockchain technology,
- More efficient stock and forex trading.

3.2 Finance 4.0

Finance 4.0 develops the framework for a new, socio-ecological finance system that promotes environmentally friendly behavior, socially responsible production, recycling, sharing of resources and more. Finance 1.0 represents a physical coin-based system, Finance 2.0 refers to the fiat currency system, Finance 3.0 refers to blockchain finance, while Finance 4.0 represents a multidimensional, real-time feedback system that unifies the blockchain (Ballandies et al., 2021: 53).

The combination of the Internet of Things (IoT) with blockchain technology and complexity science creates entirely new opportunities to address our challenges. A high quality of life for more people with fewer resources to create multidimensional complex systems in order to promote a circular economy, manage and share an incentive system, which is proposed under the label "Finance 4.0" (Dapp et al., 2019: 2).

The Finance 4.0 system is liberal, democratic, pluralistic, participatory, social and ecological. It leverages the intangible nature of knowledge, fosters combinatorial innovation, and creates opportunities for all by fostering an open and participatory production and service ecosystem. Information and communication systems that empower everyone to make better decisions, be more creative and innovative, and coordinate and collaborate with others will lead to better business models, products and services, smarter cities and smarter societies. Finance 4.0

aims to address global issues such as resource scarcity, climate change, economic disruption and technical unemployment by building a digital financial system that supports us in achieving sustainable development goals collectively (Dapp et al., 2019: 2).

Finance 4.0 (short FIN4) encompasses a socio-ecological financial system, a new economic system, and a new social contract. Regarding finance, it is proposed as a multidimensional cryptocurrency ecosystem that promotes decentralization and positive action. Concerning the economy, a new incentive scheme is proposed that protects privacy, affecting production and consumption in a way that promotes a circular and shared economy. This new system must be held together by a new kind of social contract that encourages community-based decision-making, allowing for local and personal diversity as well as locality. FIN4 is democratic, pluralistic and inclusive. It leads to better business models, products and services, smarter cities and smarter societies by leveraging information and communication systems so that everyone can make better decisions, be more creative, and coordinate or collaborate with others (Ballandies et al., 2021: 55–56). Finance 4.0, a subcategory of Industry 4.0, can support the growth of emerging and developing economies (Vida et al., 2020: 37).

3.3 Limitations of Digitalization

Digitalization or digital transformation are concepts that have recently entered our lives. In order for an efficient and effective digital transformation to be applied to businesses, businesses should be open to change and transformation, and new technologies should be accepted first by the employees (the whole organizational structure) and then by the micro-environment of the business. Managers who believe in the traditional management style are the biggest sources of resistance in the application of digitalization to businesses. Businesses that are in an effective supply chain and do not act in coordination within this chain in digitalization also have a slowing effect in the transformation process. According to Özçelik and Akçay, some of the challenges of digital transformation are as follows:

- There is no single and ready package solution. Transformation can be different in every organization.
- There is no clear answer as to what the solution is in digital transformation.
- Despite the rapid change in technologies, habits do not change at the same speed.
- Digital transformation requires transforming and managing different elements such as people, technology and processes together.

- Business and operations of organizations continue in the transformation process.
- There is no end for digital transformation.
- Digital transformation requires considering the past, present and future as a whole and drawing a roadmap accordingly.

Apart from these, it is necessary to carefully focus on limiting criteria such as competition conditions brought about by the macro environment, issues related to national or international legal regulations, time and cost losses that will occur in the transformation process, technical difficulties due to obsolete or insufficient infrastructure, and all necessary preliminary preparations should be made.

3.4 Digital Finance

Digitalization has led to direct or indirect transformations and changes in all aspects of life. The effects of technological innovations have also created a change in financial services. The effects of technological innovations have also differentiated financial services. With this differentiation, the concepts of "digital finance" or "digitalization of finance" have also become important. The benefits of traditional finance models are an undeniable fact. Thanks to the integration between Internet technology and finance in recent years, the new digital finance model, also supported by information technology, has helped to reduce the degree of information asymmetry, increased the availability of financial services, optimized resource allocation in the financial market and reduced transaction costs. In this section, rather than traditional finance models, the advantages of digital finance are discussed.

3.4.1 Concept of Digital Finance

From a practitioner's perspective, digital finance can be viewed as financial services provided through mobile phones, personal computers, the Internet, or cards connected to a trusted digital payment system. Similarly, a McKinsey report defines digital finance as "financial services provided via mobile phones, the internet, or cards." From another perspective, digital finance encompasses the vast array of new financial products, financial businesses, finance-related software, and new forms of customer communication and interaction offered by FinTech (Financial Technology) companies and innovative financial service providers. Although there is no standard definition, digital finance encompasses all products, services, technology and/or infrastructure that enable individuals and companies to access payments, savings and credit facilities via the Internet (without the need to visit a bank branch or contact a financial service provider directly) (Ozili, 2018: 330).

3.4.2 Advantages of Digital Finance

As an important component of the financial market, it can be observed that digital finance has become to occupy an important place in every aspect of daily life. Some innovative aspects of digital finance are online loan facility, Internet finance, online insurance services, mobile payment and loan inquiries. These opportunities can help increase the accessibility of financial services, improve the availability of financial services for individuals, and stimulate revenue growth by relieving individuals from liquidity constraints. Digital payment platforms have greatly reduced the transaction and time costs of financial services and increased payment and transfer efficiency for household consumption (Li et al., 2020: 319, 323; Kara and Aksu, 2020: 132–133).

The main benefit of digitalization for economic growth is to promote inclusive financing and allow groups not covered by banks to participate in formal financial systems through electronic payment platforms and technological platforms for the supply of savings and loans. sThanks to the digital solutions, entrepreneurs and businesses can reconsider their business models that can be more competitive, sustainable and better connected with other sectors of the economy (Vida et al., 2020: 37–38).

Some of the benefits of digital finance are as follows (Ozili, 2018:330):

- It provides greater financial inclusion, expansion of financial services to non-financial sectors and expansion of basic services to individuals.
- It has the potential to provide affordable, convenient and secure banking services to poor individuals in developing countries.
- It promises to increase the gross domestic product (GDP) of digitalized economies by providing convenient access to a variety of financial products and services (and credit facilities) for individuals as well as small, medium and large businesses. Hence, it improves overall spending and GDP levels.
- It can provide greater economic stability and increased financial intermediation for the economy where both customers and their families reside.
- Innovation in digital finance can have positive long-term effects on banking performance. (The adoption of SWIFT, a network-based technology infrastructure and set of standards for worldwide interbank telecommunications; (1) has major implications for long-term profitability; (2) these profitability effects are greater for small banks than for large banks; (3) exhibit significant network effects on performance.)

- It also benefits governments by providing a platform to facilitate the increase in aggregate spending, which generates higher tax revenue from the increase in the volume of financial transactions.
- It has benefits to financial and monetary system regulators, as full-scale adoption of digital finance can significantly reduce the circulation of bad (or fake) money, etc. It enables fast financial decision-making and the ability to pay and receive in seconds.

3.5 Covid-19 and Digitalization

The global epidemic, known as the Covid-19 or the coronavirus pandemic, is perhaps one of the most important events of the century we are in. The virus epidemic, which started in the city of Wuhan in China at the end of 2019, has been recognized as a pandemic by the World Health Organization and has spread throughout the world without exception (Beybur and Çetinkaya, 2020: 148). The pandemic, which gradually increased its impact in 2020, still continues its impact in many countries as the third or fourth wave in 2021. In 2020 and 2021, it has affected all social and economic life, all kinds of sectors, human lives and behaviors, and has initiated a major transformation process that will take place in the following year or years.

The fastest period of digitalization has probably been the Covid-19 pandemic period. The process of avoiding contact, rotating or remote work, distance education, less social movement and physical relationships has led to the digitalization or digital transformation of not only businesses but also people. Companies have established the necessary infrastructure systems for remote working and being constantly accessible in order to protect the health of their employees. Activities such as training, seminars, conferences and meetings started to be carried out online, with the restriction of all non-essential travels and minimizing physical accessibility. Businesses that carried out their business partially or completely through online channels before the pandemic period adapted very quickly to this change and responded quickly and effectively to increasing customer demands (Ayaydın, 2021:11–18). On the other hand, significant losses have occurred in sectors such as tourism, transportation, entertainment, non-food retail and construction, which do not have the opportunity to transfer all or most of their business to digital.

Digital businesses, which have increased their market shares thanks to new markets and customers brought about by mobile applications or online sales channels, have achieved rapid growth during the pandemic. Businesses have also captured opportunities such as increasing business awareness, experiencing e-commerce for the first time or growing e-commerce volumes (Taşel, 2020: 134–135), minimizing the negative economic conditions of the pandemic in this rapid transformation process. Apart from these, it should be noted that not all sectors were positively affected during the pandemic period. Significant losses occurred in sectors such as tourism, transportation, entertainment, non-food retail and construction, which did not have the ability to move all or most of their business to digital.

Financial transactions have been carried out almost entirely online. Speed, convenience and security, the growth of the e-commerce market, the strengthening of corporate identity through the mobile application or the website have pushed even businesses that are resistant to digitalization into this transformation.

4. Conclusion

The fact that the Internet became increasingly widespread in the mid-1990s, which resulted in new technologies that developed very rapidly in the 2000s and the start of the Industry 4.0 revolution were the most important factors of digitalization. Businesses have to benefit from digital technologies in order to stay up-to-date in the ever-increasing competitive conditions, surpass their competitors, produce fast solutions to ever-changing demands, and use advanced technologies in their production processes. In addition, it is a great advantage that digital technologies have become less costly and easier to obtain for smaller organizations. The utilization of this advantage can be achieved through digitalization, regardless of the sector, for businesses to be more prolific and to increase product quality and production efficiency.

Financial management / managers are critical in the leadership of businesses. In order to evaluate the financial management and financial technologies of companies on the concept of digitalization, it is necessary to understand the concept of digital finance and to benefit from the advantages of digital finance. Businesses whose prime objectives are profitability and aim to continuously grow by increasing this advantage have focused on financial operations and efficient management of these operations. The data provided by digitalization are important tools in making faster and more effective decisions and determining future targets more accurately.

There are also relations between the financial management and financial technologies of enterprises and financial institutions (banking, insurance, brokerage firms, factoring, financial investment consultancy institutions, etc.). Innovative services offered by financial institutions and organizations (finance applications, investment management and portfolio transactions, differentiated payment instruments, funding services, robotic-artificial intelligence services, fund management, international financial solution services, etc.) play an active role in solving many problems faced by companies in financial management. It also inspires the financial management of companies with business model innovation. In this context, the concept of digital finance is also discussed in the study.

Through digital technologies, raw material or semi-finished product purchasing processes, effective supply chain management, reducing the time to market for products, electronic sales and control can be achieved. Thanks to digital transformation, companies can contribute more to the country's economy through e-exports, internationalization, gaining competitive advantage, institutionalization and sustainable growth. Businesses and financial institutions need to be in close contact with financial technology companies (Fintech), which serve as an innovation center, have next-generation payment systems and offer up-to-date recommendations on digitalization.

In the transformation and digitalization of business processes, people will also need to be remodeled, and it will be necessary to have knowledge on subjects such as technology literacy, cyber security, cloud, artificial intelligence, augmented reality, machine learning, big data, robotic technologies and the IoT. From the perspective of finance managers, data analysis, statistical knowledge, knowledge of measurement and reporting tools, analytical thinking skills, communication and cooperation skills, high motivation, being open to development and continuous learning, crisis management knowledge, directing, coordinating, being proactive and having high level leadership skills will be imperative in businesses. It is clear from the development in the Covid-19 global pandemic process where digitalization has experienced the fastest transformation that the number of companies operating with a hybrid working style will exponentially increase, and flexible or remote working models will become widespread (Demirhan, 2021:10–19). The growth acceleration of businesses that adapt quickly to changing conditions will also increase.

References

Alam, N., Gupta, L., & Zameni, A. (2019). Digitalization and Disruption in the Financial Sector. In *Fintech and Islamic Finance*. Cham: Palgrave Macmillan. https://doi.org/10.1007/978-3-030-24666-2_1. Accessed 10 May 2021.

Ayaydın, H. (May, 2021). Dijitalleşme Kobi'lere Fırsat Penceresi Açar mı?. In Koohi, K., & Amanzholova, A. (Eds.), *v. International Kaoru Ishikawa Business Administration and Economy Congress*, Ankara.

Ballandies, M. C., Dapp, M. M., Degenhart, B. A., Helbing, D., Klauser, S., & Pardi, A. L. (2021). *Finance 4.0—A Socio-Ecological Finance System. In Finance 4.0-Towards a Socio-Ecological Finance System* (pp. 53–89). Cham: Springer.

Beybur, M., & Çetinkaya, M. (2020). Covid-19 Pandemisinin Türkiye'de Dijital Bankacilik Ürün ve Hizmetlerinin Kullanımı Üzerindeki Etkisi. *Uluslararası Batı Karadeniz Sosyal ve Beşeri Bilimler Dergisi,* 4(2), 148–163.

Bilgiç, E., Türkmenoğlu, M. A., & Koçak, A. (2020). Dijitalleşmenin Lojistik Yönetimi Bağlamında İncelenmesi. *Bitlis Eren Üniversitesi İktisadi ve İdari Bilimler Fakültesi Akademik İzdüşüm Dergisi,* 5(1), 56–69.

Brunnermeier, M. K., James, H., & Landau, J. P. (2019). *The Digitalization of Money* (No. w26300). Cambridge: National Bureau of Economic Research. Working Paper 26300.

Dapp, M. M., Klauser, S., & Ballandies, M. (2019). *Finance 4.0 Design: Technical Report.* Zurich, Switzerland: ETH Zurich.

Demirhan, M. (2021). Sektörel Bakış: Türk Bankacılık Sektöründe Dijitalleşmenin Şube Dağıtım Kanalına Etkileri. *Erciyes Akademi,* 35(1), 1–19.

Erturk, M. (2017). *İşletme Biliminin Temel İlkeleri.* İstanbul: Beta Basım Yayım.

Geisberger, E., & Broy, M. (2012). agendaCPS – *Integrierte Forschungsagenda Cyber – Physical Systems.* Berlin: Springer.

İpekten, O. B. (2019). Finansal Yönetime Giriş. B. Elmas (Ed.), *Finansal Yönetim içinde* (pp.1–19). Erzurum: Atatürk Üniversitesi Açıköğretim Fakültesi Yayını.

Kagermann, H., Wahlster, W. ve Helbig, J. (2013). *Recommendations for Implementing The Strategic Initiative Industrie 4.0,* Final Report, Acatech National Academy of Science and Engineering, 13–78.

Kara, M. A., & Aksu, T. (2020). *Pandemi Döneminde Finans Sektöründeki Teknolojik Yeniliklerin Önemi.* III. Uluslararasi Kahramanmaraş Yönetim, Ekonomi ve Siyaset Kongresi, 126, Kahramanmaraş.

Karavardar, G. (2019). Endüstri 4.0'ın İşletme Yönetimine Getirdiği Yeni Perspektif. M. Serçemeli (Ed.), *Endüstri 4.0'ın Muhasebe, Denetim Ve Finans Dünyasına Yansımaları içinde* (pp.3–22). Ankara: Gazi Kitabevi.

Kumar, K. (2018). Impact of Digitalization in Finance & Accounting. *Journal of Accounting, Finance & Marketing Technology,* 2(2), 1–9.

Li, J., Wu, Y., & Xiao, J. J. (2020). The Impact of Digital Finance on Household Consumption: Evidence from China. *Economic Modelling,* 86, 317–326.

Özçelik, A. G. M., & Akçay, V. H. (2019). Bankacılık Sektöründe Dijitalleşmenin Kariyer Platosu ile İlişkisi Özet. *Türk & İslam Dünyası Sosyal Araştırmalar Dergisi,* 6(22), 150–163.

Özgen, H., Öztürk, A. & Yalçın, A. (2001). *Temel İşletmecilik Bilgisi*. Adana: Nobel Kitabevi.

Ozili, P. K. (2018). Impact of Digital Finance on Financial Inclusion and Stability. *Borsa Istanbul Review*, 18(4), 329–340.

Parida, V. (2018). Digitalization. In Frishammar, J., & Ericsson A.(Eds.), *Adressing Social Challenges* (pp. 23–38). Sweden: Luleå University of Technology.

Taşel, F. (2020). Dijitalleşmenin Ticarete ve Ekonomiye Etkisi. *Beykoz Akademi Dergisi*, 8(2), 127–137.

Vida, I., Spaller, E., & Vasa, L. (2020). Potential Effects of Finance 4.0 on the Employment in East Africa. *Economie şi Sociologie*, (2), 29–42.

Arda TOYGAR & Senem NART

Requirements of Digital Management in the Global Supply Chain: The Case of Container Logistics

1. Introduction

The 1970s saw a significant increase in cargo volumes subject to foreign trade with the increase of global trade all over the world. Indeed, free trade and customs agreements between countries create the need for supply chain activities to be carried out on a global scale. Along with these developments around the world, the widespread use of outsourcing by companies in order to benefit from global opportunities has led to a rapid increase in the demands for all transportation systems (Kasilingam, 1998; Coyle et al., 2017). In order to meet this increasing demand in global supply chains, maritime transportation is preferred over to other transportation systems (Lam & Bai, 2016). In other words, although there are various systems such as air, sea, land and rail transportation among the transportation systems, approximately 80 % of the cargoes subject to global trade are carried out by sea trade (UNCTAD, 2019). Container logistics, which is used extensively in maritime trade, is also deemed one of the most effective methods in supply chain movements. Due to its advantages, it is an important form of maritime transportation that allows the cargo to be transported safely and securely during shipment (Ateş & Esmer, 2013).

In the shipment of many raw materials, semi-finished products or finished product groups that are subject to foreign trade from one point to another, the rate of container transportation continues to increase over the years (Çağlar & Esmer, 2015). The high increase in competition in container logistics in the recent years causes a significant decline in maritime companies' profit margins. In order to solve the resulting financial losses, maritime companies have started to provide E2E (*end to end*) services covering the entire supply chain. Maritime companies develop digital management applications with blockchain infrastructure in order to eliminate the gaps between supply chain parties in these initiatives (Kshetri, 2018; Queiroz & Wamba, 2019). However, successful management practices require a good understanding of the requirements of blockchain technology and the seamless integration of this technology into supply chains (Chang et al., 2020).

Although many companies tend to use technology with blockchain infrastructure in their supply chain management processes nowadays, there are a limited number of studies on the integration of this technology into supply chain processes in the literature (Balci, 2021). Thus, this study includes a theoretical evaluation of digital transformation in global supply chain management, particularly in the case of maritime companies, known as main logistics providers, and the shippers (foreign trade companies, freight forwarders) that create the demand. By providing an alternative to the traditional management approach in container logistics, the study is a guide for container logistics stakeholders, since it contains theoretical implications for blockchain-based management models.

2. Digitalization in Supply Chain Management

Supply chain management is an integrated system that provides cooperation and information exchange among all parts in order to obtain a product, to add value to the product obtained, and to deliver the final product to both retailers and customers by procuring raw and other materials (Min & Zhou, 2002). The chain includes not only manufacturers and suppliers, but also transportation and storage service providers, retailers and even customers (Chopra & Meindl, 2007). In order to carry out a successful supply chain management, cargo and information flows must be managed effectively throughout the entire chain (Chang et al., 2020). However, for a sustainable supply chain, it is very important for all parties to develop a strategic cooperation by providing long-term, social and economic values for a common purpose (Karakoç et al., 2020). Developments in the recent years, such as the difficulty of competition conditions within the framework of globalization, the complexity of supply chain networks and the shortening of product life cycles have made it necessary for companies to reconsider their supply chain strategies in order to be sustainable (Beamon, 1999). Although supply chain management consists of many activities, the subject of container logistics management provides the link between raw material supply, production, storage and distribution processes. In the following parts of the study, sustainable supply chain practices are evaluated in the context of container logistics.

3. Container Logistics Digital Management Requirements

Container logistics management covers all global supply chain processes between export-import factories. To explain, the cargo is stacked inside the container at the CFS (Container Freight Station) area at the export factory or in the port and is prepared for sea shipment after the export customs clearance is completed. It covers all processes from the completion of the import customs procedures after the maritime transportation is carried out to the delivery to the buyer by inland transportation (Zhang vd., 2010; Brinkmann, 2011). Supported by the globalization process and the widespread usage of the container, container logistics is a striking example of growth (Notteboom, 2012). The volume of container logistics worldwide has increased from 28.7 million TEUs in 1990 to 811.2 million TEUs in 2019 (Zairi, 1997; UNCTAD, 2020). Moreover, the increase in foreign trade volumes and the efforts of shipping companies to reduce their costs have also led to an increase in the cargo capacities of ships. Particularly between 1956 and 2020, the size and transportation volume of container ships increased significantly. While the Ideal X ship was engaged in transportation activities in 1956 with a capacity of 58 containers with 35 ft. dimensions (96 TEU), today container ships provide service with a capacity of 24,000 TEU, which is 250 times larger than the Ideal X ship (Salleh et al., 2021). The rapid increase in the carrying capacity of container ships negatively affects the management processes of companies on the supply and demand sides of the supply chain. Strategies to fill up the carrying capacity of large ships in order to save costs cause maritime companies on the supply side of the supply chain to increase their freight rates due to the pressure put on them (Notteboom, 2004). An increase in freight rates also triggers an increase in costs in all supply chain activities of foreign trade companies on the demand side (Fusillo & Haralambides, 2020).

Although the entry of the container into the shipping industry enables large-scale international trade (Singh, 2019), container logistics consists of many independent and different parties (Van Der Horst & De Langen, 2008). For example, during a single avocado shipment from Mombasa to Rotterdam in a container, 200 different information exchanges take place between 30 different parties (Godbole & Lead, 2017). Due to the fact that all these parties form the transportation chain, it is necessary to establish uninterrupted and fast collaborations between the parties (Feibert et al., 2017). However, the use of many paper documents in the system, which is a traditional management approach during the shipment of the container from the starting point to the end, causes interruptions in communication between the parties during the shipment process (Van Der Horst & De Langen, 2008; Lieber, 2017). The problems arising from these interruptions causes an uncertain and complex interaction between different and independent parties in container logistics (Caschili & Medda, 2012). In addition, companies in the global supply chain need to be fast in basic supply chain processes such as load and information flow and benefit from the technologies of the period in order to gain a sustainable advantage in competition (Yang, 2019; Toygar & İpekçi, 2020). That is, adapting to digital management in the supply chain can make container transportation transparent and allow integrated management of the physically transported containers (İpekçi & Toygar, 2020). In addition, the digitalization of port operations, which provide the connection between the land and sea in the supply chain, can reduce the use of paper in operational processes and provide fast access to information (Di Vaio & Varriale, 2020).

Blockchain is one of the important technologies that have been recently integrated into the chain so that the transactions made throughout the supply chain can be monitored and all processes can be secured (Kshetri, 2018). This technology also enables the use of smart contracts in logistics processes in order to make container operation processes more effective (Queiroz & Wamba, 2019). In this way, maritime transportation and customs documents offer important opportunities for the documentation processes required during the shipment of the container (Balci, 2021). The following section presents recent digital management trends with blockchain infrastructure used in container logistics management.

4. Blockchain Technology in Container Logistics Management

The main function of the services provided by container shipping companies is the transportation of containers between loading-discharge ports (Balci et al., 2018). However, due to the recent decrease in profitability in container transportation, the competition has gained momentum between container shipping companies that provide only maritime transportation services and freight forwarders that provide services throughout the supply chain (Balci, 2021). These rivalries cause container shipping companies to provide E2E (end to end) services throughout the entire supply chain. But the rapid spread of COVID-19 around the world is creating disruptions in global supply chains (Etemadi et al., 2021). Increased competition between the parties and the pandemic has accelerated the integration of blockchain technology into supply chain management, as in many sectors (Wang et al., 2019). The main purpose of this technology integrated into the supply chain is to establish digital connections between the parties and to ensure the mutual flow, storage and sharing of data (Wang & Sarkis, 2021). Blockchain technology allows parties to securely monitor container mobility throughout the entire supply chain from the starting point to the end (Queiroz & Wamba, 2019). In addition, blockchain plays a key role in data transfer between parties in container logistics by providing cloud-based storage of data with digital methods. In blockchain, data is stored on ledgers via decentralized blockchain systems. For this reason, modification or retrospective processing of the data is not allowed since the data stored in each block network can be viewed by anyone with a permission to access (Dong et al., 2018). No intermediary is required for this system to work. Because there are secure and transparent cloud storage systems that enable the parties, who have the switch in the supply chain, to enter data quickly when necessary (Wang et al., 2019). In the following section, examples of the use of blockchain technology in container logistics management processes since 2018 are presented.

4.1. Digital Management Trends in Container Logistics

In 2018, Maersk, world's largest container shipping company, created a global trading platform together with IBM using blockchain technology to reduce container logistics costs, make the information flow in the supply chain transparent, and prevent time loss in operational processes caused by the use of paper. On the platform called Tradelens, many parties involved in container logistics can access data in real time and share information instantly and quickly with each other (Scott, 2018).

In 2021, MSC, the world's second largest container shipping company, launched the electronic Bill of Lading (EBL) application for all its customers worldwide on its blockchain platform Wave BL. EBL enables all parties involved in the container shipment reservation to access, approve and manage the bill of lading electronically through a secure, decentralized network via a blockchain platform. Moreover, EBL enables supply chain parties to receive and transmit the bill of lading electronically without any changes or interruptions in container logistics operations (MSC, 2021; Hellenic Shipping News, 2021).

In 2018, digital technology firm Accenture created a consortium with blockchain technology to develop efficient supply chain networks, reduce the need for paper-printed shipping documents, and lower shipping costs. In order to reflect the entire supply chain, the consortium includes APL, a strong container shipping company, Kuehne+Nagel, one of the world's leading freight forwarders, and AB InBev, as a European customs organization and shipper. Within the consortium, 12 containers were shipped using the blockchain technology. The results show that blockchain technology speeds up the flow of interparty shipping documents and reduces unnecessary data entry by up to 80 % (Accenture, 2018).

5. Conclusion

The fact that commercial activities directly affect the demand, especially in container logistics, and the traditional supply chain management approach's inability to provide adequate solutions in meeting this intense demand of dynamic markets necessitated the development of new approaches and practices. As in every other field, digitalization has disrupted known practices in supply chain management and container logistics management. The positive effects of interconnected and intelligent smart networks on performance are becoming more and more important every day. Digitizing all processes in container logistics management increases the use of resources more efficiently, reduces costs, increases transparency in transportation and speed in delivery, and thus increases customer satisfaction. Blockchain technology is one of the most important initiatives in the steps taken towards digitalization at this point. This technology ensures a much more transparent freight mobility within the supply chain, enabling instant tracking of processes such as cargo documentation, transportation and management, and web-based digital interventions. The technology not only increases the reliability of the customers to the company, but also helps to facilitate uninterrupted transactions and to record data accurately. Therefore, understanding the impact of digital applications is very important in container logistics, which is one of the building blocks of the supply chain. Container logistics management, supported by the Blockchain technology infrastructure, attracts the attention of foreign trade companies by providing fast, uninterrupted and instant communication between the parties. Maritime companies benefiting from this technology also gain significant advantages in an increasingly competitive environment.

In this context, national authorities and non-governmental organizations providing support and incentives to companies that adopt digital applications in container logistics is important for an effective management. The significant costs in order to obtain these applications are undoubtedly necessary. Providing the needed financial support in the form of long-term loans by the relevant institutions and organizations will be an important incentive to grow the sector and create a bigger economic value. On the other hand, another important problem faced by companies in this field is the lack of qualified workforce. Training a workforce expert in the use of digital applications and ensuring that companies can reach a qualified workforce should be on the agenda of national authorities. In the light of all this information, conducting academic studies with qualitative and quantitative methods on digitalization in supply chain management and container logistics management will make significant contributions to both the literature and the business world.

References

Accenture. (2018). *Industry consortium successfully tests blockchain solution developed by accenture that could revolutionize ocean shipping.* https://newsroom.accenture.com/news/industry-consortium-successfully-tests-blockchain-solution-developed-by-accenture-that-could-revolutionize-ocean-shipping.htm#:~:text=NEW YORK%3B March 14%2C 2018,of millions of dollars annually. Accessed 14 March 2018.

Ateş, A., & Esmer, S. (2013). Türk Konteyner Termi̇nalleri̇ Üzeri̇nde 2009 Yili Küresel Finans Kri̇zi̇ni̇n Etki̇leri̇. *Sayıştay Dergi̇si̇,* 91, 105–125.

Balci, G. (2021). Digitalization in container shipping services: Critical resources for competitive advantage. *Journal of ETA Maritime Science*, 9(1), 3–12.

Balci, G., Cetin, I. B., & Tanyeri, M. (2018). Differentiation of container shipping services in Turkey. *Transport Policy,* 61, 26–35.

Beamon, B. M. (1999). Designing the green supply chain. *Logistics Information Management,* 12(4), 332–342.

Brinkmann, B. (2011). Operations systems of container terminals: A compendious overview. In J. W. Böse (Ed.), *Handbook of terminal planning* (pp. 25–39). New York: Springer.

Caschili, S., & Medda, F. R. (2012). A review of the maritime container shipping industry as a complex adaptive system. *Interdisciplinary Description of Complex Systems: INDECS*, 10(1), 1–15.

Chang, Y., Iakovou, E., & Shi, W. (2020). Blockchain in global supply chains and cross border trade: a critical synthesis of the state-of-the-art, challenges and opportunities. *International Journal of Production Research*, 58(7), 2082–2099.

Chopra, S., & Meindl, P. (2007). Supply chain management. Strategy, planning & operation. In *Das summa summarum des management* (pp. 265–275). New Jersey: Prentice Hall.

Coyle, J. J., Jr., C. J. L., Novack, R. A., & Gibson, B. J. (2017). *Supply chain management: A logistics perspective* (10th ed.). Boston: Cengage Learning.

Çağlar, T., & Esmer, S. (2015). Türkiye' de Boş Konteynerlerin Yeniden Konumlandırılması Sorunu Üzerine Nitel Bir Araştırma. *Mustafa Kemal Üniversitesi Sosyal Bilimler Enstitüsü Dergisi*, 12(31), 242–256.

Di Vaio, A., & Varriale, L. (2020). Digitalization in the sea-land supply chain: Experiences from Italy in rethinking the port operations within inter-organizational relationships. *Production Planning & Control,* 31(2–3), 220–232.

Dong, Z., Luo, F., & Liang, G. (2018). Blockchain: A secure, decentralized, trusted cyber infrastructure solution for future energy systems. *Journal of Modern Power Systems and Clean Energy*, 6(5), 958–967.

Etemadi, N., Borbon-Galvez, Y., Strozzi, F., & Etemadi, T. (2021). Supply chain disruption risk management with blockchain: A dynamic literature review. *Information*, 12(2), 70.

Feibert, D. C., Hansen, M. S., & Jacobsen, P. (2017). *An integrated process and digitalization perspective on the shipping supply chain: A literature review.* IEEE International Conference on Industrial Engineering and Engineering Management (IEEM), 1352–1356.

Fusillo, M., & Haralambides, H. (2020). Do carrier expectations indicate industry structure in container shipping? An econometric analysis. *Journal of Shipping and Trade*, 5(1), 1–16.

Godbole, S., & Lead, I. B. M. (2017). *How blockchain can transform global trade supply chains.* IBM Center for Blockchain Innovation IBM Research. https://www.unescap.org/sites/default/files/3_IBM Blockchain.pdf. Accessed 24 May 2021.

Hellenic Shipping News. (2021). *MSC introduces new electronic bill of lading for customers worldwide using wave bl's Platform.* https://www.hellenicshippingnews.com/msc-introduces-new-electronic-bill-of-lading-for-customers-worldwide-using-wave-bls-platform/. Accessed 29 April 2021.

İpekçi, E., & Toygar, A. (2020). *Lojistik Sektöründe Yetenek 4.0.* In S. Nart (Ed.), Çalışma Yaşamında Yetenek 4.0 (1st ed.). İstanbul: Beta Basım Yayım Dağıtım.

Karakoç, N., Eren, T., & Özcan, E. (2020). Sürdürülebilir Tedarik Zinciri Yönetimi İçin Endüstri 4.0'daki Zorlukların Değerlendirilmesi. *Endüstri Mühendisliği*, 31(2), 215–233.

Kasilingam, R. G. (1998). *Logistics and Transportation: Design and Planning* (1st ed.). Dordrecht: Kluwer Academic Publishers.

Kshetri, N. (2018). Blockchain's roles in meeting key supply chain management objectives. *International Journal of Information Management*, 39, 80–89.

Lam, J. S. L., & Bai, X. (2016). A quality function deployment approach to improve maritime supply chain resilience. *Transportation Research Part E: Logistics and Transportation Review*, 92, 16–27.

Lieber, A. (2017). *Trust in trade: Announcing a new blockchain partner.* IBM. https://www.ibm.com/blogs/blockchain/2017/03/trust-trade-announcing-new-blockchain-partner/#:~:text=IBM has a new blockchain,to improve efficiencies in trade. Accessed 9 March 2017.

Min, H., & Zhou, G. (2002). Supply chain modeling: Past, present and future. *Computers and Industrial Engineering*, 43, 1–2.

MSC. (2021). *Save time and reduce costs with msc electronic bill of lading* (ebl). Mediterranean Shipping Company. https://www.msc.com/prt/news/2021-april/msc-electronic-bill-of-lading-ebl-now-available-fo. Accessed 28 April 2021.

Notteboom, T. E. (2004). Container shipping and ports: An overview. *Review of Network Economics,* 3(2), 86–106.

Notteboom, T. E. (2012). Container Shipping. In W. K. Talley (ed.), *The Blackwell Companion to Maritime Economics* (1st ed., pp. 230–262). Blackwell Publishing Ltd. https://doi.org/10.1002/9781444345667.ch12. Accessed 24 January 2021.

Queiroz, M. M., & Wamba, S. F. (2019). Blockchain adoption challenges in supply chain: An empirical investigation of the main drivers in India and the USA. *International Journal of Information Management*, 46, 70–82.

Salleh, N. H. M., Zulkifli, N., & Jeevan, J. (2021). The emergence of very large container vessel (VLCV) in maritime trade: Implications on the Malaysian seaport operations. *WMU Journal of Maritime Affairs*, 20(1), 41–61.

Scott, T. (2018). *TradeLens: How IBM and Maersk Are Sharing Blockchain to Build a Global Trade Platform*. IBM. https://www.ibm.com/blogs/think/2018/11/tradelens-how-ibm-and-maersk-are-sharing-blockchain-to-build-a-global-trade-platform/. Accessed 28 November 2018.

Singh, L. (2019). The metal box that transformed global trade: The innovative vision of Malcom McLean behind the container revolution. *Legacy*, 19(1), 31–45.

Toygar, A., & İpekçi, E. (2020). Tedarik Zinciri Yönetiminde Yetenek 4.0. In S. Nart (Ed.), *Çalışma Yaşamında Yetenek 4.0* (1st ed.). İstanbul: Beta Basım Yayım Dağıtım.

UNCTAD. (2019). *Review of Maritime Transport*. https://unctad.org/system/files/official-document/rmt2019_en.pdf. Accessed 31 January 2020.

UNCTAD. (2020). *Review of maritime transport* – 2020. https://unctad.org/system/files/official-document/rmt2020_en.pdf. Accessed 7 July 2021.

Van Der Horst, M. R., & De Langen, P. W. (2008). Coordination in hinterland transport chains: A major challenge for the seaport community. *Maritime Economics & Logistics*, 10(1), 108–129.

Wang, X., Yang, W., Noor, S., Chen, C., Guo, M., & Van Dam, K. H. (2019). Blockchain-based smart contract for energy demand management. *Energy Procedia*, 158, 2719–2724.

Wang, Y., & Sarkis, J. (2021). Emerging digitalisation technologies in freight transport and logistics: Current trends and future directions. *Transportation Research Part E: Logistics and Transportation Review,* 148, 1–8.

Yang, C. S. (2019). Maritime shipping digitalization: Blockchain-based technology applications, future improvements, and intention to use. *Transportation Research Part E:*, 131(108), 117.

Zairi, M. (1997). Business process management: A boundaryless approach to modern competitiveness. *Business Process Management Journal,* 3(1), 64–80.

Zhang, R., Yun, W. Y., & Kopfer, H. (2010). Heuristic-based truck scheduling for inland container transportation. *OR Spectrum*, 32(3), 787–808.

Emre İPEKÇİ

Digital Transformation in Logistics Activities

1. Introduction

The twenty-first century was a period when digital technologies multiplied having gained great momentum. The emerging technologies during this period quickly penetrated the lives of both individuals and businesses. Digital technologies have got a foothold in, more or less, all sectors. Some sectors have benefited more quickly from what digitalization has brought due to their structure, while others have taken longer to transform digitally. Logistics and related sectors have rapidly adopted emerging technologies and incorporated them into their daily operations.

Logistics is a critical process for the smooth operation of supply chains when evaluated from the viewpoint of multidimensional and multinational enterprises. Today's holistic and sustainable supply chain management approach covers the entire product life cycle (Avelar-Sosa et al., 2019). For this reason, reverse logistics systems also occupy an important place concerning closed-loop supply chains, which plan both forward and backward flow of products.

Although logistics are based on the smooth implementation of product movement, it is also quite crucial that the data generated in all processes is visible. This data needs to be seen by every element involved in the supply chain that makes up the chain, especially customers, suppliers and production lines. Data, such as product delivery date for customers, estimated time when raw materials will reach the production line for production planners, and inventory information for sellers is critical for businesses. Obtaining this data is only possible with the smooth management of the flow of product and information that occurs in logistics processes. This enables the intensive use of digital technologies in the logistics sector. This section focuses on the place of digitalization in the logistics sector. After investigating the digital transformation and technologies that have occurred in the logistics sector from past to present, the possible effects of emerging technologies on the logistics sector in the near future and in the following years and how new digital trends can guide logistics were discussed.

2. Logistics and Digitalization

Logistics is a set of services consisting of transportation in particular, storage, inventory management, order management, stock management, customs, inspection-surveillance and other value-added works (Rushton et al., 2014). Businesses buy what they need from these services from one or more logistics companies through outsourcing. Especially when faced with a multi-layered logistics network design, the number of companies throughout the system receiving services increases, and it becomes more important that the data produced is easily accessible and remains interpretable. This has enabled digital technologies to gain a solid place in the logistics sector. Today, businesses need faster and more accurate information flow, particularly with full-time production systems finding application areas in many different sectors. In order to ensure this flow, information communication technologies should be included in logistics processes.

The presence of information systems in the field of logistics began to be felt more intensely from the second half of the twentieth century. It can be said that the first traces of digitalization in logistics occurred through the transmission of information processed into barcodes to computers through electronic data exchange systems. With the processing of this information by computers, material requirements planning (MRP) software emerged. These software can be seen as the ancestor of today's supply chain software (Schroeder and Goldstein, 2018). Since the 1990s, international transport companies implementing vehicle and equipment-tracking systems can be considered the first applications of ensuring visibility for both businesses and consumers. Today, road fleet owners can instantly access and control many data such as the instantaneous position of the vehicle, fuel consumption, the condition of the tires, the internal temperature of the transport unit, by means of GPS-based electronic cards mounted on vehicles (Kanarachos et al., 2019). Supply chains are designed in a wide range, from field to table, thanks to the systems used today in different modes of transport. Table 1 provides examples of significant digital transformations in logistics from past to present.

Table 1. Significant developments in logistics and supply chain from past to present

2020	**Industry 4.0 applications, augmented reality, smart factories and use of robots**
2018	Announcement of the blockchain-based Tradelens system, developed by Maersk and IBM.
2013	Amazon's filing for a patent for the system, which shortens delivery times by estimating what consumers will buy before making a purchase.
2004	Walmart begins using RFID tags with its 100 largest suppliers.
2000	Using global outsourcing for complex supply chains.
1999	Alibaba's first e-commerce post.
1994	Amazon's first e-commerce post.
1990	The emergence of the first ERP systems.
1979	FedEx announces a real-time tracking system.
1975	Walmart begins using IBM for stock management and distribution.
1974	The first barcode scanned in the US.
1973	Toyota's successful implementation of the just-in-time production system.
1956	The first EDI transfer was sent on the transatlantic line.

Source: Adapted by the author into Turkish based on Herold et al. (2021).

When evaluating digital applications in the logistics sector, addressing the process from a multidimensional point of view makes it more understandable both from the perspective of logistics companies and from the viewpoint of manufacturing enterprises. For example, while applications such as vehicle tracking and fleet management used by an enterprise performing international transportation to provide visibility to the customers belong to the implementation side of logistics, systems employed by a manufacturing business for tracking inventory fall under daily operational processes. For this reason, logistics information systems will be more comprehensible when they are considered in two separate categories as distribution and storage systems, and production and order systems.

Table 2. Logistics information systems

Distribution and Storage Systems	Production and Order Systems
Vehicle Tracking Systems	Material Requirements Planning (MRP)
Geographic Information Systems	Enterprise Resource Planning (ERP)
Maintenance Management Systems	Production Resources Planning (MRP II)
Driver Tracking Systems	Order Management Systems
Route Planning Systems	Customer Relationship Management Systems
Warehouse and Inventory Management Systems	Network Design Systems

Source: Created by the author.

The systems in the table are systems that have been used for many years in the field of logistics and offer businesses visibility in all areas they need. Although some of these systems can be more diversified and divided into subcategories according to the demands and expectations of enterprises, they are sufficient to express the overall image. It must still be noted that there are various different technologies used today. Furthermore, new technologies entering our lives together with Industry 4.0 have started to create their own application ecosystems. These systems will also be mentioned in the following sections. It is also worth noting that the systems on the left side of the table are mostly used by logistics service providers, while the systems on the right side are used by manufacturing businesses.

3. Logistics Information Systems

The main purpose of information systems used in logistics is to successfully manage all related processes by providing visibility to enterprises. Data needed to ensure visibility is collected from the environment through physical systems. In order to make sense and use the collected data, software are needed. Data generated in logistics processes can be collected by means of different channels (hardware) such as infrared sensors, barcode readers, hand-held terminals, computers, Internet-connected devices, as well as be uploaded to the system by employees. Software and applications that interpret the collected data underpin information systems (Helo and Szekely, 2005). For example, warehouse personnel who collect products in the warehouse in accordance with the customer's order read the barcode of each product they receive from the shelf to the hand-held terminal, informing the system that the product is removed from inventory and the order is prepared. The delivery note, arranged after the products from the order are collected and packed for shipment, is a reflection of the system that the products are sent from the warehouse to the customer. As can be deduced from the example, any data generated in logistics processes is actually a critical success factor for proper management and visibility of an entire supply chain. In order for the system to function correctly, the data must be fully collected and should be interpreted with the correct software after entering the system.

In Table 2, information systems used in logistics were considered in two separate categories: systems for distribution and storage and systems for production and order. When evaluated in the framework of outsourcing in logistics, while software in the first group are used by logistics companies that offer moving and storage services to businesses, systems targeting production and order are used by businesses. *Lead logistics provider (LLP), fourth party logistics provider*

(4PL) and *fifth party logistics provider (5PL)* companies, which stand as advanced versions of outsourcing, can offer services at every stage falling outside the core activities of manufacturing businesses. These companies can provide integrated services to businesses by accessing their customers' all relevant information systems infrastructure. In short, thanks to information systems, some logistics businesses have become able to provide services today at every stage outside of production.

3.1. Distribution and Storage Systems

The software that will be examined under this heading are related to the movement of products. Warehouses are one of the largest data sources where the data needed in the supply chain is integrated into the system. Although warehouses are places where products halt during movement, the new-generation understanding of supply chain views warehouses as places where there is zero-kilometer transport per hour. This understanding is an indication that warehouses are in fact places that need to be managed more dynamically. Although warehouses are places where products are kept, prolonging this wait causes businesses to incur high costs. For this reason, any value-added operation that will be brought to the product should be carried out quickly in warehouses and the inventory turnover rate of the products should be kept high (İpekçi and Toygar, 2020). The work of transporting the right product to the right place, at the right time and at the right cost – one of the generally accepted truths of logistics – is also carried out thanks to the systems under this heading. The level reached by today's information technologies makes it possible to provide instant information throughout the entire movement within the product's supply chain network.

Vehicle Tracking Systems: Regardless of the type of transport used, it is quite essential for businesses to have location information visible during product movement. Since other modes other than road transport act according to a certain tariff or program, there are no major changes in the estimated delivery times provided to businesses, except for force majeure. Road transport is more open to external factors. Therefore, it is rather difficult to comply with the transit times committed by the logistics service provider. This makes instant location tracking of vehicles mandatory for both businesses and logistics companies. With GPS and GSM systems added to road vehicles, instant tracking of vehicles is possible. Thanks to the advanced systems used today, in addition to the instantaneous position of the vehicle, more data such as the speed of the vehicle, fuel status, engine speed, tire wear status, and the internal temperature of the vehicle can be accessed. Furthermore, thanks to equipment placed externally inside transport units such as containers and trailers, the flow of information provided is not interrupted even when the transport mode changes between the first exit and final destination of the transport container (Fort et al., 2018).

Geographic Information Systems: Geographic information systems are systems that can be employed in many different areas. In logistics processes, they can be used in areas such as designing distribution networks and real-time route planning. Thanks to a system, which can work integrated with vehicle tracking systems and similar software, optimization-based processes such as cargo-courier route planning and instant vehicle routes can be managed (Karabulut and Ocalir-Akunal, 2015). Owing to these software, significant amounts of fuel can be saved, especially when calculated annually in fleet management.

Maintenance Management Systems: For businesses that have a road fleet, repairs, maintenance and fixing of vehicles should be monitored regularly. These systems are used for tracking parts of vehicles that must be changed periodically according to mileage and engine operating hours, especially in large fleets. Thanks to maintenance systems, tire wear in the vehicle is managed in different processes such as tracking papers and documents that need to be renewed for the vehicle. Planned maintenance is important in managing customer relationships correctly, as it minimizes potential problems and prevents businesses from facing unexpected situations.

Driver Tracking Systems: Although the effects of digitalization are widely seen in the logistics sector, the need for humans in certain areas persists. Although currently work is being done on driverless truck projects, this technology is still in its infancy. Drivers are an important part of fleet management. For this reason, they often have to be watched over by logistics companies. The purpose of these systems is to monitor whether drivers follow both general traffic rules and the rules set by the business. In addition, tracking of drivers' licenses and permits, current visa status for the countries they will be transporting, and controlling of driver and vehicle assignments are also done through this system.

Route Planning Systems: Transportation is the area where the most expenses incur among logistics costs. Routes must be kept at the optimum level in order to minimize transport costs for businesses. These systems usually work integrated with geographic information systems, providing businesses with current road status and traffic data obtained from different sources, as well as different routes that can change instantly. It is especially important for these systems to be used by micro-distribution businesses to save fuel and time.

Warehouse and Inventory Management Systems: Warehouses are areas where raw materials or semi-finished products that will enter production and final products that come out of production are stored. Warehouses also allow value-added transactions that do not change the nature of the products to be carried out on products before they are offered for sale. All these activities lead to warehouses being the second largest logistics cost item after transportation within the product sales price (Engblom et al. 2012). Reducing storage costs within the chain is important for businesses to maintain their presence in competitive market conditions. Warehouse management systems generally record the movement of products coming to and leaving the warehouse. These systems work together with other systems used within an enterprise to provide instant inventory tracking. In this way, out-of-stock sales in enterprises are prevented, production continuity is ensured and possible disruptions in the supply chain are avoided. Complete and accurate use of hardware, such as hand-held terminals and barcode readers, are also essential for the smooth operation of warehouse management systems.

Today, many businesses are outsourcing and transferring the management of their warehouses to logistics service providers who are experts in their field. Enterprises can transfer the management of their own or leased warehouses to logistics companies, as well as transfer the storage needs and inventory management to logistics enterprises completely. In both cases, logistics operators are responsible for managing the processes. Logistics operators provide information sharing by making accessible all the data they need to their customers instantly.

3.2. Production and Ordering Systems

Competition between enterprises increases day by day and reaches different dimensions. As market conditions become more severe every year, consumer demands are also being diversified. While businesses that want to continue their existence focus more on their main fields of activity, they buy every operation outside of their main field of activity from companies that are experts in their fields. Logistics is also one of the areas where businesses most resort to outsourcing. Thanks to the standard reached by information systems, each data created in logistics processes can be transferred to enterprises instantly. Under this heading, some systems for production and order will be expounded upon.

Material Requirements Planning (MRP): Businesses use various methods when planning their production. Production plans are created according to these methods and demand estimates. MRP systems are systems that answer questions about when and in what quantity the inputs needed for production should be ordered and when they should be stored on the production line (Yaman, 2017). In order for MRP systems to give accurate results, they must work integrated with warehouse and inventory management systems, since MRPs need data such as inventory records, production plans and pending shipments. Although the history of MRP systems dates back to the 1970s, thanks to changes that they have undergone from year to year, today they are used by manufacturing enterprises together with different versions (MRP II, Closed Loop MRP, etc.). Today, MRP systems have been replaced by more advanced enterprise resource planning systems.

Production Resources Planning (MRP II): These are systems formed by the inclusion of processes such as marketing, finance and capacity planning in MRPs. It is a system that allows the company's top management to present reports such as business plans, purchase reports and inventory plans, thus increasing visibility in the supply chain. MRP software have been the beginning of today's enterprise resource planning software by carrying out planning of the material as well as the labor force and other elements necessary for production.

Enterprise Resource Planning (ERP): ERP is a comprehensive software used to manage all processes belonging to a business, especially production, sales, marketing, purchasing, and accounting (Yaman, 2017). These systems, which allow you to consider all the functions of the enterprise from a holistic point of view, can be offered to enterprises as a whole by their developers, as well as to enterprises to use only the modules they request. These systems, which allow management to consider the entire business from a holistic point of view, are one of the best examples of the progress that digitalization in logistics has accomplished from the past to the present. ERP provides businesses with a high level of visibility through the simultaneous connection between different business processes.

Network Design Systems: As the scale of businesses grows, supply chains become more layered and complex. Here, the production processes of products and how many components they have are especially vital. Businesses can position their production facilities in different countries or cities, as well as offer them for sale in different markets. In this case, choosing the location of the facility becomes an important decision. In a general sense, many different elements such as factories, retail points, warehouses with different functions (collection center, distribution center, etc.) are found together within a supply chain. The flow of raw materials or finished products between all these components that make up the supply chain is very important to ensure that logistics costs are kept at an optimal level. Network design systems are needed to manage the volumes of warehouses, to decide on plants to be added to or removed from the chain, as well as the production capacities of factories. Network design should be planned as multi-layered for both logistics and manufacturing enterprises. Network design systems in the supply chain guide businesses in the process of making strategic decisions.

4. Industry 4.0 and Its Effects on Logistics Technologies

Many technological developments that have emerged from the past to the present have found their application in logistics. Industry 4.0 is the new industrial revolution in which intelligent factories are at the center of production, the need for people is greatly reduced, and production lines are connected to each other through the Internet of things (Toygar and İpekçi, 2020). Although manufacturing systems are the focus of Industry 4.0, the technologies that have emerged with this new revolution have taken the steps of digitalization in the logistics and supply chain further. While blockchain ensures that data is shared more securely and faster, each link in the Internet of things supply chain is connected, big data analysis enables more accurate demand forecasts and production plans, 3D printers have started to radically change the structure of production (Scrauf and Berttram, 2016).

In today's market conditions, where supply chains are competitive, the most basic way to build agile supply chain networks is to share data just in time, without errors and securely. Blockchain technology, which stores data piecemeal in a virtual environment and prepares it where it is needed, turning it into a whole if necessary, will be one of the indispensable technologies of enterprises in this period when cyber data theft is increasing.

Each of the Industry 4.0 technologies has a separate task in establishing supply chain and logistics networks. While *cloud platforms* are reducing data storage costs, *smart sensors* and *mobile technologies* serve different monitoring solutions. Also, with the help of these technologies, *cyber physical* systems make it possiblc to managc production lincs with virtual computing infrastructurc. With the increased processing power in computer technology, *augmented reality* enables faster, smoother and less cost-effective labor in warehouses, factories and intermediate assembly decks (Schrauf and Berttram, 2018). As a result, Industry 4.0 is the end point of digitalization in production.

5. Conclusion

In order for supply chains to be successful, information exchange must be efficient. Supply chains that are structured in a traditional manner have difficulties in dealing with demand fluctuations that are difficult to predict. Information technologies provide both businesses and their customers with the data they need, ensuring that logistics processes are visible, while providing the opportunity to fight changes in demand faster. For this reason, the existence of digital technologies in all areas of logistics has become a necessity. In addition, logistics services are necessary not only for trade, but also for the functioning of everyday life to continue smoothly. Factors such as increasing consumer demand and expectations, environmental concerns, and the emergence of value-based food supply chains make it a necessity to record and present every stage of the product movement to consumers. When all these factors are evaluated together, the importance of information technologies in logistics and supply chain is once again demonstrated. However, logistics is an area where each technological development can quickly find a response or adapt itself. Today, new technologies that have emerged with Industry 4.0 also find their own response in logistics processes. Achieving this transformation has gone far beyond being a choice for businesses. As the need for humans decreases in physical processes, digital transformation opens up new business spaces. In the future, businesses' chances of survival will be proportional to the extent to which they have implemented this digital transformation.

References

Avelar-Sosa, L., García-Alcaraz, J. L., & Maldonado-Macías, A. A. (2019). *Evaluation of Supply Chain Performance A Manufacturing Industry Approach.* Ciudad Juárez: Springer.

Engblom, J., Solakivi, T., JuusoTöyli, & Ojala, L. (2012). Multiple-method Analysis of Logistics Costs. *International Journal of Production Economics*, 29–35.

Fort, H. E., Oya, G. J., Chavero, M. F., & Carvajal, G. R. (2018). Intelligent Containers Based on a Low-Power Sensor Network and a Non-Invasive Acquisition System for Management and Tracking of Goods. *IEEE Transactions On Intelligent Transportation Systems*, 2734–2738.

Helo, P., & Szekely, B. (2005). Logistics Information Systems: An Analysis of Software Solutions for Supply Chain Co-ordination. *Industrial Management & Data Systems*, 5–18.

Herold, D. M., Cwiklicki, M., Pilch, K., & Mikl, J. (2021). The Emergence and Adoption of Digitalization in the Logistics and Supply Chain Industry: An Institutional Perspective. *Journal of Enterprise Information Management*, 1917–1938.

İpekçi, E., & Toygar, A. (2020). Lojistik Sektöründe Yetenek 4.0. S. Nart (Dü.) içinde, *Çalışma Yaşamında Yetenek 4.0* (s. 249–268). İstanbul: Beta.

Kanarachos, S., Mathew, J., & Fitzpatrick, E. M. (2019). Instantaneous Vehicle Fuel Consumption Estimation Using Smartphones and Recurrent Neural Networks. *Expert Systems with Applications*, 436–447.

Karabulut, S., & Ocalir-Akunal, E. V. (2015). Geographical Information System Based Environmental Risk Analysis for Road Transportation of Hazmats.

Journal of the Faculty of Engineering and Architecture of Gazi University, 351–359.

Rushton, A., Croucher, P., & Baker, P. (2014). *The Handbook of Logistics and Distribution Management*. Londra: Kogan Page.

Schrauf, S., & Berttram, P. (2018). How digitization makes the supply chain more efficient, agile, and customer-focused. *Price Waterhouse Cooper*.

Schroeder, R. G., & Goldstein, S. M. (2018). *Operations Management in the Supply Chain Decisions and Cases*. New York: McGraw-Hill Education.

Toygar, A., & İpekçi, E. (2020). Tedarik Zinciri Yönetiminde Yetenek 4.0. *Çalışma Yaşamında Yetenek 4.0* (s. 119–144). içinde İstanbul: Beta.

Yaman, R. (2017). *Üretim Planlama Kontrol ve Bütünleştirme*. Ankara: Nobel Yayınevi.

Oğuzhan KIVRAK, Mustafa Zahid GÜRBÜZ & Aysun GÜRAN

Management and Digitalization in the Service Industry

1. Introduction

Social habits and lifestyles are changing significantly with the processing and interpretation of information, highlighting experiences, and technological developments. Digitization, which accelerated with Industry 4.0, has affected all sectors with new concepts and developing technology. The service sector, which is under the influence of digitalization, has started to overtake the agricultural and industrial sectors in the last century. This applies not only to developed countries, but also to developing countries. The main reason for this situation is the developments in technology, but there are other factors as well. These can be exemplified as the increase in incomes, people having more free time, women's participation in labor force employment, changes in people's living standards, and the emergence of new and more useful products (Kıratlı, 2018: 147).

Many businesses apply business-specific solutions and technologies for the problems of their sector. Some of these technologies include systems such as online video conferencing, virtual private network (vpn), remote computer-based training, project management and version control system. Due to the Covid-19 outbreak, there has been a noticeable change in the use of these systems in the service industry. The reason for this change is the changed living standards due to measures such as travel restrictions, social distancing, and curfews. One of these changes, the self-checkout process, appears in the retail sector. In this period where people are wary of contacting each other, users can scan the products they want to buy into the system themselves and make payments (Yıldırım and Taştekin, 2020: 77). Furthermore, with the innovations made in retail sector during the pandemic, the products purchased from the market can be delivered to the desired place in a very short time with contact-free delivery options (e.g., online payment, no-contact delivery at the door) (Gençtürk and Öztürkoğlu, 2020: 51).

Banking is another sector that is not accustomed to the "Remote Working" system with its use of digital opportunities, and is undergoing a restructuring of its normal business and life cycle. Banks with tens of thousands of employees have adapted to a remote working system in order to ensure the health of their employees (Başaran and Ünal, 2021: 655). One of these assurances is that performance interviews with employees and job interviews with job candidates have been moved to a virtual environment. While choosing the video conferencing application, those that meet the security criteria of the banks were preferred.

The first part of this section details the concept of management in the service industry and application areas of video conferencing within the framework of the relevant literature. The second part presents an evaluation of how multiple video conferencing applications are integrated with the help of a common platform.

2. Management in the Service Industry

As a concept, service can be defined as the benefit that consumers buy without taking ownership of the systems that originate from their living standards and solve their problems (Dalgıç, 2013: 3). Another definition of service must have three characteristics which are intangibility, heterogeneity, and inseparability (Parasuraman et al., 1985; 42). To sum up, it can be defined as intangible activities that provide benefits to the user, offered for sale at a certain price so that service users can meet their needs by purchasing them (Sayım & Aydın, 2015). It is possible to define the service industry as the area where these activities are offered by the businesses and the income is generated.

The service industry grows each day. For this reason, companies operating in the service industry are in fierce competition to retain their existing customers and acquire new customers. These companies, which can provide their services as long as they have customers, have to take into account the expectations, perceptions and experiences of their customers in order to protect and expand their field of activity. The perception and the user experience that the quality of service, an abstract concept, will create in the customer are intangible. For this reason, the quality and satisfaction of the services in the industry are completely dependent on the perception of the customer. In the management of this perception, there are new elements that need to be improved and developed in the management approach of the enterprises, even if the enterprises have practices that comply with the rules that employees and customers are satisfied with. One of these new elements is the social media platform that has become a part of our daily life. In these environments where time and place limits are removed, corporate identity of businesses can be transferred to digital environments with low cost. The perceptions of satisfaction, behaviors and choices of people who use these platforms can be affected by a shared short message or a content. In addition, dealing with individuals quickly and solving their problems through these platforms will increase trust and loyalty to the business (Ceng, 2018: 665).

Many fields from agriculture to education, medicine to art has seen the impact of creative destruction of the digital transformation experienced by the developments in technology. However, this process has accelerated especially during the Covid-19 pandemic. Due to travel restrictions, isolations, quarantines, curfews, and the holiday of all educational institutions from kindergartens to universities, many sectors have come to a standstill and businesses have had profound effects (Kestane, 2021: 94). Technologies that support the continuation of work without being side-by-side, such as remote working and teleconference meetings, which are part of digital transformation and are not implemented by businesses, have started to be established by companies as infrastructure. Especially at the point of communicating with customers, the most suitable technology has been integrated into the company's structure among the various opportunities offered by the digitalization process.

One of the institutions where a digital transformation is seen is universities. Online learning, which was already a practice in some universities before the pandemic, became a compulsory practice due to the pandemic. The fact that online learning provides a flexible, comfortable and location-independent learning environment has enabled the education process to continue without interruption (Mercan, 2018: 12). Another sector where digital transformation is experienced is banking. Banks that have switched to open banking with the digital transformation have thus started to issue new products. The concept of open banking is the sharing of the data in the databases of the banks within the framework determined by the laws. In addition to technologies such as machine learning, behavior analysis, churn analysis, they offer new products to their customers and add a new and fast communication channel with contact-free payment and online video calling technologies (Bilgel and Aksyon, 2019). Especially for the customers who cannot go to the bank during the pandemic, with the video call feature integrated into the mobile application, relevant processes were moved to the digital environment. Similar to the other sectors, bank employees continued their work without any security problems and without going to a branch or office, from their homes with virtual private network (VPN) technology.

3. Video Conferencing Applications

Video conference is a communication channel that provides simultaneous transmission of audio, video and data between two or more people (Correia et al.,

2020: 432). Thanks to this communication channel, it is possible to communicate over the Internet from different physical locations. Video conferencing applications using Internet protocols can be widely used in almost every area where human interaction occurs. Video conferencing applications developed by more than one company have missing or extra features in contrast to each other. While some applications are less secure than others, some applications have features such as recording the meeting and muting and unmuting the participants (Billingsley, 2020: 275). These applications, which have different price policies, are used in different areas in line with the needs.

Kılıç (2017: 207) states that video conferencing applications that can be used in the field of health have helped communication between patients and doctors can be established without time and place restrictions, and thus patients can receive service more easily. For example, Kılıç (2017: 207) explains that with the tele-medicine system, a psychiatrist could offer sessions from their home at the weekend with a video conference system. They also show that patients who were discharged or terminally ill could receive support from their caregivers by using video conferencing application. Thus, video conferencing applications have brought significant improvements in factors such as patients' waiting time, length of stay and general health expenses.

Kapucu and Uşun (2019: 10) examined online education practices in the teaching of common compulsory courses at 119 state universities in Turkey starting from the 2018 to 2019 academic year. As a result of the study, it was taken into consideration to give common compulsory courses of state universities in Turkey with distance education applications. As it is known, educational institutions in Turkey have switched to the distance education model, especially during the pandemic. Thanks to the video conferencing applications used in this model, the education continued. During this period, there was a significant increase in demand for open and distance education. In addition, the importance of open and distance education services in the society has started to be noticed. Can (2020: 11–53) shows that the open and distance education system in our country should be strengthened in terms of infrastructure, access, security, content, design, implementation, quality, legislation and pedagogy. In this sense, it may be important to design integrated video conferencing systems in order to maintain the distance education system on a healthier basis.

Video conferencing applications have started to be used in judicial law in different countries. Yerdelen (2019: 272) mentions the advantages and disadvantages of using the (SEGBİS) method, which is a video conferencing application, in the field of criminal procedure. Acar and Gürsoy (2012: 113–114) provides information on the use of the "Audio Video Recording and Video Conference System" in courts in Turkey, which is included in the National Judicial Network System, which is a component of the e-justice project. In the study, it is stated that this technological system accelerates the judicial process and provides gains from time and workforce. Taner and Yıldırım (2021: 233) noted that the use of video conferencing applications in legal systems provides many advantages such as saving transfer costs and completing the proceedings in a reasonable time. It was also stated in their studies that this system could be limited by many warranties within the scope of the right to a fair trial.

Video conferencing applications have started to be widely used not only in fields such as health, education and law, but also in sports activities. Examining the contribution of the use of communication technologies in sports education to people's sports tendency, Yüzel and Devecioğlu (2012: 12) stated that some studies emphasized that computer-assisted education has positive effects on the learning of basketball and volleyball skills. Recently, many sports facilities have not been able to serve due to the impact of COVID-19. The trainings given in clubs and sports facilities during normal times, when the conditions are suitable in terms of health, started to be given with video conference trainings during the pandemic period. Drawing attention to the health problems that may occur as a result of lack of exercise and inactivity, especially during the COVID-19 pandemic, which affected the whole world, Çelik and Yenal (2020: 257) emphasized the importance of exercise during this period. They indicated that Internet tools and video conferencing applications that minimize physical contact can reach everywhere unhindered in terms of performing physical activities at any time and personal training.

Integrating different video conferencing applications that facilitate many areas from health to sports, and education, banking and law to our daily life will undoubtedly benefit us in many ways. In the next section, an integrated video conferencing application software prepared by the authors will be discussed to maximize these benefits.

4. The Integrated Video Conferencing Application

This section details the platform developed by the authors, which brings together video conferencing applications. On this platform, companies can start a conference in line with the platform owned by their customers, add participants, and receive participant reports by controlling various video conferencing applications from a single point.

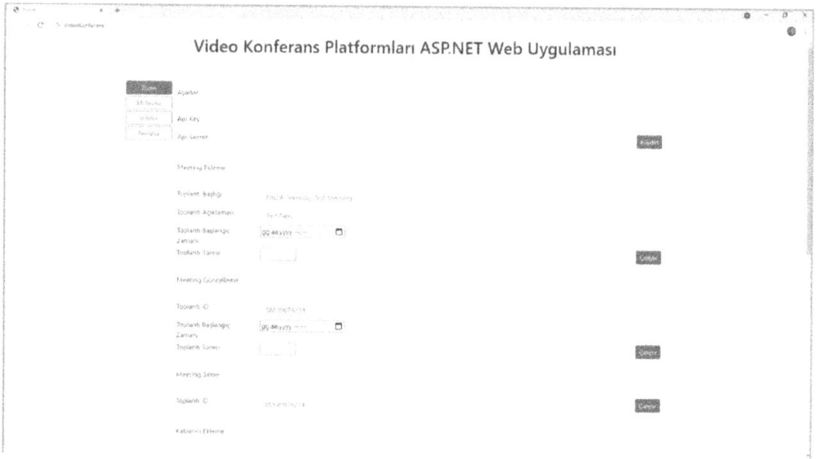

Figure 1. Test page of the proposed integrated video conferencing application

Figure 1 shows a web application that brings together four video conferencing applications. The video conferencing applications mentioned here are Zoom, Microsoft Teams, Cisco Webex, and Perculus. These applications offer REST services for integration. In this way, developers can integrate these services into their own projects. However, due to the unique nature of each platform, developers deal with separate documents and service calls for each. This greatly extends the development process. Adding a new application to the system becomes a costly task. In this developed system, a development kit that can access to all platforms with a single documentation and service structure has been prepared.

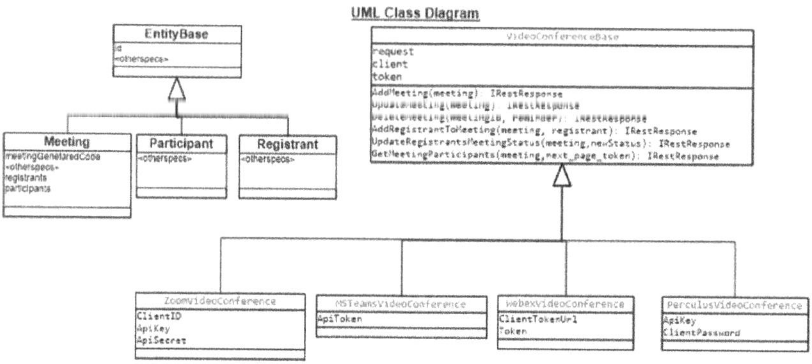

Figure 2. UML diagram of the proposed system

The UML class diagram of the developed system is shown in Figure 2. The Clean Architecture structure was adopted while designing the Object model of the system. All objects declaring entities in this architecture are derived from an EntityBase base class. In addition, the VideoConferenceBase abstract class has been prepared, which offers a common contract for video conferencing applications. Within the platform-specific classes derived from this abstract class, the necessary methods have been created to meet the conditions of the base class, and the integration module has been prepared. This project was packaged as a software development kit (SDK) for later testing. A web application was prepared as in Figure 1 for the tests and it was confirmed that all methods were working for each conference application. The SDK, packaging and verification processes of which have been completed successfully, is now being used by a service provider in the education sector.

5. Conclusion

The advantages brought by digitalization open the doors of a new world for all sectors. Therefore, if companies want to maintain their advantage in the competition, they must adapt to new concepts and new technologies. In the twenty-first century, competition is based not only on the final output produced, but also on innovation and the ability to adapt quickly to new developments. As seen during the pandemic period, companies that survived this period with the least damage and grew even more are the ones who can quickly switch to digitalization and, in short, keep up with the future (Sayar, 2019: 69). There may be more than one solution and application throughout this adaptation process. For this reason, integrated applications that will support more than one solution in the applied technology will provide advantages to companies both in terms of speed and cost.

As the world focuses less and less on the physical location, communication via video conferencing will increase even more. Features such as making calls in an efficient and secure manner, ease of use, and the price may be the reasons why applications prefer each other. In this case, instead of integrating each application into the business, it will be advantageous to prefer applications that bring all conference applications together at a single point. Thus, transitions between video conferencing applications will be easier.

The integrated video conferencing application, developed in the light of this information, accelerated the digitalization process of companies and provided an advantage at the cost. This application was implemented by a real customer and the mentioned benefits were observed. The implementing agency stated in their feedback that the application has accelerated the software development process by 75 %.

References

Acar, S., Gürsoy, H. (2012). Türkiye Mahkemelerinde Sesli Görüntülü Kayıt ve Video Konferans Sistemi Uygulamasına Geçiş: Ceza Mahkemeleri Örneği. *Ankara Barosu Dergisi*, (4), 109–137.

Aksoy, B., Bilgel, D. (2019). Finansal Teknoloji Şirketleri ve Geleceğin Bankacılığı: Açık Bankacılık . *Avrupa Bilim ve Teknoloji Dergisi*, (17), 1097–1105 . DOI: 10.31590/ejosat.646196.

Başaran, E. Y., Ünal, H. T. (2021). Covid – 19 Pandemi Döneminde Özel Bankaların Çalışan Deneyimi Tasarımı. *International Journal Of Social, Journal Of Social, Humanities and Administrative Sciences*, 7(39), 654–672.

Billingsley, L. (2020). Using Video Conferencing Applications to Share the Death Experience During the COVID-19 Pandemic. *Journal of Radiology Nursing*, 39(4), 275–277, ISSN 1546-0843, https://doi.org/10.1016/j.jradnu.2020.08.001. Accessed 12 May 2021.

Can, E. (2020). Coronavirüs (Covid-19) pandemisi ve pedagojik yansımaları: Türkiye'de açık ve uzaktan eğitim uygulamaları. *Açıköğretim Uygulamaları ve Araştırmaları Dergisi*, 6(2), 11–53.

Çelik, F., Yenal, T. H. (2020). Covid-19 ve Hareketsiz Yaşam. *Akdeniz Spor Bilimleri Dergisi*, 3(2), 249–259.

Ceng, E. (2018). Algı Yönetimi Aracı Olarak Twitter Kullanımına İlişkin Siyasal Bir Analiz, *Erciyes İletişim Dergisi*, 5(4), 663–689, Jul. 2018, doi:10.17680/erciyesiletisim.419956.

Correia, A., Liu, C., Xu, F. (2020). Evaluating Videoconferencing Systems for the Quality of the Educational Experience. *Distance Education*, 41(4), 429–452, DOI: 10.1080/01587919.2020.1821607.

Dalgıç, A. (2013). Hizmet Sektöründe Hizmet Kalitesinin Ölçümü ve Hizmet Kalitesini Etkileyen Faktörler Antalya'da Hizmet Kalitesi Ölçümüne Yönelik Bir Uygulama, *Yüksek Lisans Tezi, Adnan Menderes Üniversitesi, Sosyal Bilimler Enstitüsü İşletme Anabilim Dalı, Yüksek Lisans Tezi*, Aydın.

Gençtürk, S., Öztürkoğlu, Y. (2020). Yeni Nesil Perakendecilik: KOVID-19 Sürecinde Marketten Eve Hizmet İnovasyonu Araştırması. *Journal of Entrepreneurship and Innovation Management*, 9(2), 49–69. Retrieved from https://dergipark.org.tr/en/pub/jeim/issue/60046/868140. Accessed 17 May 2021.

Kestane, Ü. S. (2021), The Effects of the Black Swan Pandemic on Turkish Companies and their Previsions for Face-to-Face Sales in the Near Future. *International Journalof Social, Political and Economic Research*, 8(1), 89–110.

Kılıç, T. (2017). E-sağlık, iyi uygulama örneği; Hollanda. *Gümüşhane Üniversitesi Sağlık Bilimleri Dergisi*, 6(3), 203–217.

Kıratlı, F. (2018). Dünya ve Türkiye'de Hizmet Ticareti Gelişimi. *İktisadi İdari ve Siyasal Araştırmalar Dergisi*, 4. DOI:10.25204/İktisad.426125.

Mercan, A. (2018). Üniversite Öğrencilerinin Uzaktan Eğitim İle İlgili Görüşleri ve Hazır Bulunuşlukları: Afyon Kocatepe Üniversitesi Fen Edebiyat Fakültesi Örneği. *Afyon Kocatepe Üniversitesi, İnternet ve Bilişim Teknolojileri Yönetimi Anabilim Dalı, Yüksek Lisans Tezi*, Afyon.

Parasuraman, A., Zeithaml, V.A., Berry, L.L. (1985). A Conceptual Model of Service Quality and Its Implications for Future Research. *Journal of Marketing*, 49, Fall.

Sayar, S. (2019). Dijitalleşme ile Yeni Oluşan Kavramlar: Endüstri 4.0, IOT ve Blockchain Uygulamaları, *Uluslararası Ticaret ve Lojistik Yönetimi Anabilim Dalı Lojistik ve Tedarik Zinciri Yönetimi Yüksek Lisans Programı*, Yüksek Lisans Tezi, İstanbul.

Sayım, F., Aydın, V. (2015). Hizmet Sektörü Özellikleri Ve Sistematik Olmayan Risklerin Sektör Menkul Kıymetleri İle Etkileşimine Dair Teorik Bir Çalışma. *Dumlupınar Üniversitesi Sosyal Bilimler Dergisi*, (29). Retrieved from https://dergipark.org.tr/en/pub/dpusbe/issue/4771/65667. Accessed 17 May 2021.

Taner, F. G., Yıldırım, A. (2021). Suç İsnadına veya Medeni Hak ve Yükümlülüklere İlişkin Uyuşmazlıklarda Duruşmaya Video Konferans Yöntemiyle Uzaktan Katılma. *Ankara Üniversitesi Hukuk Fakültesi Dergisi*, 70(1), 229–293.

Ünal, K, S. (2021). The Effects of the Black Swan Pandemic on Turkısh Companies and their Previsions for Face - to - Face Sales in the Near Future. *International Journal of Social, Political and Economic Research*, 8(1), 89–110. https://doi.org/10.46291/IJOSPERvol8iss1pp89-110. Accessed 28 April 2021.

Yerdelen, E. (2019). Ceza Muhakemesinde Video Konferans Yönteminin (Segbis) Kullanımı. *Bilişim Hukuku Dergisi*, 1(2), 271–287.

Yıldırım, F., Taştekin, K. (2020). Perakende Yönetiminde Teknoloji Kullanımının Algılanan Hizmet Kalitesindeki Önemi: Gıda Perakendeciliği Üzerine Bir Araştırma. *İstanbul Ticaret Üniversitesi Girişimcilik Dergisi*, 3(6), 75–88. Retrieved from https://dergipark.org.tr/tr/pub/tje/issue/56620/788408. Accessed 17 May 2021.

Umut YILDIRIM & Arda TOYGAR

An Evaluation of the Factors Affecting Risk Management Processes in the Maritime Sector

1. Introduction

In the twenty-first century, the spread of customs liberalization agreements and the globalization process has enabled the disappearance of cultural differences and borders. In this way, supplier and customer networks of multinational companies entering the global market contribute to the rapid growth and change of global resources (Toygar & İpekçi, 2020). Because national companies, benefiting from the advantages of globalization, can supply the raw materials required for production through outsourcing and sell their value-added goods in international markets. However, in order to benefit from the opportunities brought by globalization and achieve sustainable cost savings in foreign trade processes, intercontinental long-distance circulation of high-tonnage cargoes should be carried out at low costs (Açık, 2020). This requirement causes the international circulation of goods subject to global trade such as food, energy and raw materials to be carried out by maritime transportation at a rate of 80 % (UNCTAD, 2020). Although maritime transportation leads the most intensive use rate in global foreign trade processes, the long transit times in this transportation system directly affect the supply chain planning of foreign trade companies. Companies that carry out rapid production and shipment planning in the globalization process demand the supplying of resources to be performed collectively in order to avoid interruptions in the supply chain processes. In order to meet these demands, maritime companies increase the number of ships they operate (Geman & Ohana, 2008; Helmy & Shrabia, 2016; İpekçi & Toygar, 2020). As a matter of fact, 11.08 billion tons of cargo was handled worldwide, with the number of the fleet of commercial ships reaching 98,140 in 2020 (UNCTAD, 2020). The rise in maritime trade volumes in recent years also increases the potential risk factors in the seas. A total of 19,418 incidents involving maritime accidents, deaths and injuries were reported between 2014 and 2019 (EMSA, 2020). The rapid increase in accidents and risk factors at sea necessitates the development of Risk Management that adheres to international standards. For this reason, international organizations take many decisions and develop various practices to ensure maritime safety. Unfortunately, safety practices are only valued and become the focus of attention on a global scale following major maritime accidents[1] (Wang, 2006). In addition, most[2] of the rules and arrangements in the regulations are based on past events and experiences (Kristiansen, 2005). In other words, the practices developed to reduce the dangers at sea are organized on the basis of past accidents (IMO, 2008). For instance, after the Exxon Valdez ship crashed into Prince William Sound's Bligh Reef in 1989, 10.8 million gallons of crude oil spilled into the sea, almost destroying the ecosystem in the region. According to the reports of the accident, the company operating the ship had stopped re-evaluating the environmental preparation plans required within the scope of RM a few weeks before the accident (Mitroff & Pauchant, 1990).

Accidents are likely to occur again in cases where RM rules and practices prepared by international authorities are not followed. However, the rules developed by international authorities cannot ensure a high level of protection for seafarers and the environment significantly reduce the likelihood of adverse events occurring (Mearns et al., 2003). In addition, despite international rules and regulations, risk factors in the maritime profession continue to pose a threat to maritime safety (Akhtar & Utne, 2014). Because, although RM in maritime is a basic concept related to practices to stay safe at sea, the maritime profession has a unique structure that cannot be handled with theoretical methods (Kennedy & Kirwan, 1998). For this reason, RM in the maritime industry is an important issue and is seen as the main field of study in the literature (Kulkarni et al., 2020; Fu et al., 2021). In this study, the human factor and financial uncertainties are examined as the riskiest factors in maritime trade. The study aims to be a guide for the relevant literature and maritime trade parties, since it includes the main hazards that may pose a risk factor in maritime trade and recommendations for RM practices.

1 *"Titanic-1912, Amoco Cadiz-1978, Herald of Enterprise-1987, Exxon Valdez-1989, Erica-1999, Prestige-2002".*

2 *"ILLC 66 (International Load Line Convention), SOLAS 74 (International Convention For the Safety of Life at Sea), MARPOL 73/78 (International Convention for the Prevention of Pollution from Ships), COLREG 72 (International Regulations for Preventing Collisions at Sea Convention) and STCW 78/95 (The International Convention on Standards of Training, Certification and Watchkeeping for Seafarers)".*

2. Risk Management in Maritime Transportation

Understanding the concepts of RM at sea is vital. Within this framework, risk is the possibility of harm occurring and danger refers to the center of damage. In other words, risk is the probability of danger occurring. RM, on the other hand, can be defined as the process that includes the determination of risk and its possible effects (Papanikolau, 2009). RM in maritime industry should include methods developed to prevent accidents at sea and to minimize risks that may pose a danger to life, property, and environmental safety. RM practices that meet this requirement enable the understanding of hazards that may pose as a risk factor in order to prevent crises and, most importantly, to ensure safety at sea (Zhang et al., 2016). For this reason, RM has a high level of importance in the development of managerial decisions of companies in the maritime industry (Haimes, 2009).

Maritime transportation is more global, volatile, and open to risks than other sectors due to its internal dynamics (Li & Wonham, 1999). Thus, RM in maritime transportation aims to prepare response systems to prevent accidents and keep risks related to human factors, ecology, or the safety of cargo at low levels and further develop these systems, as they can be created for different purposes in each sector (Kristiansen, 2005). The main method developed to reduce risks in maritime is the regulation of the ISM (International Safety Management) Code (Hänninen et al., 2014). The ISM Code was adopted by the International Maritime Organization (IMO) in November 1993 in order to operate ships in safe conditions and to prevent threats that will pose a risk factor in the seas. Following the Estonian shipwreck incident in 1994, at the SOLAS Conference in May 1994, the ISM Code was added to SOLAS Chapter IX, regardless of the year of construction of the ships, making it mandatory for passenger ships. As of 1 July 2002, it has been made compulsory for all ships[3] (IMO, 2010).

Maritime transportation poses many dangers to human life and environmental safety. Many inspections have been developed to keep this dangerous structure of maritime under control. These inspections help the prevention of risk factors at sea and the development of effective RM practices. There are substantial financial penalties for loss of life and property, as well as damage to the cargo and the environment due to non-compliance with the inspections (Z. Yang et al., 2018). In order to determine the adequacy of RM practices, three basic questions are asked to maritime companies: "*Are the seafarers well trained? Are*

3 For all passenger and high-speed ships and other ship types, there is a requirement to be 500 grt (gross tonnage) and above.

system inspections done regularly? Are accidents followed through with analysis and implementation of reactive measures?" (Kristiansen, 2005). Inspections carried out in the context of the ISM Code are executed periodically. The following parts are evaluated within the scope of inspections (IMO, 1995):

- Evaluating whether the Safety Management System (SMS) complies with ISM requirements,
- Assessing the adequacy of the maritime company's management systems,
- Assessing the compliance of the ship's management systems with the rules and regulations,
- Assessing the effectiveness of the maritime company's management systems in complying with other rules and regulations,
- Assessing whether recommended safety practices have been taken into account.

In addition to the systematic process of RM in maritime, the identification of dangers that may pose a risk is among the most important processes (Harrington & Niehaus, 2003; Lim et al., 2018). Therefore, the next section details the evaluation of human and financial factors that can create risk factors in maritime trade.

3. Risk Elements in the Maritime Sector

3.1. The Human Element

Despite the fact that seafarers have to be educated at international standards, the human factor is the leading risk factor in the maritime profession (Kuronen & Tapaninen, 2010; Yıldırım et al., 2019). Moreover, according to many studies in the literature, majority of accidents at sea are caused by the human factor (Hetherington et al., 2006; Martins & C., 2010; Mullai & Paulsson, 2011). According to the statistics, human factor is the cause of 75 % of the accidents that occur in maritime transportation in just one year, totaling a loss of $1.6 billion (Allianz, 2018). One of the main reasons for the human factor to come to the fore in accidents is the difficult working conditions of the maritime profession. In addition to the fact that maritime work is among the most demanding occupational groups in the world, working on ships carries a 1.3 times higher risk of death compared to occupations on land (Rinne et al., 2021). Seafaring is one of the dangerous occupations that can cause work accidents, injuries and various diseases due to its difficult working conditions (ILO, 2006). Moreover, seafaring requires keeping a 24-hour work schedule. In other words, seafarers are in the same indoor environment during their working and resting periods on the ship (Exarchopoulos et al., 2018). Due to this type of social isolation, seafarers must be mentally and physically healthy (Carter, 2005). However, seafaring, which is among the most difficult occupational groups in the world, deteriorates the mental health of seafarers (Jezewska & Iversen, 2012). Seafarers with mental health problems also frequently experience negative events such as assault, murder, or suicide on ships (Roberts & Marlow, 2005). All these working conditions, which cause the mental health of seafarers to deteriorate, cause a significant increase in the dangers that may pose as a risk factor on ships (Carotenuto et al., 2012).

In addition to the risk factors involved in sea voyages, there are also frequently encountered factors in the operation of ships. The next section details this as financial uncertainty in the maritime sector, which poses great threats to the operation of ships.

3.2. Financial Uncertainty

Another important danger that creates a risk factor for maritime companies is financial uncertainties (Notteboom & Lam, 2014). The rapid growth of the maritime trade and the developments in recent years cause maritime companies to develop managerial strategies in response to financial risks. Because of the insufficient RM systems, maritime businesses are forced to sell their assets and restructure (Choi et al., 2018). Furthermore, negative events in maritime trade cause interruptions in the supply chains of thousands of companies. For example, in March 2021, a 400-meter-long container ship ran aground in the Suez Canal, which is on the world's busiest trade routes, causing the canal to be closed to ship traffic for a week. Data from Lloyd's List Intelligence (2021) show that this accident hindered the international circulation of cargoes, which were worth approximately $9.6 billion, carried by ships passing through the Suez Canal in one day. Every economic crisis in maritime trade tests the dynamics of the industry. The 2008–2009 financial crisis especially caused great uncertainties regarding the maritime trade, causing many maritime companies to go bankrupt. COVID-19, which still has a huge impact today, has similar features to the crises in the past periods (UNCTAD, 2020). However, maritime companies have developed various RM practices in order to prevent financial losses by taking important lessons from the dangers of the past. The most important practice developed to reduce the financial effects of COVID-19 is to keep low-carrying capacity ships idle at anchorage areas, and to carry out commercial activities with high-carrying capacity ships. Although this practice has maintained the financial stability of companies against minor crises in the recent past, it does not have the same positive effect today. Because high tonnage ships cannot find cargo at the planned rate, they increase the fluctuations in freight and, therefore, reduce the profits of maritime companies (Fusillo & Haralambides, 2020). Today, this management practice has started to cause financial uncertainties in maritime transportation (Notteboom et al., 2021). As a matter of fact, the strategy of operating large-tonnage ships is among the main reasons for the bankruptcy of the world's seventh largest container shipping company (Shin et al., 2019). Today, practices have been updated with various methods in order to reduce the destructive effects of financial uncertainties. These changes aim to solve the empty capacity problems of high-tonnage ships by establishing strategic alliances between competing maritime companies (Yang, 2020). Another risk factor that causes financial uncertainty in maritime trade is fuel (bunker) costs. Fuel costs of ships constitute more than half of all voyage costs (Alizadeh & Nomikos, 2009). As of January 1, 2020, the reduction of sulfur rate from ships' fuels to 0.5 % by IMO has negatively affected the voyage costs of ships by causing fuel costs to further increase. Maritime companies have also been increasing their freight costs in order to balance the increasing margin (UNCTAD, 2020).

4. Results and Recommendations

Maritime trade is one of the most important links of the supply chain, providing the intercontinental circulation of cargo and other components in global trade activities. Although maritime transport has many advantages in global trade, it also comes with numerous risk factors. This is due to the fact that 98,140 ships carrying out their transportation activities are faced with conflicts, aground, sinking, flooding and similar dangers at any moment. Determining the risk factors at sea is extremely important for the RM of the maritime trade parties. This means that it will be possible to improve safety in the industry by knowing the risks of seafaring, one of the most dangerous professions in the world, in which approximately 1.65 million seafarers are involved (ICS, 2019; UNCTAD, 2020).

RM in maritime trade should become a priority in the principal management approach. In other words, it is beneficial to carry out ship operations with a safe management approach. Moreover, managers in decision-making roles regarding RM on board and on land need to not only follow rules and procedures, but also encourage seafarers through leading by example to achieve their set safety objectives. Rules and regulations that ensure safety and security in maritime transportation have been developed over time, taking into account the accidents experienced in the past. These rules and regulations primarily focus on the consequences of accidents arising from the risk factor in terms of safety. As can be seen from the results of the accident report, this method alone is not effective.

Rather than focusing only on results, international authorities and maritime companies should evaluate all the identified risks inherent in shipping and take safety measures against these risks. Furthermore, it is necessary to develop cooperation between international authorities and maritime companies in order to understand the main causes of the risk factors in the maritime profession and to propose solutions. Finally, it is important for the authorities to develop encouraging practices and increase university-industry cooperation in order to prevent dangers that pose as a risk factor in the sea, and to develop effective RM for maritime companies.

In the history of the maritime industry, there have been many financial crises that could pose as a risk factor. RM practices developed in previous crises are still being carried out by maritime companies. Although these practices prevented financial losses at the time they were developed, they are not valid today. In the maritime sector, where high-carrying capacity ship operations are widespread, many maritime companies that cannot keep up with the pressures from companies with strong financial structures have to end their commerce. Moreover, maritime companies lose their advantages in their commercial routes by merging with their global rival companies in order to provide capacity management of high-carrying capacity ships. Furthermore, keeping low-carrying capacity ships at anchorage areas causes maritime transportation to slow down in many connection routes that are not on the main trade routes, and major disruptions in the supply chain processes of most foreign trade companies in the region. It is essential to learn from past crises. But the maritime industry has a dynamic and constantly evolving structure. It is important to pay attention to demands of the customer in order to develop sustainable RM practices in maritime businesses. For this reason, as a necessary method for solving the problem of financial uncertainty, maritime companies should take an active role in the entire supply chain processes, not only in the transportation part.

References

Açık, A. (2020). The impact of uncertainty on international trade: An evidence from container traffic in Turkish ports. *Journal of Politics, Economy and Management (JOPEM)*, *3*(2), 1–10.

Akhtar, M. J., & Utne, I. B. (2014). Human fatigue's effect on the risk of maritime groundings–A Bayesian network modeling approach. *Safety Science*, *62*, 427–440.

Alizadeh, A. H., & Nomikos, N. K. (2009). *Shipping Derivatives and Risk Management*. Palgrave Macmillan.

Allianz. (2018). *Safety and shipping review 2018: An annual review of trends and developments in shipping losses and safety.* https://www.agcs.allianz.com/content/dam/onemarketing/agcs/agcs/reports/AGCS-Safety-Shipping-Review-2018.pdf. Accessed 5 June 2021.

Carotenuto, A., Molino, I., Fasanaro, A. M., & Amenta, F. (2012). Psychological stress in seafarers: A review. *International Maritime Health, 63*(4), 188–194.

Carter, T. (2005). Working at sea and psychosocial health problems. *Travel Medicine and Infectious Disease, 3*(2), 61–65. https://doi.org/10.1016/j.tmaid.2004.09.005. Accessed 25 May 2021.

Choi, J. S., Kim, H. K., & Han, J. H. (2018). Development of early warning index in Korean shipping industry by using signal approach. *Maritime Policy & Management, 45*(8), 1007–1020.

EMSA. (2020). *Annual overview of marine casualties and incidents.* http://www.emsa.europa.eu/newsroom/latest-news/item/4266-annual-overview-of-marine-casualties-and-incidents-2020.html. Accessed 25 May 2021.

Exarchopoulos, G., Zhang, P., Pryce-Roberts, N., & Zhao, M. (2018). Seafarers' welfare: A critical review of the related legal issues under the Maritime Labour Convention 2006. *Marine Policy, 93*(April), 62–70. https://doi.org/10.1016/j.marpol.2018.04.005. Accessed 5 June 2021.

Fu, S., Goerlandt, F., & Xi, Y. (2021). Arctic shipping risk management: A bibliometric analysis and a systematic review of risk influencing factors of navigational accidents. *Safety Science, 139*, 105254.

Fusillo, M., & Haralambides, H. (2020). Do carrier expectations indicate industry structure in container shipping? An econometric analysis. *Journal of Shipping and Trade, 5*(1), 1–16.

Geman, H., & Ohana, S. (2008). Mean-Reversion and Structural Breaks in Crude Oil, Copper, and Shipping. In H. Geman (Ed.), *Risk Management in Commodity Markets: From Shipping to Agriculturals and Energy* (pp. 183–206). John Wiley & Sons Inc. Publication.

Haimes, Y. Y. (2009). *Risk Modeling, Assessment, and Management* (3rd ed.). John Wiley & Sons Inc. Publication. https://doi.org/10.1002/9780470422489. Accessed 5 June 2021.

Hänninen, M., Banda, O., & Kujala, P. (2014). Bayesian network model of maritime safety management. *Expert System with Applications, 41*(17), 7837–7846.

Harrington, S. E., & Niehaus, G. R. (2003). *Risk Management and Insurance* (2nd ed.). McGraw Hill.

Helmy, S., & Shrabia, A. (2016). Mega container ships, pros, cons and its implication recession. *Journal of Shipping and Ocean Engineering, 6*, 284–290.

Hetherington, C., Flin, R., & Mearns, K. (2006). Safety in shipping: The human element. *Journal of Safety Research, 37*(4), 401–411.

ICS. (2019). *Shipping and world trade: Global supply and demand for seafarers.* https://www.ics-shipping.org/shipping-facts/shipping-and-world-trade/global-supply-and-demand-for-seafarers. Accessed 25 June 2021.

ILO. (2006). *Guidelines for implementing the occupational safety and health provisions of the maritime labour convention.* https://www.ilo.org/wcmsp5/groups/public/---ed_dialogue/---sector/documents/normativeinstrument/wcms_325319.pdf. Accessed 25 June 2021.

IMO. (1995). *Guidelines on Implementation of the ISM Code by Administrations, resolution A.788(19).* International Maritime Organization. https://www cdn.imo.org/localresources/en/KnowledgeCentre/IndexofIMOResolutions/AssemblyDocuments/A.788(19).pdf. Accessed 7 July 2021.

IMO. (2008). *Code of the international standards and recommended practices for a safety investigation into a marine casualty or marine incident.* http://emsa.europa.eu/retro/Docs/marine_casualties/msc-mepc_3-circ_2.pdf. Accessed 7 July 2021.

IMO. (2010). *ISM code international safety management code and guidelines on implementation of the ISM Code.* https://www.imo.org/en/OurWork/HumanElement/Pages/ISMCode.aspx. Accessed 7 July 2021.

İpekçi, E., & Toygar, A. (2020). Lojistik sektöründe yetenek 4.0. In S. Nart (Ed.), *Çalışma Yaşamında Yetenek 4.0* (pp. 249–268). Beta Basım Yayım Dağıtım.

Jezewska, M., & Iversen, R. (2012). Stress and fatigue at sea versus quality of life. *International Maritime Health, 63*(2), 106–115.

Kennedy, R., & Kirwan, B. (1998). Development of a hazard and operability-based method for identifying safety management vulnerabilities in high risk systems. *Safety Science, 30*(3), 249–274.

Kristiansen, S. (2005). *Maritime Transportation Safety Management and Risk Analysis* (1st ed.). Elsevier Butterworth-Heinemann.

Kulkarni, K., Goerlandt, F., Li, J., Banda, O. V., & Kujala, P. (2020). Preventing shipping accidents: Past, present, and future of waterway risk management with Baltic Sea focus. *Safety Science, 129*, 104798.

Kuronen, J., & Tapaninen, U. (2010). Evaluation of maritime safety policy instruments. *WMU Journal of Maritime Affairs, 9*(1), 45–61.

Li, K. X., & Wonham, J. (1999). Who is safe and who is at risk: A study of 20-year-record on accident total loss in different flags. *Maritime Policy & Management, 26*(2), 137–144.

Lim, G. J., Cho, J., Bora, S., Biobaku, T., & Parsaei, H. (2018). Models and computational algorithms for maritime risk analysis: A review. *Annals of Operations Research*, *271*(2), 765–786.

Lloyd's List Intelligence. (2021). *Suez Canal remains blocked despite efforts to refloat grounded Ever Given*. https://lloydslist.maritimeintelligence.informa.com/LL1136229/Suez-Canal-remains-blocked-despite-efforts-to-refloat-grounded-Ever-Given. Accessed 5 June 2021.

Martins, M. R., & Maturana, M. C. (2010). Human error contribution in collision and grounding of oil tankers. *Risk Analysis*, *30*(4), 674–698.

Mearns, K., Whitaker, S. M., & Flin, R. (2003). Safety climate, safety management practice and safety performance in offshore environments. *Safety Science*, *41*(8), 641–680.

Mitroff, I. I., & Pauchant, T. C. (1990). *We're So Big and Powerful Nothing Bad Can Happen to Us: An Investigation of America's Crisis Prone Corporations*. Birch Lane Press.

Mullai, A., & Paulsson, U. (2011). A grounded theory model for analysis of marine accidents. *Accident Analysis & Prevention*, *43*(4), 1590–1603.

Notteboom, T., & Lam, J. S. L. (2014). Dealing with uncertainty and volatility in shipping and ports. *Maritime Policy & Management*, *41*(7), 611–614.

Notteboom, T., Pallis, T., & Rodrigue, J. P. (2021). Disruptions and resilience in global container shipping and ports: The COVID-19 pandemic versus the 2008–2009 financial crisis. *Maritime Economics & Logistics*, *1*, 1–32.

Papanikolau, A. (2009). *Risk-Based Ship Design: Methods, Tools and Applications*. Springer.

Rinne, H., Laaksonen, M., Notkola, V., & Shemeikka, R. (2021). Mortality among seafarers: A register-based follow-up study. *Occupational Medicine*, *70*(2), 119–122. https://doi.org/10.1093/OCCMED/KQAA002. Accessed 5 June 2021.

Roberts, S. E., & Marlow, P. B. (2005). Traumatic work related mortality among seafarers employed in British Merchant Shipping, 1976–2002. *Occupational And Environmental Medicine*, *62*(3), 172–180.

Shin, S. H., Lee, P. T. W., & Lee, S. W. (2019). Lessons from bankruptcy of Hanjin Shipping Company in chartering. *Maritime Policy & Management*, *46*(2), 36–155.

Toygar, A., & İpekçi, E. (2020). Tedarik zinciri yönetiminde yetenek 4.0. In S. Nart (Ed.), *Çalışma Yaşamında Yetenek 4.0* (1st ed., pp. 119–143). Beta Basım Yayım Dağıtım.

UNCTAD. (2020). *Review of maritime transport 2020*. https://unctad.org/system/files/official-document/rmt2020_en.pdf. Accessed 7 July 2021.

Wang, J. (2006). Maritime risk assessment and its current status. *Quality and Reliability Engineering International*, *22*, 3–19.

Yang, C. S. (2020). An evaluation of alliance motives, shipping alliances, and alliance performance in Taiwan. *International Journal of Shipping and Transport Logistics*, *12*(5), 445–461.

Yang, Z., Yang, Z., Yin, J., & Qu, Z. (2018). A risk-based game model for rational inspections in port state control. *Transportation Research Part E: Logistics and Transportation Review*, *118*, 477–495.

Yıldırım, U., Başar, E., & Uğurlu, Ö. (2019). Assessment of collisions and grounding accidents with human factors analysis and classification system (HFACS) and statistical methods. *Safety Science*, *119*(November 2016), 412–425. https://doi.org/10.1016/j.ssci.2017.09.022. Accessed 5 June 2021.

Zhang, J., Teixeira, A. P., Soares, G. C., Yan, X., & Liu, K. (2016). Maritime transportation risk assessment of tianjin port with bayesian belief networks. *Risk Analysis*, *36*(6), 1171–1187.

Aysun KANBUR & Ibrahim A. H. MOHAMED

The Path to Innovation: Discovering Intellectual Capital

1. Introduction

Last decades of the twentieth century have experienced remarkable changes in business enterprises, which were represented by the growing interest in knowledge-based resources (also known as intangible assets). It has been observed that large organizations take more interest in intellectual capital (IC) investments (Carnerio, 2000). IC created a new type of economy known as the knowledge economy, which depends more on information, skills, technology, experience, and innovation. It can be claimed that any organization's innovative potential largely relies on its IC (Nonaka & Takeuchi, 1995). For managing IC efficiently in any knowledge-based society, the focus should be directed towards needed intangible assets (Parpandel, 2013).

Through the growing importance of investment in IC, organizations accept extra responsibilities as necessary to augment their existing IC levels. Investment in IC can create a difference because it will encourage creative employees and idea promotion for value generation. It is also essential to make and enforce some rules for smooth working and management; otherwise, the efforts of innovation might become futile if diseconomies exceed the advantages of higher productivity (Najem, 2008). IC is a leading creator of wealth and competitive advantage. IC is pivotal for managing knowledge but once it is well-managed, it creates remarkable synergies and efficiencies (Wang, Chang, Huang & Wang, 2011). The relation between IC and value enhancement is complex. Nowadays, the governments, senior managers, economic institutions, and investors realized the important nature of this relation (Zeghal & Maaloul, 2010). In OECD countries, knowledge-based economies created a structural change from the classic method that depended on tangible assets to activities of modern innovation (OECD, 2006). Many organizations are currently investing in the training of employees, R&D, administrative systems, etc. (OECD, 2008). They are IC investments, which grow and become more useful than any other kind of investment (Zeghal & Maaloul, 2010).

In the last few decades, most researchers expressed belief in the causal relationship between R&D spending and innovation; however, the IC-innovation relationship is a way more complex than the traditional focus on R&D investment (Walliser & Mignon, 2015). Global competition, and changing business scenarios are critical business factors because they always demand from enterprises to initiate some value addition. Innovation is, therefore, essential for sustainable competitive advantage (Jacobs & Heracleous, 2005). It is believed that IC creates innovation, which improves efficiencies and turns them into competencies that help an organization to prolong its existence and outcompete some of its rivals (Kamara, Anumba & Carrillo, 2002). IC and innovation are two crucial and vital resources, which improve an organization's performance and they do so through knowledge, employees' skills, experiences, and newly designed task performance methodologies. Thus, IC indicates the idea of value and helps to keep organizations' innovativeness for a long time.

2. Intellectual Capital

In the twentieth century, the conventional focus was on the physical assets known as tangible assets, which were considered as the main factors behind wealth. During the twenty-first century, wealth resides in intangible assets called intellectual capital (IC). Competitive organizations are developing and building IC for gaining a competitive edge (Gupta & Singh, 2015). Intangible assets are more vital than tangible assets (Wang, Chang, Huang & Wang, 2011). During that period when human capital was the core focus, many studies pointed to intangible assets. These studies on intangible assets, knowledge, and human resources were later followed by studies on IC (Santoso, 2011). IC not only includes the minds of workers but the intangible structures they work in and that makes an organization's function (Fazlagic, 2005).

IC transforms raw substances into final goods and creates value out of them (Stewart & Ruckdeschel, 1998). It includes intellectual property, information, and experience used to create an organization's wealth (Kannan & Aulbur, 2004). Many explanations of IC were presented by many authors and researchers and it is still trying to be defined. There is no agreement on IC definition; however, experts believe that intangible assets significantly contribute to organizational wealth. Intellectuals have wealth-creating capacities, which add value to an organization (Carroll & Tansey, 2000). In the new economy, IC means employees, who can convert and integrate their knowledge for the production of goods/services for the creation of value (Pulic, 2008). IC is a priceless resource for any organization.

There are different views by authors and researchers about determining components of IC. Ultimately, being frequently cited in researches related to

IC, Subramaniam and Youndt (2005) determined three components of IC as human capital, social capital, and organizational capital. Human capital includes the knowledge, abilities, and skills of every on-the-job employee (Youndt, Subramaniam & Snell, 2004). Social capital focuses on mutual respect and the link between the people (Nahapiet & Ghoshal, 1998). Organizational capital consists of knowledge assets like patents/copyrights, trademarks, processes, models, legal paperwork, knowledge artifacts, information technology networks including software, and/or administration systems (Stewart & Ruckdeschel, 1998). Organizational capital exists even if all workers leave (Hansen, Nohria & Tierney, 1999). Thinking from different viewpoints, many IC scholars observed that they see IC as a strategic instrument, which has the potential to increase an organization's value (Subramaniam & Youndt, 2005).

In many organizations, IC is considered as the most valuable resource, therefore, that should be managed with more attention and differently than other resources. IC can fill the book value and market value gap but it depends on the ability to add "real value" to an organization (Andriessen, 2004). It is confirmed in the literature that IC is positively linked with performance (Wang & Chang, 2005; Nimtrakoon, 2015), value creation (Berzkalne & Zelgalve, 2014), and return on assets/return on investment (Santoso, 2011). IC represents the definitive principle for increasing innovation and creativity in business organizations (Khalique, Shaari, Isa & Samad 2013). As a result, organizations should manage IC through which their values would be improved and balance would be created between them, which has an important effect on creating value, enhancing innovation, and competitive advantage (Jahanian & Salehi, 2013).

3. Innovation

The concept of innovation has been taken from the Latin word *innovare*, which means recover or interested in novelty, newness, or renewal in human activity; therefore, innovation is quite necessary for humanity (Likar, Fatur & Mrgole, 2013). Innovation is a strategy to attain some kind of competitive edge to meet the market requirements (Lord-Tarte, 2012; Kanbur & Şen, 2020). The term "innovation" is also used for referring to innovative practices (such as making use of ideas for resolving problems) and referring to the innovative procedural findings, which can either be a radical finding or a breakthrough (Likar, Fatur & Mrgole, 2013). Oslo Manual (2005) suggests that innovation means designing an improved good or service, a new method for marketing, an improved business practice, or a method to improve external relations. Here, the term "innovation" is R&D-related and it deals with new products (Armbruster, Bikfalvi, Kinkel &

Lay, 2008). Most organizations' demand for growth is higher. So, effective innovation provides a solution to the need for sustainable value-based growth (Lord-Tarte, 2012).

Prevalent models of innovation can be described in terms of linear models on one side and open and closed models on the other side. Many authors and scholars have written about linear models for decades (Oliveira, 2014). After many years, linear models transformed into environmental models. Demand for the transformation led to other forms of interaction, which resulted in "open innovation" that transformed into "mental models" (Godin & Lane, 2013). Then the idea of the open innovation model gained attention. Open innovation is the model or paradigm which presumes that organizations should rely on external ideas in their quest to develop internal ideas and advance their technique for value creation (Chesbrough, 2006). The innovative process is a complex activity because it demands a combination of various internal/external sources (Kanbur & Kanbur, 2014). Internal sources have the most significant effect on the organizations' innovation and organizations mostly rely on in-house knowledge obtained through R&D efforts, continuous improvement, and internal training/human resources development programs (Svetina & Prodan, 2008). On the other hand, external innovation sources have become important elements to the internal capabilities of the companies (Chesbrough, 2006).

Innovation types have been defined in such a different way and understanding each type is difficult (Rowley, Baregheh & Sambrook, 2011). The first effort to promote innovation was made in 1934 when "Schumpeter" presented a very early model containing five innovation types (new goods, new methods of production, new places to sell, newer supply sources, and new organization methods) (Hagedoorn, 1996; Günday, Ulusoy, Kılıç & Alpkan, 2011). According to the review of innovation differences in the literature, OECD Oslo Manual (2005) which introduced four innovation types can be accepted as a reference source for the classification of types of innovation. Product innovation is the execution of a good product or service. Process innovation includes important changes in production, technology, software, or even in the procedures or techniques. Marketing innovation is implemented in a new way of marketing. Organizational innovation is a process of using new/latest organizational methods (Oslo Manual, 2005). There are many key factors behind successful innovation, but organizational success depends on innovation type and proportionality between features of the innovative process (Boer & During, 2001). If organizations want to continue growing in the competition, they should invest in different innovation types, because it has different results (Simpson, Siguaw & Enz, 2006).

4. Relationship Between Intellectual Capital and Innovation

Organizations are trying to survive in a competitive business environment where the winds of change blow faster. The innovation moves taken in this process stand out in the success of the companies. The reasoned action theory assumes that individuals are rational beings and that they always behave in the way they intend (Hoewe & Sherrick, 2015). Intention is a cognitive explanation of the readiness to perform a behavior (Houran & Lange, 2013). The reasoned action theory can be explanatory in an organization's decision to move towards innovation. Innovation involves the intention of being innovative as a multidimensional concept. In addition, the intention of innovation should be supported by the right infrastructure (Dobni, 2008). For an organization, there will be many factors that influence performing innovation. Many factors can be effective in an organization's innovation decisions such as the organization's marketing strategy, talents of its employees, financial structure, technological capacity, R&D investments, organization size, management approach, organizational structure, sector in which it operates, innovation perspective, past innovation experiences, continuity of innovation activities, relationships with suppliers, job satisfaction levels of employees and the level of competition in the market it operates. The innovation power of a system depends on the collection of resources (customers, suppliers, information providers, intermediaries, private and public institutions, etc.) (Erdem, Gül & Gül, 2013). Resource-based theory suggests that there is a relationship between competitive advantage and the resources and capabilities used (Shan, Luo, Zhou & Wei, 2019). In the context of performance and competition, successful innovation as a pillar of organizational success can be attributed to the use of resources in terms of resource-based theory. The survival and growth of an organization depend largely on how it creates new resources, how it develops existing ones, and how it maintains its core capabilities (Ray, Muhanna & Barney, 2005; Yang, 2008). Companies seek to explore and develop their intangible resources as well as their physical and financial resources, and these intangible resources are seen as IC (Özdemir, 2017). The creation and maintenance of intangible resources for competitive advantage shows the connection between IC and resource-based theory. The accepted common view about IC is the acceptance of IC as a source. Different types of IC represent different types of intangible resources (Navas-Lopez, Alama-Salazar, Martin-de-Castro & Lopez-Saez, 2006).

The investigation of the sources of innovation has been the subject of numerous researches. The most striking aspect in terms of human resources is human capital (İpek, 2018). The knowledge, skills, and ability of human capital can be considered as an important resource for the innovation moves of companies. The importance of transactive memory structures with the support of individual-level draws attention to the ability of the teams and organizations (that come together with goal congruence) to convert the knowledge to the result (Kaya, 2013). According to the transactive memory theory, a transactive information system is a collective information processing system (Tsai, Joe, Chen, Lin, Ma & Du, 2016). Being related to the cognition of the group, transactive memory theory focuses on the relationship between individuals' memory systems. According to the theory, individuals in an ongoing relationship develop a specialized division of labor on the coding, storage, and retrieval of information in different substantive domains (Hollingshead, 1998). A transactive memory system is a domain-specific knowledge that individuals have and is a sharing in which a group understands who knows what. The development of a transactive memory system depends on the mechanisms of the recognition of expertise, access to information, and information retrieval. According to the transactive memory theory, individuals do not take the responsibility of storing and processing information, but instead acquire information from whoever they perceived as an expert (Huang, Barbour, Su & Contractor, 2013). A transactive memory system has a direct effect on performance (Hollingshead, 1998). Transactive memory has a significant impact on R&D capabilities (Kaya, 2013). Therefore, transactive memory theory can be explanatory for the transformation of the gains of human capital into innovation.

Human capital is a social wealth consisting of the sum of knowledge, skills, talents, and experiences gained. Social capital, on the other hand, is a social wealth consisting of the sum of elements such as interpersonal relations, networks, bonds, communication, assistance, solidarity, values, and trust. Human capital and social capital are integral and complementary to each other (Aktan, Tunç & Yay, 2017). The theoretical framework of social capital has developed based on social network theory. Social network theories can be considered as Granovetter's Strength of Weak Ties Theory, Burt's Structural Hole Theory, Coleman's Social Closure Theory, and Lin's Social Resources Theory (Özdemir, 2008). Networks help to understand the flow of information and ideas and the interdependence between technology and the diffusion of innovation (Steen, Macaulay & Kastelle, 2011). Granovetter's contribution to the social network theory by addressing network ties is that a weaker tie creates more new information for the network actor than a strong tie. When analyzed in terms of network ties, R&D network ties among companies improve their innovation performance (Bertrand-Cloodt, Hagedoorn & Kranenburg, 2011). On the other hand, in terms of economic development, regions are economically successful primarily when they have sufficient innovative actors (companies, research institutes, public agencies, etc.) and secondly when there are intensive networks between these actors (Yokura, Matsubara & Sternberg, 2013). Different social networks affect innovation and lead to the diffusion of innovation in different ways (Kong & Bi, 2014).

A critical success factor in innovation management is strategy. To be successful in the innovation management process, companies with innovative cultures need to provide adaption between their innovation strategies and organizational structures (Ecevit Satı & Işık, 2011). Incompatibility between strategy and organizational structure will prevent the organization from achieving its goals efficiently. Concerning strategy-structure cohesion, in the literature, the harmonization of strategy and organizational structure has been an important discussion topic (Efil & Çubukcu, 2018). From this point of view, organizational structure can be decisive in innovation formation. The explaining role of structural capital in the process of the formation of new ideas and innovation management are emphasized (Aramburu, Saenz & Blanco, 2015).

To understand IC and its significance for innovation, what scholars have put forward so far were also examined in this study. Being as components of IC human capital, social capital and organizational capital have a positive and significant correlation with different types of innovation. Previous researches in the literature claimed the positive relationship between IC and innovation (Subramaniam & Youndt, 2005; Zerenler, Hasiloğlu & Sezgin, 2008; Ghorbani, Mofaredi & Bashiriyan, 2012; Dumay, Rooney & Marini, 2013; El Telbani, 2013; Al-Fawaeer, 2013; Agostini, Nosella & Filippini, 2017). Thus, IC can be confirmed as a significant factor to promote innovation, and a source to create competitive advantage/s (Parpandel, 2013).

5. Conclusion

Innovation is now more important than ever in the highly competitive world that we live in. The world around us is changing so quickly in the digitalization era and innovation becomes a strategic tool for organizations to survive. It is apprehensible to those who know what innovation means. At the core, innovation is not only the invention but also the introduction of something new. This can involve getting it into the market. Innovation provides a competitive edge and organizational sustainability. It is a priority for improvements. Based on its outcomes, it is inevitably one of the most important concerns of organizations. There are myriad of different reasons that are forcing organizations to be innovative. Therefore, being innovative should be a part of any organization regardless of how big it is. Leading organizations owe their continued success to innovation. Thus, innovation can be accepted as a universal truth grounded in success.

Millennials are operating in an innovative business environment and they recognize the need to innovate. Organizations seek ways for formulating and building innovation. It's important to understand that the drivers needed to develop innovation skills should be strengthened to achieve innovation. Questions have arisen concerning how to innovate and what is required to become innovative. Intellectual capital is expected as the main driver of innovation. To instill an innovation culture in an organization, it is required to be aware of the resources. Innovative organizations utilize resources and capabilities which are crucial to accomplish the goals and carry out the activities. Based on the categorization of assets, different kinds of resources may be divided into two broad types as tangible and intangible. In today's business world, the focus of organizations should shift from tangible to intangible capital.

Intellectual capital is a critical factor for improving performance, innovating and creating value. Intangibles are important for the reason that they have higher utility for an organization and they are hard for competitors to reproduce or copy, which gives an organization a sustainable competitive advantage resource. Through intangible investments, organizations acquire knowledge assets that increase their innovativeness. The relationship between intellectual capital and innovation should be understood because the key question in the innovation path which has been raised many times is "after all which resources really drives organizations towards innovation". In order to innovate, you have to be willing to explore intellectual capital.

References

Agostini, L., Nosella, A., & Filippini, R. (2017). Does intellectual capital allow improving innovation performance? A quantitative analysis in the SME context. *Journal of Intellectual Capital*, 18(2), 400–418.

Aktan, C. C., Tunç, M., & Yay, S. (2017). Exploring the relationship and complementary roles between human capital and social capital. *Ekonomi Bilimleri Dergisi*, 9(1), 81–103.

Al-Fawaeer, M. A. (2013). The intellectual capital investment and its impact on organizational innovation: An empirical study on Jordanian Industrial Public Shareholding Listed Companies (JIPSLC). *International Business Research*, 6(10), 119–131.

Andriessen, D. (2004). IC valuation and measurement: Classifying the state of the art. *Journal of Intellectual Capital*, 5(2), 230–242.

Aramburu, N., Saenz, J., & Blanco, C. (2015). Structural capital, innovation capability and company performance in technology-based Colombian firms. *Cuadernos de Gestion*, 15(1), 39–60.

Armbruster, H., Bikfalvi, A., Kinkel, S., & Lay, G. (2008). Organizational innovation: The challenge of measuring non-technical innovation in large-scale surveys. *Technovation*, 28(10), 644–657.

Bertrand-Cloodt, D., Hagedoorn, J., & Kranenburg, H. (2011). The strength of R&D network ties in high-tech sectors – a multi-dimensional analysis of the effects of tie strength on innovation performance. *Technology Analysis & Strategic Management*, 23(10), 1015–1030.

Berzkalne, I., & Zelgalve, E. (2014). Intellectual capital and company value. *Procedia-Social and Behavioral Sciences*, 110, 887–896.

Boer, H., & During, W. E. (2001). Innovation, what innovation? A comparison between product, process and organisational innovation. *International Journal of Technology Management*, 22(1–3), 83–107.

Carnerio, A. (2000). How does knowledge management influence innovation and competitiveness? *Journal of Knowledge Management*, 4(2), 87–98.

Carroll, R. F., & Tansey, R. R. (2000). Intellectual capital in the new internet economy – Its meaning, measurement and management for enhancing quality. *Journal of Intellectual Capital*, 1(4), 296–312.

Chesbrough, H. W. (2006). Open innovation: A new paradigm for understanding industrial innovation. In Chesbrough, H. W., Vanhaverbeke, W., & West, J. (Eds.), *Open innovation: Researching a new paradigm* (pp. 1–12). Oxford: Oxford University Press.

Dobni, C. B. (2008). Measuring innovation culture in organizations: The development and validation of a generalized innovation culture construct using exploratory factor analysis. *European Journal of Innovation Management*, 11(4), 539–559.

Dumay, J., Rooney, J., & Marini, L. (2013). An intellectual capital-based differentiation theory of innovation practice. *Journal of Intellectual Capital*, 14(4), 608–633.

Ecevit Satı, Z., & Işık, Ö. (2011). The synergy of innovation and strategic management: Strategic innovation. *Celal Bayar University, Journal of Social Sciences*, 9(2), 538–559.

Efil, İ., & Çubukcu, M. (2018). Strategy-Structure fit in organizations and examples from implementation. *"IS, GUC" Industrial Relations and Human Resources Journal*, 20(1), 101–128.

El Telbani, N. (2013). The relationship between intellectual capital and innovation in Jawwal Company-Gaza. *Jordan Journal of Business Administration*, 9(3), 619–649.

Erdem, B., Gül, K., & Gül, M. (2013). The relationship between market orientation, innovation orientation and firm performance: A research in four and five star hotels in Ankara. *Journal of Business Research-Turk*, 5(2), 74–104.

Fazlagic, A. (2005). *Measuring the intellectual capital of a university. Trends in the management of human resources in higher education.* Poland: IMHE.

Ghorbani, M., Mofaredi, B., & Bashiriyan, S. (2012). Study of the relationship between intellectual capital management and organizational innovation in the banks. *African Journal of Business Management*, 6(15), 5208–5217.

Godin, B., & Lane, J. P. (2013). Pushes and pulls: Hi(S)tory of the demand pull model of innovation. *Science, Technology & Human Values*, 38(5), 621–654.

Günday, G., Ulusoy, G., Kılıç, K., & Alpkan, L. (2011). Effects of innovation types on firm performance. *Int. Journal of Production Economics*, 133(2), 662–676.

Gupta, M., & Singh, T. (2015). Intellectual capital & firm profitability: An empirical study on the IT sector listed in NSE. *Global Journal of Multidisciplinary Studies*, 4(4), 105–108.

Hagedoorn, J. (1996). Innovation and entrepreneurship: Schumpeter revisited. *Industrial and Corporate Change*, 5(3), 883–896.

Hansen, M. T., Nohria, N., & Tierney, T. (1999). What's your strategy for managing knowledge? *Harvard Business Review*, 77(2), 106–116.

Hoewe, J., & Sherrick, B. (2015). Using the theory of reasoned action and structural equation modeling to study the influence of news media in an experimental context. *Atlantic Journal of Communication*, 23(5), 237–253.

Hollingshead, A. B. (1998). Communication, learning, and retrieval in transactive memory systems. *Journal of Experimental Social Psychology*, 34(5), 423–442.

Houran, J., & Lange, R. (2013). Applying the theory of reasoned action to a computerized test of intuition, part II: Decision-making in a hidden test of PSI. *Journal of the Society for Psychical Research*, 77(913), 236–251.

Huang, M., Barbour, J., Su, C., & Contractor, N. (2013). Why do group members provide information to digital knowledge repositories? A multilevel application of transactive memory theory. *Journal of the American Society for Information Science and Technology*, 64(3), 540–557.

İpek, İ. (2018) The resource-based view within the export context: An integrative review of empirical studies. *Journal of Global Marketing*, 31(3), 157–179.

Jacobs, C. D., & Heracleous, L. T. (2005). Answers for questions to come: Reflective dialogue as an enabler of strategic innovation. *Journal of Organizational Change Management*, 18(4), 338–352.

Jahanian, R., & Salehi, R. (2013). Managing intellectual capital in organizations. *International Journal of Human Resource Studies*, 3(4), 121–127.

Kamara, J. M., Anumba, C. J., & Carrillo, P M. (2002). A clever approach to selecting a knowledge management strategy. *International Journal of Project Management*, 20(3), 205–211.

Kanbur, A., & Kanbur, E. (2014). Investigation of white collar differences between levels of innovation sources of use. *Journal of International Management and Social Researches*, 1(1), 10–23.

Kanbur, E., & Şen, S. (2020). The effect of perceived overqualification on innovative behavior: The mediating role of perceived leader support. *Third Sector Social Economic Review*, 55(2), 1060–1077.

Kannan, G., & Aulbur, W. G. (2004). Intellectual capital: Measurement effectiveness. *Journal of Intellectual Capital*, 5(3), 389–413.

Kaya, N. (2013). Organizational learning and memory transition of the R&D impact on skills and how the increase network map can be self-regalated? *Kahramanmaras Sutcu Imam University, Faculty of Economics and Administrative Sciences Journal*, 3(2), 115–124.

Khalique, M., Shaari, J. A. N., Isa, A. H. B. M., & Samad, N. B. (2013). Impact of intellectual capital on the organizational performance of Islamic banking sector in Malaysia. *Asian Journal of Finance & Accounting*, 5(2), 75–83.

Kong, D. Y., & Bi, X. H. (2014). Impact of social network and business model on innovation diffusion of electric vehicles in China. *Mathematical Problems in Engineering*, 2014(1), 1–7.

Likar, B., Fatur, p., & Mrgole, U. (2013). *Innovation management*. Ljubljana, Slovenia: Korona plus – Institute for Innovation and Technology.

Lord-Tarte, E. (2012). *Innovation and the development of the Canadian wine industry*. Doct. Dissert., Telfer School of Management University, Ottawa.

Nahapiet, J., & Ghoshal, S. (1998). Social capital, intellectual capital, and the organizational advantage. *Academy of Management Review*, 23(2), 242–266.

Najem, N. (2008). *Knowledge management: Concepts, strategies, processes*. Amman, Jordan: Dar Alwaraaq.

Navas-Lopez, J. E., Alama-Salazar, E., Martin-de-Castro, G., & Lopez-Saez, P. (2006) Organizational capital as competitive advantage of the firm. *Journal of Intellectual Capital*, 7(3), 324–337.

Nimtrakoon, S. (2015). The relationship between intellectual capital, firms' market value and financial performance: Empirical evidence from the ASIAN Countries. *Journal of Intellectual Capital*, 16(3), 587–618.

Nonaka, I., & Takeuchi, H. (1995). *The knowledge creating company*. New York: Oxford University Press.

OECD. (2006). *Creating value from intellectual assets*. Paris: OECD Publishing.

OECD. (2008). *Intellectual assets and value creation – synthesis report.* Paris: OECD Publishing.

Oliveira, M. B. (2014). Technology and basic science: The linear model of innovation. *Scientle Studia*, 12, 129–146.

Oslo Manual. (2005). *Guidelines for collecting and interpreting innovation data.* Third Edition, A Joint Publication of OECD and Eurostat.

Özdemir, A. (2008). The relationship between social capital and knowledge creation with the perspective of social network features: A field survey on academics. *Anadolu University Journal of Social Sciences*, 8(2), 81–102.

Özdemir, B. (2017). Validity and reliability testing of intellectual capital scale: An empirical study in top 1000 industrial enterprises of Turkey. *The Journal of Academic Social Science Studies*, 61, 363–372.

Parpandel, D. E. (2013). The role of intellectual capital in knowledge-based society. *Management Strategies Journal*, 19(1), 47–52.

Pulic, A. (2008). *The principles of intellectual capital efficiency – A Brief Description*. Zagreb: Croatian Intellectual Capital Center.

Ray, G., Muhanna, W. A., & Barney, J. B. (2005). Information technology and the performance of the customer service process: A resource-based analysis. *MIS Quarterly*, 29(4), 625–652.

Rowley, J., Baregheh, A., & Sambrook, S. (2011). Towards an innovation-type mapping tool. *Management Decision*, 49(1), 73–86.

Santoso, E. (2011). *Intellectual capital in Indonesia: The influence on financial performance of banking industry*. Doct. Dissert., University of Phoenix, USA.

Shan, S., Luo, Y., Zhou, Y., & Wei, Y. (2019). Big data analysis adaptation and enterprises' competitive advantages: The perspective of dynamic capability and resource-based theories. *Technology Analysis & Strategic Management*, 31(4), 406–420.

Simpson, P. M., Siguaw, J. A., & Enz, C. A. (2006). Innovation orientation outcomes: The good and the bad. *Journal of Business Research*, 59(10), 1133–1141.

Steen, J., Macaulay, S., & Kastelle, T. (2011). Small worlds: The best network structure for innovation? *Prometheus*, 29(1), 39–50.

Stewart, T., & Ruckdeschel, C. (1998). Intellectual capital: The new wealth of organizations. *Performance Improvement*, 37(7), 56–59.

Subramaniam, M., & Youndt, M. A. (2005). The influence of intellectual capital on the types of innovative capabilities. *Academy of Management Journal*, 48(3), 450–463.

Svetina, A. C., & Prodan, I. (2008). How internal and external sources of knowledge contribute to firms' innovation performance. *Managing Global Transitions*, 6(3), 277–299.

Tsai, Y. H., Joe, S. W., Chen, M. L., Lin, C. P., Ma, H. C., & Du, J. W. (2016). Assessing team performance: Moderating roles of transactive memory, hypercompetition, and emotional regulation. *Human Perf.*, 29(2), 89–105.

Walliser, E., & Mignon, S. (2015). General presentation: Society of knowledge, intellectual capital and innovation. *Journal of Innovation Economics & Management*, (2), 3–11.

Wang, W. Y., & Chang, C. (2005). Intellectual capital and performance in causal models: Evidence from the information technology industry in Taiwan. *Journal of Intellectual Capital*, 6(2), 222–236.

Wang, C. N., Chang, Y. L., Huang, Q. H., & Wang, C. H. (2011). Assessment on intellectual capital management for Taiwanese pharmaceutical industry: Using GRA and MPI. *African Journal of Business Management*, 5(7), 2950–2958.

Yang, Y. F. (2008). The roles of human resources, information technology, and marketing knowledge capabilities in performance: An extension of the resource-based theory perspective. *Social Behavior and Personality: An International Journal*, 36(9), 1269–1282.

Yokura, Y., Matsubara, H., & Sternberg, R. (2013). R&D networks and regional innovation: A social network analysis of joint research projects in Japan. *Area, Royal Geographical Society*, 45(4), 493–503.

Youndt, M. A., Subramaniam, M., & Snell, S. A. (2004). Intellectual capital profiles: An examination of investments and returns. *Journal of Management Studies*, 41(2), 335–361.

Zeghal, D., & Maaloul, A. (2010). Analysing value added as an indicator of intellectual capital and its consequences on company performance. *Journal of Intellectual Capital*, 11(1), 39–60.

Zerenler, M., Hasiloğlu, S. B., & Sezgin, M. (2008). Intellectual capital and innovation performance: Empirical evidence in the Turkish automotive supplier. *Journal of Technology Management & Innovation*, 3(4), 31–40.

Maruf GÖGEBAKAN & Serkan AKOĞUL

A New Approach to Clustering the Human Development Index in Terms of Business Management Using Gaussian Mixture Models

1. Introduction

The Human Development Index (HDI) was created by the United Nations (UN) to determine countries' levels of development based on indicators of health (expected life expectancy at birth), education (length of adult education, expected duration of child education) and economic (national income per capita). Human, development is defined by the average success of long and healthy living, economic standard ownership indicators that can ensure good education and wealth (UNDP, 2021). The Human, Development Index of countries is formed by taking the geometric mean of the health (Life Expectancy at Birth [LEB]), education (Mean Years of Schooling [MYS] and Expected Years of Schooling [EYS]) and economic (GNI per capita [GNI]) indicators (UNDP Technical Note, 2021). With the averages of these indicators, the countries' development indicators have been determined by taking into account not only the economic but also the health and education components.

Different infrastructure indicators that affect people's living conditions also make a significant impact on human development. Although there are many indicators impacting human development, health, education, and economy have been identified as the most significant influence values (Sudirman and Hapsara, 2021).

HDI has been consistently criticized since its initial publication and alternative forms of classification and calculation have been proposed (Noorbakhsh, 1998). There are many different indexes derived from countries' human development. Yakunina and Bychkov constructed a reliable regression model among countries using four variables that make up the HDI (Yakunina and Bychkov, 2015). In order to highlight people's living conditions, indicators obtained from municipal services in the field of life were added to HDI indicators and the Municipal Human Development Index (MHDI) was created (Yero et al., 2021).

The probability of including the variables of HDI in the calculation of human development is a significant problem. Semi-HDI calculations were obtained using the probability weights of variables. Countries are classified by variables, using different variables predominantly (Omrani et al., 2020).

Karagiannis and Karagiannis proposed a weighting algorithm based on Shannon's Entropy with a linear combination of inputs. The suggested method uses the effect of variables on different probability weights. Variable weighting and decision criteria were compared and graded. With suggestion of this different weighting, the HDI classification method can be considered as an alternative to the classification method obtained by using equally weighted variables (Karagiannis and Karagiannis, 2020).

In his study, Dogru (2017) proposed two-component finite mixture models created using normal distribution, t-distribution, skew normal distribution, and skew t-distributions as an alternative to the classification method obtained by the UN of HDI data (Dogru, 2017).

In this study, GMM was used to classify multivariate HDI data. Each variable in the HDI data was examined with one-component normal mixture models (U-GMM). The number and structure of mixture models that can be formed by a variable structure in a mixed structure have been revealed. As an alternative to the classification of the geometric mean of variables proposed by the UN based on quarters, classes formed by variables with different probability weights with GMM were obtained. With the new method proposed, ranking and class memberships of countries were changed. Countries' HDI classes and rankings in these classes help to improve their relations in many fields, such as trade, marketing, logistics and well-being share.

The chapter is designed as follows. In Section 2, we define the finite mixture model and give the maximum likelihood (ML) estimation using the Expectation-Maximization (EM) algorithm of this model. In Section 3.1, we select the number of clusters using model-based clustering for HDI data set. In Section 3.2, we obtain the best model for HDI data set by comparing the mixture models based on the GMM. We provide some conclusions in Section 4.

2. Data and Method

2.1. Data

In this study, four variables belonging to three basic indicators in the HDI data set were used as an indicator of the human development of countries for 2020. The UN-published HDI includes health, education and economic dimensions used to identify human development. Accordingly, the health category consists of a single variable, "Life Expectancy at Birth (LEB)," and the education dimension of two variables, "Expected Years of Schooling (EYS)" and "Mean Years of

Schooling (MYS)," while the economic dimension comprises of one variable, "GNI per capita (GNI)." The geometric average of the normalized variables of these three basic dimensions gives countries an HDI score (Roser, 2014; UNDP, 2021). According to this calculation method, the arithmetic mean of the variables of expected education duration and average training duration was obtained first, and then the three obtained variables were normalized between [0–1] using the formula $\frac{X_i - X_{min}}{X_{max} - X_{min}}$. Three normalized variables were obtained by geometric mean of HDI scores as $HDI = \sqrt[3]{\left(I_H I_E I_{GNI}\right)}$. The United Nations determined HDI scores for 189 countries by 4 classes according to quartiles and named the country scores as Very High (VH), High (H), Medium (M) and Low (L) classes.

2.2. Method

2.2.1 Model-Based Clustering

Bayes-based clustering approaches produce quite good results to uncover the components contained in each variable of multivariate distributions (Fraley and Raftery 2003). Single-component normal mixture distributions are used to determine the number of components in each variable using the information criteria (Gogebakan and Erol 2018). Single variable normal mixture model is formulated as

$$f\left(x;\theta_j\right) = \sum_{j=1}^{g} \pi_j f_j\left(x;\mu_j,\sigma_j\right) \tag{1}$$

Here g represents the number of mixed components of the univariate distribution, while π_j represents the combined probability weights. Probability density functions of univariate normal mixture distributions is formulated as

$$f\left(x;\mu,\sigma^2\right) = \frac{1}{\sigma\sqrt{2\pi}} exp\left\{-\frac{1}{2}\frac{\left(x-\mu\right)^2}{\sigma^2}\right\}, x \in \mathbb{R} \tag{2}$$

Here, it is obtained as the mean vector of the variable based on observation values μ and standard deviation σ.

2.2.2 Finite Mixture Distributions

Finite mixture models are calculated by linear combination of a finite number of probability density functions. These mixture models are among the very essential methods in modeling and analyzing heterogeneous data sets with more than one mixture distribution in the variables. It is well known that finite mixture models are a very powerful computational method used in supervised and unsupervised classification/clustering methods, data mining, pattern recognition, image processing, and machine learning problems (Titterington et al., 1985; McLachlan and Basford, 1988; McLachlan and Peel, 2000; Bishop, 2006).

Finite mixed distributions are assumed to have n observation and p-dimensional $y=\left(y_1^{\,T}, y_2^{\,T}, \ldots, y_n^{\,T}\right)^T$ data structure.

Clustering analysis based on a mixture of multivariate distributions examines the identification of clusters/components formed by subgroups of different distributions of variables. Each set of finite mixture distributions is expressed by a parametric mathematical model.

Probability density function of finite mixture distribution models is formulated as

$$f\left(x_i;\theta\right)=\sum_{j=1}^{g}\pi_j f_j\left(x_i;\psi_j\right) \tag{3}$$

Here, as $0<\pi_j<1$ and $\sum_{i=1}^{g}\pi_j=1$, π_j represents probability mixing weight, while $\psi_j=\left(\mu_j, £_j\right)$ represents the unknown parameter vector. Probability density function of multivariate normal distributions is formulated as

$$f_j\left(x_i;\mu_j,£_j\right)=\frac{1}{\left(2\pi\right)^{\frac{p}{2}}\left|£_j\right|^{\frac{1}{2}}}exp\left\{-\frac{1}{2}\left(x_i-\mu_j\right)^T £_j^{-1}\left(x_i-\mu_j\right)\right\} \tag{4}$$

Here, $\theta_j=\pi_1,\ldots,\pi_k,\psi_1,\ldots,\psi_k$ vectors are multi-variable parameter vectors of Gaussian mixture distributions in unknown vector space.

Log-likelihood (Log-L) function based on density functions of Gaussian mixture models (GMM) is formulated as

$$logL(\text{¤}) = \sum_{i=1}^{n} log\left(\sum_{j=1}^{k} \pi_j f_j\left(x_i;\theta_j\right)\right) \tag{5}$$

The probability that the Log-L function's $\boldsymbol{x}_i$ observations belong to a composite component f_j is calculated as

$$\tau_j\left(\boldsymbol{x}_i;\Psi\right) = \pi_j \Phi_j\left(\boldsymbol{x}_i;\text{¼}_j,\text{£}_j\right) / \sum_{m=1}^{k} \pi_m \Phi_j\left(\boldsymbol{x}_i;\text{¼}_m,\text{£}_m\right) \tag{6}$$

Here, maximum probability estimates of θ_j elements in ψ unknown parameter space calculated by the EM algorithm are obtained by iterations of

$$\pi_j^{(m+1)} = \sum_{i=1}^{n} \frac{\tau_j\left(y_i;\Psi^{(m)}\right)}{n} \tag{7}$$

$$\text{¼}_j^{(m+1)} = \frac{1}{\sum_{i=1}^{n} \tau_j\left(\boldsymbol{x}_i;\Psi^{(m)}\right)} \sum_{i=1}^{n} \tau_j\left(\boldsymbol{x}_i;\Psi^{(m)}\right)\boldsymbol{x}_i \tag{8}$$

$$\text{£}_j^{(m+1)} = \frac{1}{\sum_{i=1}^{n} \tau_j\left(\boldsymbol{x}_i;\Psi^{(m)}\right)} \sum_{i-1}^{n} \tilde{\ }_j\left(\boldsymbol{x}_i;\Psi^{(m)}\right)\left(\boldsymbol{x}_i - \text{¼}_j^{(m+1)}\right)\left(\boldsymbol{x}_i - \text{¼}_j^{(m+1)}\right)^T \tag{9}$$

(McLachlan et al., 2004).

2.2.3 Determining the Number of Components by GMM

In multivariable finite mixture models, it is a difficult and significant problem to uncover significant subgroups in the data. The homogeneous or heterogeneous nature of the variables in the data set determines the number of clusters. Homogeneous variables include observations from a single (one) normal distribution. The absence of homogeneous variables in a mixed structure increases the probability that they will be included in each set that can occur. Heterogeneous variables are variables formed by observations from at least two or more normal distributions with different parameters. The number of normal mixtures of heterogeneous variables indicates the number of components of that variable. Therefore, the sets formed by multivariate normal mixture distributions must correspond to the subcomponent of at least one variable (Fraley and Raftery, 1998). A range can be obtained for the number of sets that can be formed by the component numbers of heterogeneous variables. The number of components in heterogeneous variables should be displayed as k_j as $j = 1,\dots,n$, minimum and maximum cluster numbers calculated using the equations $C_{min} = max\{k_j\}$ and $C_{max} = \prod_{j=1}^{p} k_j$ respectively, indicate the range of alternating sets that may occur. The number of all alternative mixture models that can occur based on the resulting cluster numbers is achieved by $M_{Total} = 2^{\prod_{j=1}^{n} k_j} - 1$ (Gögebakan and Servi, 2019).

In this study, the Mclust package in R software was used to estimate the number of components in normal mixture models (Bouveyron et al., 2019). The component count estimate in normal mixture models is calculated using information criteria based on the Likelihood function.

Information criteria for component count estimation in normal mixture models is formulated as

$$2logL(\psi) - C \tag{10}$$

Here C is called the penalty term and is usually calculated based on the number of free parameters in the model (d) and the number of observations (n) (McLachlan and Rathnayake, 2014). The maximum number of components that make the information criterion is determined as the appropriate number of components. Log-L value in component count estimation with Mclust package, Bayesian information criterion (BIC) (Schwarz 1978) and Integrated complete-data likelihood criterion (ICL) (Biernacki et al., 2000) values were used. BIC value is calculated through the equation

$$\text{BIC} = 2logL(\hat{\psi}) - dlog(n) \tag{11}$$

Here, the number of individual parameters is calculated with $d=(k-1)+(kp)+kp\left(\frac{k+1}{2}\right)$ (Bozdoğan 1994).

ICL value,

$$ICL = BIC + 2\sum_{i=1}^{n}\sum_{k=1}^{G} c_{ik}\log\left(z_{ik}\right) \tag{12}$$

where z_{ik} is the conditional probability that x_i arises from the kth mixture component, and c_{ik} = 1 if the ith unit is assigned to cluster k and 0 otherwise. ICL penalises the BIC through an entropy term which measures clusters overlap.

The number and alternative set of mixed models that multivariate heterogeneous normal mixed distributions can form is a combinatorial problem. The sequences of sets according to the components of variables represent the geometry of the alternate mixture model. Combinatoric equation in the p-dimensional data set for the number and sequence of alternative mixed models is as follows

$$f\left(n_k;c\right)=\sum_{i_1,i_2,\ldots,i_k=0}^{n_1,n_2,\ldots,n_k}\left(-1\right)^{\sum_{k=1}^{p} i_k}\binom{n_1}{i_1}\binom{n_2}{i_2}\cdots\binom{n_k}{i_k}\binom{\left(n_1-i_1\right)\left(n_2-i_2\right)\ldots\left(n_k-i_k\right)}{c} \tag{13}$$

(Gögebakan 2020). Here, n_k represents the number of components in variables and c represents the number of alternate clusters in the mixture model.

3. Findings

3.1. Classification-Based Variable Selection with Univariate Normal Mixture Models

In multivariate normal mixture models, Single Variable Normal Mixed Models (U-GMM), which is a single variable Bayesian approach, are used in order to determine the number of mixture components for each variable (Gogebakan, 2020). The number of components of single variable normal distributions is determined by the use of information criteria, such as BIC and ICL calculated from the Log-L value (Akogul and Erisoglu, 2017).

According to the U-GMM method, the number of components obtained based on the Log-L, BIC, and ICL values for the Mclust (Scrucca et al., 2016) and LEB (Life Expectancy of Birth) variable as shown in Table 1.

Table 1. Mclust model V (univariate, unequal variance) with 3 components for LEB variable.

# Components	Log-L	BIC	ICL
3	-623.5075	-1288.949	-1338.926

According to the U-GMM method, there are three components with Mclust for the LEB variable in the HDI data set. A graph of BIC values according to the component number of the HDI score is shown in Figure 1(a) and a plot of the 3-component GMM is shown in Figure 1(b).

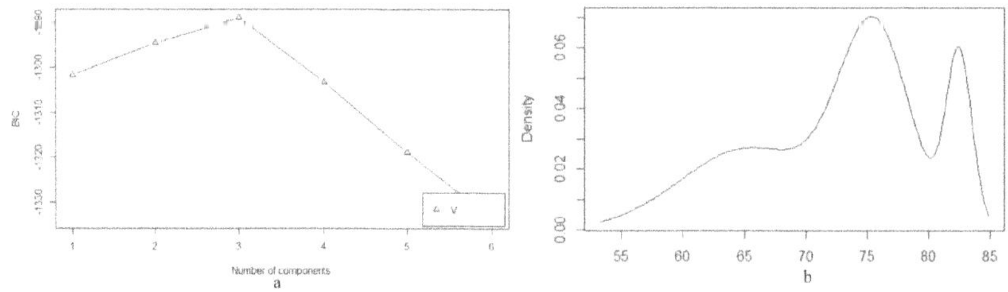

Figure 1. For the LEB variable, (a) BIC values based on component numbers, (b) 3-component GMM chart

According to the U-GMM method, the number of components obtained based on the Log-L, BIC and ICL values for the Mclust and EYS (Expected Years of Schooling) variable is shown in Table 2.

Table 2. Mclust model V with 1 component for MYS variable.

# Components	Log-L	BIC	ICL
1	-471.5457	-953.575	-953.575

According to the U-GMM method, there is 1 component for the EYS variable in the HDI data set with Mclust. A graph of BIC values according to the component number of the EYS variable is shown in Figures 2(a) and 2(b) is a graph of a 1-component GMM.

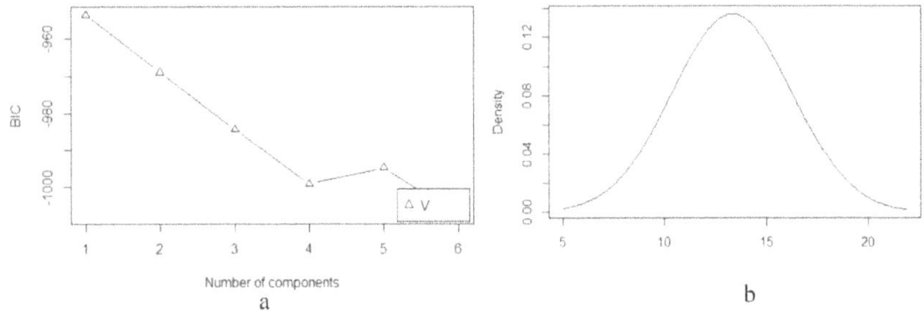

Figure 2. For the EYS variable; (a) BIC values according to the number of components, (b) GMM graph with 1 component

According to the U-GMM method, the number of components obtained based on the Log-L, BIC and ICL values for the Mclust and MYS (Mean years of schooling) variable is shown in Table 3.

Table 3. Mclust model V with 2 components for average training time variable.

# Components	Log-L	BIC	ICL
2	-471.5457	-953.575	-953.575

According to the U-GMM method, there are two components with Mclust for the MYS variable in the HDI data set. A graph of BIC values according to the number of components of the MYS variable is shown in Figures 3(a) and 3(b) is a graph of a 2-component GMM.

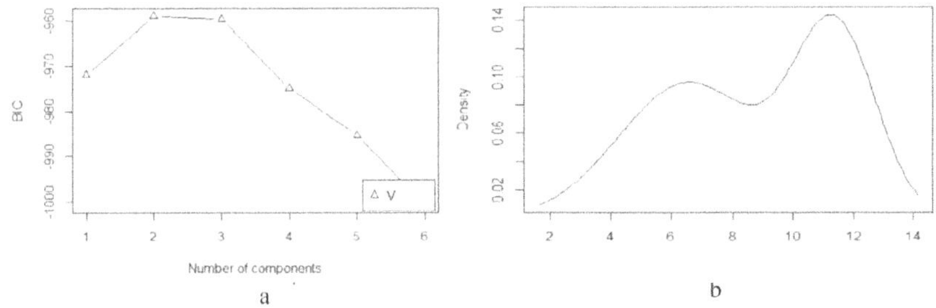

Figure 3. For MYS: (a) BIC values based on component numbers, (b) 2-component GMM chart

According to the U-GMM method, the number of components based on Log-L, BIC, and ICL values for the Mclust and GNI (GNI per capita) variable is shown in Table 4.

Table 4. Mclust model V with 3 components for GNI variable.

# Components	Log-L	BIC	ICL
3	-2060.159	-4162.252	-4207.957

According to the U-GMM method, there are three components with Mclust for the GNI variable in the HDI data set. A graph of BIC values according to the component number of the GNI variable is shown in Figures 4(a) and 4(b) of a 3-component GMM chart.

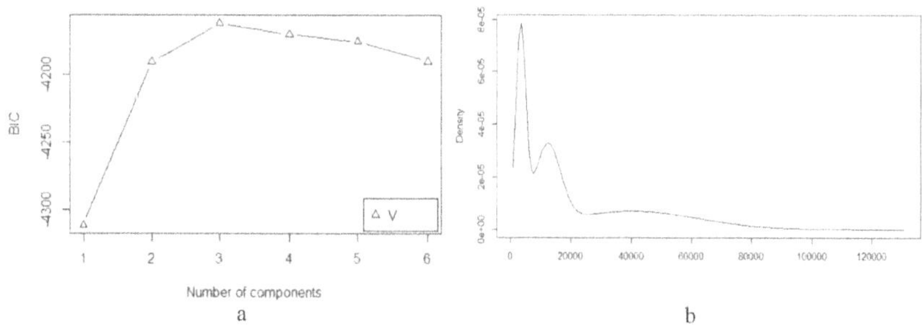

Figure 4. For GNI variable, (a) BIC values based on component numbers, (b) 3-component GMM chart

3.2. Number of Mixture Models and Alternative Mixture Models Based on Number of Variable Components

Component counts for the four variables in the HDI data set according to the U-GMM method were obtained. Minimum number of sets for all possible normal mixture models based on component numbers of variables is obtained as $C_{min} = max\{k_j\} = max\{k_1, k_2, k_3, k_4\} = max\{3,1,2,3\} = 3$ and maximum number of clusters as $C_{max} = \prod_{j=1}^{p} k_j = \prod_{j=1}^{4} k_1 k_2 k_3 k_4 = \prod_{j=1}^{4} 3.1.2.3 = 18$. The range for the number of sets that can occur in the mixture model based on the number of components of the variables is determined as $3 \leq C \leq 18$. The number of mixture models that can occur based on the number of components is calculated as $M_{Total} = 2^{\prod_{j=1}^{n} k_j} - 1 = 2^{\prod_{j=1}^{4} k_1 k_2 k_3 k_4} - 12^{18} - 1 = 262143$.

In normal mixture models, each component of variables is associated with at least one set center. The number of alternate sets is calculated combinatorically according to the sets corresponding to the components of the variables and their alternate locations. For alternative set numbers, $3 \leq C \leq 18$ the numbers of appropriate mixture models that can occur according to the range of cluster numbers are shown in Table 5.

Table 5. All possible mixture model and appropriate mixture model numbers based on the number of components in variables

Number of components in mixture model	Number of all mixture models	Number of suitable mixture models
1	18	-
2	153	-
3	816	36
4	3,060	702
5	8,568	4,176
6	18,564	13,122
7	31,824	27,072
8	43,758	40,779
9	48,620	47,298
10	43,758	43,362
11	31,824	31,752
12	18,564	18,558
13	8,568	85,68
14	3,060	3,060
15	816	816
16	153	153
17	18	18
18	1	1
Total	**262,143**	**239,473**

3.3. Modeling of HDI Data Set with GMM and Determination of the Number of Alternative Clusters for HDI Score

In real-life problems, most of the variants have a normal distribution. The use of normal distributions in modeling problems provides advantages in terms of applicability and computability. In addition, different probability density and variables in the components can be found in a heterogeneous structure in real-world applications. In the classification and clustering of multivariate data set, solutions containing the GMM are used (Frühwirth-Schnatter, 2006).

The four-variable HDI data set has been modeled with GMM. Table 6 shows the correct classification rate (CCR) and Adjusted Rand Index (Adj RI) values for the four groups selected based on Log-L, BIC, and ICL values, and the four classes set by the UN.

Table 6. Log-L, BIC, ICL, CCR and Adjusted Rand Index (Adj RI) values for four classes Mclust model EVI (diagonal, equal volume, varying shape) with 4 components

# Components	Log-L	BIC	ICL	CCR	Adj-RI
4	-3287.743	-6743.222	-6771.944	0.5185	0.4166

A chart of BIC values for different types of covariance matrices (Scrucca et al., 2016) for the HDI data according to the component numbers is shown in Figure 5. According to Figure 5, the maximum BIC value component number is set as 4 and EVI covariance structure.

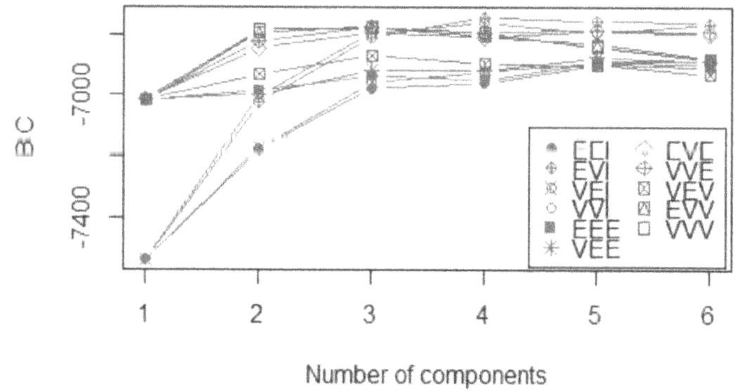

Figure 5. BIC values for different types of covariance matrices for HDI data according to the number of components

According to HDI data, class memberships of countries assigned to 3 classes were obtained for 189 countries. Table 7 shows the correct assignment numbers and the cross-accuracy table for the countries assigned with the GMM to four classes.

Table 7. Cross-correctness of countries according to four classes

	Real			
Estimate	**VH**	**H**	**M**	**L**
VH	34	0	0	0
H	0	31	14	0
M	32	22	0	0
L	0	0	23	33

Figure 6 shows the scattering of each country for four clusters in terms of variables.

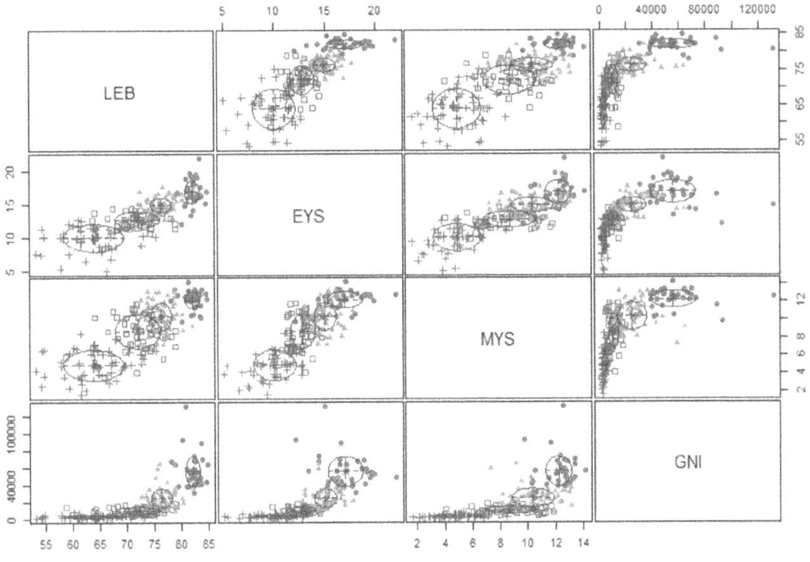

Figure 6. Dispersion chart of four clusters of countries in terms of variables

The HDI data set was modeled with 4-component GMM and the CCR value calculated according to the 4 classes specified by the UN was found to be 0.5185.

In other words, the probability of assigning a country to the correct class is 51.85 %.

In this study, model-based classification was developed as an alternative to the method in which the UN obtains a geometric average score and determines classes with quartiles. Alternative classes have been put in place for UN-endorsed grades by modeling the HDI score with U-GMM. The HDI score is obtained with 3 components with the U-GMM with a "V" covariance. Log-L, BIC and ICL values obtained with "V" model covariance are shown in Table 8.

Table 8. Log-L, BIC and ICL values of HDI score for U-GMM (Mclust V model with three components)

# Components	Log-L	BIC	ICL
3	116.2638	190.5936	159.2354

The number of classes with U-GMM and the number of observations assigned to classes are given in Table 9.

Table 9. Observation numbers falling into three classes in HDI data set

Class	High (H)	Medium (M)	Low (L)
# observations	27	102	60

According to the U-GMM method for HDI score, there were 3 components with Mclust. A graph of BIC values according to the component number of the HDI score is shown in Figure 7(a) and a plot of the 3-component GMM is shown in Figure 7(b).

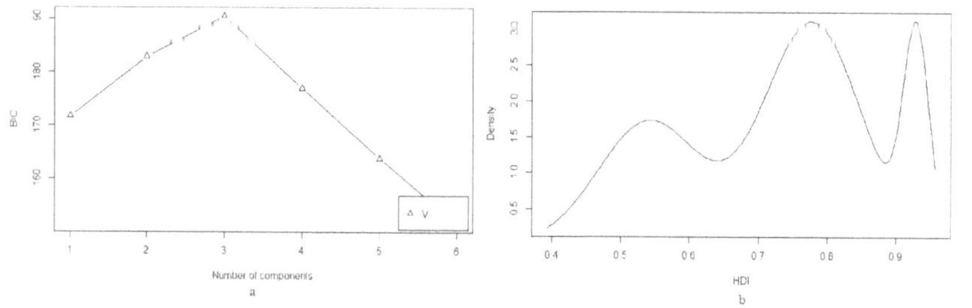

Figure 7. A graph of BIC values according to the component number of the HDI score is shown in Figure 7(a) and a plot of the 3-component GMM is shown in Figure 7(b)

Taking into account Table 9 and Figure 7(b), the HDI score has been sectioned into three classes in an increasing manner (L, M and H).

HDI data was modeled using “VVV-ellipsoidal, varying volume, shape, and orientation model” covariance structured GMM, and the number of components was determined as three according to Log-L, BIC and ICL values. The obtained model assigns countries to three clusters and provides Table 10 with the CCR, Adj RI, Log-L, BIC, and ICL values.

Table 10. Log-L, BIC, ICL, CCR and Adj Ri values for three classes (Mclust VVV ellipsoidal, varying volume, shape, and orientation model with 3 components)

# Components	Log-L	BIC	ICL	DSO (CCR)	Adj-RI
3	-3273.603	-6777.843	-6796.488	0.9365	0.8287

Figure 8 shows the graph of BIC values according to the number of components of “VVV” covariance matrix types for HDI data. According to Figure 8, the number of components with a maximum BIC value is determined as 3.

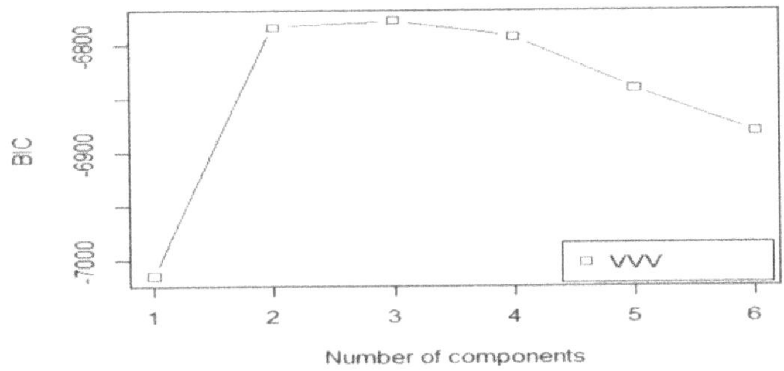

Figure 8. BIC values based on component numbers for HDI data

According to HDI data, class memberships of countries assigned to 3 classes were obtained for 189 countries. Accurate assignment numbers and cross-accuracy table of countries assigned to three classes with GMM are given in Table 11.

Table 11. Cross-accuracy of countries according to three classes

	Real		
Estimate	**H**	**M**	**L**
H	27	11	0
M	0	90	0
L	0	1	60

Figure 9 shows the scatter chart of countries for three clusters in terms of variables.

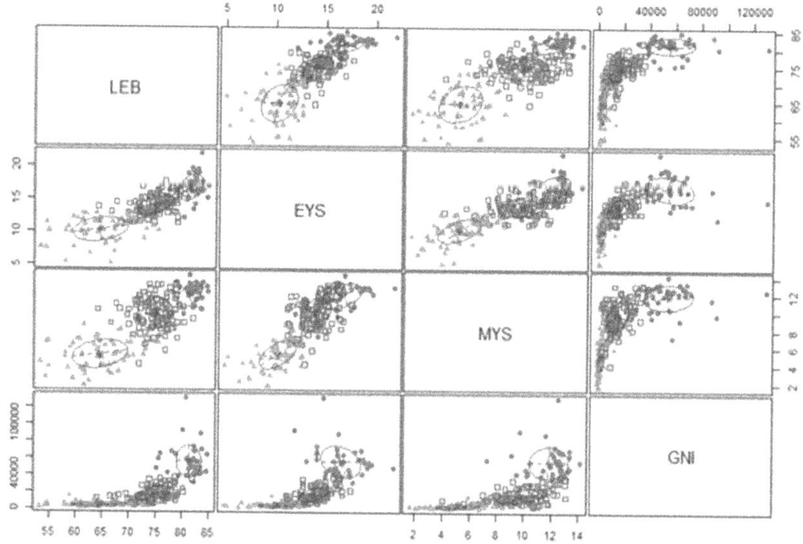

Figure 9. Scattering graph of three sets in terms of variables of countries

The HDI data set was modeled with a 3-component GMM and the CCR value calculated according to the proposed three classes for the HDI score was found to be 0.9365. Thus, the probability that any country will be assigned to the correct class is 93.65 %.

4. Conclusion

In this study, a new model was proposed in determining the number of classes for the HDI data set with GMM in finite mixture models. Parameters for determining the number of components for four variables in human development data were determined by the EM algorithm, and the best number of components was obtained using the BIC and ICL information criteria. The number of mixture models that can occur according to the number of components in human development variables has been determined.

Component numbers and class memberships of mixture models based on the GMM method in the Mclust package were obtained. According to the four classes determined by the United Nations by quartiles, the accuracy level is 51.85 % when class memberships and the correct classification rate are obtained with GMM. Three classes were obtained when the HDI score was modeled with GMM as an alternative to the number of BM classes. High, medium and low grades were given, and the countries' membership was determined (Appendix 1).

HDI data was modeled using GMM with "VVV" covariance structure and the appropriate number of clusters was determined as three. With the GMM, countries were assigned to clusters and the correct classification ratio according to the three clusters proposed for the HDI score was 93.65 %. A more appropriate method was found to be the GMM and the 3-component classification model, which have a higher success rate compared to the 4-component classification model obtained using quartiles.

The new class and rankings of countries show the level of development in the world according to the UN. With technological advances, such as digitalization, artificial intelligence, blockchain, Industry 4.0, countries receive a greater share of prosperity according to their rankings. For this reason, countries want to rank better with regards to the HDI classes and rankings in terms of businesses, management of enterprises and investment decisions of enterprises.

The study proposes new classes based on GMM, rather than the quadrant-based classification proposed by the UN, for the human development score of countries derived from the 2020 HDI data set. The humanitarian development levels of countries submitted and proposed by the UN are given in Appendix 1. The newly proposed three-cluster classes (H, M and L) again classify countries in a decreasing fashion according to their level of development. When HDI data was modeled with GMM, it was determined that the classification success was higher compared to the three proposed sets.

References

Akogul, S., & Erisoglu, M. (2017). An approach for determining the number of clusters in a model-based cluster analysis. *Entropy, 19*(9), 452.

Biernacki, C., Celeux, G., & Govaert, G. (2000). Assessing a mixture model for clustering with the integrated completed likelihood. *IEEE Transactions on Pattern Analysis and Machine Intelligence, 22*(7), 719–725.

Bishop, C. M. (2006). *Pattern Recognition and Machine Learning.* Singapore: Springer.

Bouveyron, C., Celeux, G., Murphy, T. B., & Raftery, A. E. (2019). *Model-Based Clustering and Classification for Data Science: With Applications in R* (Vol. 50). Cambridge, U.K.: Cambridge University Press.

Bozdogan, H. (1994) Mixture-model cluster analysis using model selection criteria and a new informational measure of complexity. In *Proceedings of the First US/Japan Conference on the Frontiers of Statistical Modeling: An Informational Approach.* Berlin, Germany: Springer, pp. 69–113.

Dogru, F. Z. (2017). Modeling Human Development Index using finite mixtures of distributions. *Anadolu Üniversitesi Bilim Ve Teknoloji Dergisi A-Uygulamalı Bilimler ve Mühendislik, 18*(2), 403–418.

Fraley, C., & Raftery, A. E. (1998). How many clusters? Which clustering method? Answers via model-based cluster analysis. *The Computer Journal, 41*(8), 578–588.

Fraley, C., & Raftery, A. E. (2003). Enhanced model-based clustering, density estimation, and discriminant analysis software: MCLUST. *Journal of Classification, 20*(2), 263–286.

Frühwirth-Schnatter, S. (2006). *Finite Mixture and Markov Switching Models.* New York: Springer.

Gogebakan, M., & Erol, H. (2018). A new semi-supervised classification method based on mixture model clustering for classification of multispectral data. *Journal of the Indian Society of Remote Sensing, 46*(8), 1323–1331.

Gogebakan, M., & Servı, T. (2019). Genetik Algoritma Kullanılarak Verilerin Karma Normal Modele Dayalı Kümelenmesi. *Erciyes Üniversitesi Fen Bilimleri Enstitüsü Fen Bilimleri Dergisi, 35*(3), 12–23.

Gogebakan, M. (2020). Gauss Karma Modellerin Özellikleri ve Modele Dayalı Kümeleme. *Bitlis Eren Üniversitesi Fen Bilimleri Dergisi, 9*(3), 1377–1388.

Karagiannis, R., & Karagiannis, G. (2020). Constructing composite indicators with Shannon entropy: The case of Human Development Index. *Socio-Economic Planning Sciences, 70*, 100701.

McLachlan, G. J., Basford, K. E. (1988). *Mixture Models: Inference and Application to Clustering.* New York: Marcel Dekker.

McLachlan, G. J., Peel, D. (2000). *Finite Mixture Models.* New York: Wiley.

McLachlan, G. J., Krishnan, T., & Ng, S. K. (2004). *The EM algorithm* (No. 2004, 24). Papers.

McLachlan, G. J., & Rathnayake, S. (2014). On the number of components in a Gaussian mixture model. *Wiley Interdisciplinary Reviews: Data Mining and Knowledge Discovery*, *4*(5), 341–355.

Noorbakhsh, F. (1998). A modified Human Development Index. *World Development, 26*(3), 517–528.

Omrani, H., Alizadeh, A., & Amini, M. (2020). A new approach based on BWM and MULTIMOORA methods for calculating semi-human development index: An application for provinces of Iran. *Socio-Economic Planning Sciences, 70*, 100689.

Roser, M. (2014). Human development index (HDI). *Our World in Data.*

Schwarz, G. (1978). Estimating the dimension of a model. *Ann. Statist., 6*, 461–464.

Scrucca, L., Fop, M., Murphy, T. B., & Raftery, A. E. (2016). mclust 5: Clustering, classification and density estimation using Gaussian finite mixture models. *The R Journal, 8/1*, 289–317.

Sudirman, & Hapsara, O. (2021). Analysis of the Human Development Index in Jambi City. *Advances in Economics, Business and Management Research, 168*, 264–268.

Titterington, D. M., Smith, A. F. M., Markov, U. E. (1985). *Statistical Analysis of Finite Mixture Distributions.* New York: Wiley.

UNDP. (2021). *United Nations Development Programme Human Development Reports.* Human Development Index (HDI): http://hdr.undp.org/en/content/human-development-index-hdi. Accessed 11 April 2021.

Yakunina, R., & Bychkov, G. (2015). Correlation analysis of the components of the Human Development Index across countries. *Procedia Economics and Finance, 24*, 766–771.

Yero, E., Sacco, N., & Nicoletti, M. (2021). Effect of the Municipal Human Development Index on the results of the 2018 Brazilian presidential elections. *Expert Systems with Applications, 168*, 114305.

Appendix 1. Class memberships according to United Nations HDI scores for 189 countries by quartiles (Class 1) and proposed GMM (Class 2).

Number	Country	Class1	Class2	Number	Country	Class1	Class2	Number	Country	Class1	Class2
1	Norway	VH	H	**64**	Kuwait	VH	M	**127**	Guatemala	M	M
2	Ireland	VH	H	**65**	Serbia	VH	M	**128**	Nicaragua	M	M
3	Switzerland	VH	H	**66**	Mauritius	VH	M	**129**	Bhutan	M	M
4	Hong Kong, China	VH	H	**67**	Seychelles	H	M	**130**	Namibia	M	L
5	Iceland	VH	H	**68**	Trinidad and Tobago	H	M	**131**	India	M	L
6	Germany	VH	H	**69**	Albania	H	M	**132**	Honduras	M	L
7	Sweden	VH	H	**70**	Cuba	H	M	**133**	Bangladesh	M	L
8	Australia	VH	H	**71**	Iran	H	M	**134**	Kiribati	M	L
9	Netherlands	VH	H	**72**	Sri Lanka	H	M	**135**	Sao Tome and Principe	M	L
10	Denmark	VH	H	**73**	Bosnia and Herzegovina	H	M	**136**	Micronesia	M	L
11	Finland	VH	H	**74**	Grenada	H	M	**137**	Laos	M	L
12	Singapore	VH	H	**75**	Mexico	H	M	**138**	Eswatini	M	L
13	United Kingdom	VH	H	**76**	Saint Kitts and Nevis	H	M	**139**	Ghana	M	L
14	Belgium	VH	H	**77**	Ukraine	H	M	**140**	Vanuatu	M	L
15	New Zealand	VH	H	**78**	Antigua and Barbuda	H	M	**141**	Timor-Leste	M	L
16	Canada	VH	H	**79**	Peru	H	M	**142**	Nepal	M	L
17	United States	VH	H	**80**	Thailand	H	M	**143**	Kenya	M	L
18	Austria	VH	H	**81**	Armenia	H	M	**144**	Cambodia	M	L

Number	Country	Class1	Class2	Number	Country	Class1	Class2	Number	Country	Class1	Class2
19	Israel	VH	H	**82**	North Macedonia	H	M	**145**	Equatorial Guinea	M	L
20	Japan	VH	H	**83**	Columbia	H	M	**146**	Zambia	M	L
21	Liechtenstein	VH	H	**84**	Brazil	H	M	**147**	Myanmar	M	L
22	Slovenia	VH	H	**85**	China	H	M	**148**	Angola	M	L
23	Korea	VH	H	**86**	Ecuador	H	M	**149**	Congo	M	L
24	Luxembourg	VH	H	**87**	Saint Lucia	H	M	**150**	Zimbabwe	M	L
25	Spain	VH	H	**88**	Azerbaijan	H	M	**151**	Solomon Islands	M	L
26	France	VH	H	**89**	Dominican Republic	H	M	**152**	Syrian Arab Republic	M	L
27	Czechia	VH	H	**90**	Moldova	H	M	**153**	Cameroon	M	L
28	Maltese	VH	M	**91**	Algeria	H	M	**154**	Pakistan	M	L
29	Estonia	VH	M	**92**	Lebanon	H	M	**155**	Papua New Guinea	M	L
30	Italy	VH	M	**93**	Fiji	H	M	**156**	Comoros	M	L
31	United Arab Emirates	VH	M	**94**	Dominica	H	M	**157**	Mauritania	L	L
32	References	VH	M	**95**	Maldives	H	M	**158**	Benin	L	L
33	Cyprus	VH	M	**96**	Tunisia	H	M	**159**	Uganda	L	L
34	Lithuania	VH	M	**97**	Saint Vincent and the Grenadines	H	M	**160**	Rwanda	L	L
35	Poland	VH	M	**98**	Suriname	H	M	**161**	Nigeria	L	L
36	Andorra	VH	M	**99**	Mongolia	H	M	**162**	Cote d'ivoire	L	L

(*continued on next page*)

Appendix 1. Continued

Number	Country	Class1	Class2	Number	Country	Class1	Class2	Number	Country	Class1	Class2
37	Latvia	VH	M	**100**	Botswana	H	M	**163**	Tanzania	L	L
38	Portugal	VH	M	**101**	Jamaica	H	M	**164**	Madagascar	L	L
39	Slovakia	VH	M	**102**	Jordan	H	M	**165**	Lesotho	L	L
40	Hungary	VH	M	**103**	Paraguay	H	M	**166**	Djibouti	L	L
41	Saudi Arabia	VH	M	**104**	Tonga	H	M	**167**	Togo	L	L
42	Bahrain	VH	M	**105**	Libya	H	M	**168**	Senegal	L	L
43	Chile	VH	M	**106**	Uzbekistan	H	M	**169**	Afghanistan	L	L
44	Croatia	VH	M	**107**	Bolivia	H	M	**170**	Haitian	L	L
45	Qatar	VH	M	**108**	Indonesia	H	M	**171**	Sudan	L	L
46	Argentina	VH	M	**109**	Philippines	H	M	**172**	Gambia	L	L
47	Brunei Darussalam	VH	M	**110**	Belize	H	M	**173**	Ethiopia	L	L
48	Montenegro	VH	M	**111**	Samoa	H	M	**174**	Malawi	L	L
49	Romania	VH	M	**112**	Turkmenistan	H	M	**175**	Congo	L	L
50	Palau	VH	M	**113**	Venezuela	H	M	**176**	Guinea-Bissau	L	L
51	Kazakhstan	VH	M	**114**	South Africa	H	M	**177**	Liberia	L	L
52	Russian Federation	VH	M	**115**	Palestine, State of	H	M	**178**	Guinea	L	L
53	Belarus	VH	M	**116**	Egypt	H	M	**179**	Yemen	L	L
54	Turkey	VH	M	**117**	Marshall Islands	H	M	**180**	Eritrea	L	L
55	Uruguay	VH	M	**118**	Viet Nam	H	M	**181**	Mozambique	L	L
56	Bulgaria	VH	M	**119**	Gabon	H	M	**182**	Burkina Faso	L	L
57	Panama	VH	M	**120**	Kyrgyzstan	M	M	**183**	Sierra Leone	L	L

Number	Country	Class1	Class2	Number	Country	Class1	Class2	Number	Country	Class1	Class2
58	Bahamas	VH	M	**121**	Morocco	M	M	**184**	Mali	L	L
59	Barbados	VH	M	**122**	Guyana	M	M	**185**	Burundi	L	L
60	Oman	VH	M	**123**	Iraq	M	M	**186**	South Sudan	L	L
61	Georgia	VH	M	**124**	El Salvador	M	M	**187**	Chad	L	L
62	Costa Rica	VH	M	**125**	Tajikistan	M	M	**188**	Central African Republic	L	L
63	Malaysia	VH	M	**126**	Cabo Verde	M	M	**189**	Niger	L	L

Remzi GÖK, Aviral Kumar TİWARİ & Şener İLTER

International Co-movement of Stock Markets during Crisis and Non-crisis Periods[1]

1. Introduction

The integration of international stock markets has been increasingly examined by investors for making financial decisions as well as by policymakers responsible for maintaining financial stability through policies that diminish the destabilizing effects of regional or global economic crises. Since Markowitz's (1952) pioneering study, it has been recognized that the total risk of a portfolio can be reduced through investing in different sectors and/or international stock markets (Aloui and Hkiri, 2014); however, the extant literature has shown that the benefits of international asset allocation and portfolio diversification depend on the degree of integration between the local and other stock markets during the holding periods (Tiwari et al., 2016; Albulescu et al., 2017; Das et al., 2018).

The structure of financial markets has changed most significantly due to financial deregulation, globalization, international trade, advances in communication technology, and economic and monetary integration (Baele, 2002), and these have reduced the benefits of international portfolio investment (Dajcman, 2013). Consequently, co-movement among stock markets is of interest to investors and researchers as they can examine whether the relationship between different markets changes over time, during both crisis and non-crisis periods. By allocating resources more efficiently and reducing macroeconomic volatility, the integration and development of financial markets could promote economic growth (Hatemi-J, 2012) in developing countries. However, as emerging markets mature, their sensitivity to the volatility of global markets increases (Neaime, 2006), and investment gains from international diversification reduces (Lucey and Voronkova, 2004). Moreover, as Neaime (2006) highlights, the more (less) regulated a stock market, the less (more) exposure to financial shock it faces. Furthermore, as geographic distance increases, market co-movements get weaker (Forbes and Rigobon, 2002). Similarly, the degree of co-movement is also

1 This chapter is an extended version of the abstract presented at the "III. International Symposium of Economy, Politics and Administration" in 10–12 October 2019, Diyarbakır.

related to the size and structure of markets. Forbes and Rigobon (2002) argue that the relationship is not homogenous over time; in other words, as stated by Dimitriou et al. (2013), the interdependency is stronger in bearish rather than bullish markets due to shifts in global risk aversion and investor behavior during the crisis period. Lucey and Zhang (2010) maintain that countries with smaller (greater) cultural differences or the same religion exhibit higher (lower) co-movement, indicating that the convergence of investing behavior leads to a confluence of market movement. Yarovaya and Lau (2016) report that the contagion hypothesis suggests increasing co-movement between emerging and developed stock markets due to financial shocks to developed countries during crisis periods, while the decoupling hypothesis assumes a lower sensitivity of emerging markets to developed markets with a strong reverse direction of spillovers from the former to the latter after a crisis because of the changing role of those stock markets in the world economy.

Further relevant literature includes Mandaci and Torun (2007), Alkulaib et al. (2009), Kenourgios and Samitas (2011), Hatemi-J (2012), Demiralay and Ulusoy (2017), and Al-Yahyaee et al. (2019). Mandaci and Torun (2007) provided evidence in favor of international portfolio diversification gains by investing in Turkey, Russia, South Africa, and Korea. They emphasized arbitrage opportunities for Turkish investors investing in Russia, South Africa, Korea, and Poland, and for Brazilian, Russian, Korean, and South African investors investing in Turkey. Alkulaib et al. (2009) studied the relationship among Middle East and North African countries and found a bidirectional causal relationship between the Turkish and Lebanese equity markets. Kenourgios and Samitas (2011) documented that the Balkan stock markets were cointegrated, and this dependence was strengthened in relation to the international stock market indexes like S&P500(US), FTSE100(UK), DAX(Germany), and ASE GI(Greece), confirming herding behavior during the 2007–2009 Global Financial Crisis (GFC). By employing cointegration tests, Benli et al. (2012) showed evidence of significant common stochastic trends between the 14 EU stock markets and Istanbul Stock Exchange 100 Index (ISE100), and the absence of portfolio diversification benefits in Turkey for long-term global investors. Hatemi-J (2012) revealed evidence supporting co-movement between the Morgan Stanley Capital International (MSCI) stock price index and the UAE stock market in bearish markets. By adopting an EGARCH model, Demiralay and Ulusoy (2017) presented evidence in favor of the hypothesis of recoupling for emerging markets. They stated that the linkage became stronger during the GFC, indicating that these markets were not immune to the shocks arising from developed financial markets. Vuran and Türkay (2017) highlighted the opportunity for long-term portfolio diversification among selected stock markets in BRICS and MIST groups for international investors and portfolio managers. Additionally, they stated that there was significant evidence that the fluctuations in the KOSPI (South Korea), Shanghai (China), and JSE (South Africa) stock indices were predictable for Turkish investors. In contrast, the reverse prediction was given for Brazilian, Mexican, and South African investors. Al-Yahyaee et al. (2019) revealed that the collapse of Lehman Brothers had significant causal impacts for stock market returns of the US and the five GIPSI countries (Greece, Ireland, Portugal, Spain, and Italy), reducing opportunities for portfolio diversification for investors from those countries.

In addition to the time-domain approaches, the use of wavelets, a novel method, has received considerable interest from researchers and investors during recent years as it enables us to investigate the co-movement of stock markets during different periods. Given that stock markets comprise many agents with varying periods of trading, it appears to be necessary to apply a different approach that is suitable for detecting co-movement and causal relations at different time scales. This can demonstrate short-run fluctuations at higher frequencies for short-term investors who give weightage to speculative activities, and long-run movements at lower frequencies for long-term investors who concentrate on price fundamentals. The literature on stock market co-movements includes Lee (2004), Gallegati (2005), Rua and Nunes (2009), Graham et al. (2012), Dajcman (2013), Aloui and Hkiri (2014), Dima et al. (2015), Tiwari et al. (2016), Yilmaz and Unal (2016), Albulescu et al. (2017), and Das et al. (2018). Of those, Gallegati (2005) studied the co-movements of the five MENA stock markets, including Egypt, Israel, Jordan, Morocco, and Turkey, through both unconditional correlations and maximal overlap discrete wavelet transform (MODWT) based wavelet correlations. The findings of the first method showed that MENA stock markets were neither regionally nor internationally integrated from 1997 to 2005. However, the second method showed that the Turkish market had positive correlation with the Israeli market at almost all the time scales, and with the Egyptian market only at the longest wavelet scales. Graham et al. (2012) investigated the integration between the US and 22 emerging stock markets contained in the MSCI Emerging Market (MSCI-EM) Index for the period of 2001–2010. The author reported low co-movement between MSCI USA and the five emerging European stock markets, including the Czech Republic, Hungary, Poland, Russia, and Turkey at higher frequencies, suggesting significant portfolio diversification benefits for US investors in the short term. There was a consistent change in the pattern after 2006, which coincided with the onset of the GFC. In a related paper, Yilmaz and Unal (2016) analyzed the integration of S&P500 and

FTSE100 stock markets with 11 Asian equity markets, including AXJO, AXPJ, BIST100, HIS IDX, KLSE, 1368.KL, KOSPI, N225, RTS, Shenzhen, and 0050. TW. First, they found that the US and UK markets had a significant impact on Asian equity markets at varying magnitudes and frequencies, suggesting the presence of substantial portfolio diversification and risk elimination benefits for UK and US investors in the short and medium terms. Specifically, there was a strong co-movement and bidirectional causal relationship between the pairs of BIST100-S&P500 and BIST100-FTSE100 stock markets at higher frequencies (corresponding to [0–64] daily periods) in 2006–2012 and at lower frequencies (corresponding to [512–1024] daily periods) in 2005–2009. Utilizing the wavelet-based correlation and covariance method, Das et al. (2018) revisited the issues of contagion, co-movement, and changes in correlation structure between developed and emerging markets for the period of January 1999–November 2016 using daily closing prices. During the GFC, they found evidence of stronger and weaker co-movement relationships for the emerging equity markets at higher frequencies in Europe and Middle Eastern countries and at lower frequencies in Latin American countries. Further, the study showed that the correlation structure between all emerging markets and the MSCI World Index (MSCI-WI) had permanently changed in the post GFC era, suggesting diversification benefits in the long run.

The effects of the ongoing COVID-19 pandemic as a source of systematic risk have been widely investigated by researchers and policymakers. Much research has investigated the impact of COVID-19 on local and global stock markets. Salisu et al. (2020) show that the hedging effectiveness or sensitivity of emerging stock markets to pandemics and epidemics, including Severe Acute Respiratory Syndrome (SARS), Middle East Respiratory syndrome (MERS), Ebola and Zika virus, and COVID-19, is higher than developed stock markets. David et al. (2021) reveal similar results, and higher volatilities for the 11 key financial indices and conclude that stock markets showed fast and sustainable recovery from the diseases, except for COVID-19 during the first 79-day period. Topcu and Gulal (2020) find that the negative impact of COVID-19 was largest for Asian emerging markets and lowest for emerging markets in Europe during the first half of 2020. Uddin et al. (2020) show evidence of a strong and increasing tendency of co-movements between Asian financial markets arising from COVID-19 over the higher horizons. Results from Okorie and Lin (2021) support the short-lived fractal contagion effect of COVID-19 on the stock markets in the top 32 coronavirus-affected countries. Akhtaruzzaman et al. (2021) show that the magnitude of increase in conditional correlations between Chinese and G7 countries' market returns were considerably higher for financial firms, and that China and Japan were the net transmitters of spillovers during the period studied.

This study examines stock market co-movements between the BIST100 index and 18 stock markets over the sample period of October 2005–February 2021, with 776 weekly average prices. The cointegration test demonstrates international portfolio diversification gains for Turkish investors in 12 out of 18 countries. The results of the VECM reveal that the BIST100 index unidirectionally Granger-causes DAX, TSX, JSE, MERVAL, and MOEX indices in the short run and/or long run, while the reverse causality from the NIKKEI225 and MOEX indices become evident in the short run only. The application of wavelet coherence analysis provides strong evidence for co-movements and lead/lag relationships during the financial crises in the lower frequency bands and during the COVID-19 pandemic in the higher frequency bands, indicating an absence of portfolio diversification benefits and arbitrage opportunities for investors living in Turkey or other countries.

Concerning the methodology employed and the application, the contribution of this study to the existing literature on markets behaviors is two-fold. We employ both standard econometric tools and wavelets to improve our understanding of short-, medium-, and long-run dynamics of interrelations, as these markets' dynamics are the result of the interaction of agents with different trading objectives and investment periods. We analyze portfolio diversification to achieve better risk-return trade-offs from a domestic point of view, namely, for Turkish investors' foreign portfolio investments in both developed and emerging countries, and non-domiciled investors' portfolio investments in Turkey.

The chapter proceeds as follows – Section 2 explains the methodology including the literature on wavelet coherence analysis. In Sections 3 and 4, we describe our variables and present the results. Section 5 concludes the chapter and provides implications.

2. Methodology

Before proceeding further, it should be emphasized that the technical details of the Maki unit root test (2012) and Kapetanios cointegration test (2005) are left for the reader to understand for conciseness. Similarly, given that the use of wavelet analysis is a well-established approach in the literature, we will briefly discuss the essential methods of wavelet coherence and wavelet phase difference for our purposes.

Assuming two time series of X and Y, the cross-wavelet spectrum of these variables can be defined as:

$$W_n^{XY}(d) = W_n^X(d) W_n^Y * (d) \tag{1}$$

Here, $W_n^X(d)$ and $W_n^Y(d)$ represent the wavelet transforms of *X* and *Y*, while $W_n^Y * (d)$ denotes the complex conjugate of $W_n^Y(d)$.

The squared wavelet coherency can be defined as the absolute value squared of the smoothed cross-wavelet spectrum, normalized by the smoothed wavelet power spectra, given by:

$$R_n^2(d) = \frac{\left| S\left(\frac{1}{d} W_n^{XY}(d)\right) \right|^2}{S\left(\frac{1}{d}\left|W_n^X(d)\right|^2\right) . S\left(\frac{1}{d}\left|W_n^Y(d)\right|^2\right)}, \tag{2}$$

where *S* is a smoothing operator in both scale and time, and $0 \leq R_n^2(d) \leq 1$. The higher (lower) is the value of $R_n^2(d)$, the stronger (weaker) is the co-movement between *X* and *Y*.

The wavelet-coherence phase difference can be written using equation (1) in conjunction with equation (2):

$$\phi_{x,y}(d) = \frac{1}{\tan}\left(\frac{\mathcal{J}\left(\left(\frac{1}{d} W_n^{XY}(d)\right)\right)}{\Re\left(\left(\frac{1}{d} W_n^{XY}(d)\right)\right)} \right), \tag{3}$$

where the $\mathcal{J}$ and $\Re$ parameters represent the imaginary and smoothed real parts of the smooth power spectrum, respectively.

The phase difference indicates the direction of linkage and lead-lag interdependence between the market returns. In other words, the phase difference is represented by the orientation of the arrows ([←,→] [↗,↘] [↙,↖]). The first two arrows, for example, indicate a phase-difference of π and zero, with no lead/lag relationship, respectively. The arrows pointing leftward [←] show that the underlying stock returns are out-of-phase with a negative relation, whereas the arrows pointing rightward [→] shows that the underlying stock returns are in-phase with a positive movement at a specific time-frequency. If the phase-difference, ϕ_{xy}, ranges between 0 and $-\pi/2$, namely, if the arrows point right-up

[↗], then the financial time series of x= DL_BIST100 and y= DL_SP500 are in-phase and move together, with returns of BIST100 leading returns of S&P500. If $\phi_{xy} \in (-\pi, -\pi/2)$, that is, [↙], this indicates that the variables are out-of-phase and move in the reverse direction, again with DL_BIST100 leading DL_SP500. Similarly, the left-up [↖] and right-down [↘] arrows indicate that DL_SP500 leads DL_BIST100 with a negative and positive correlation, since they are out-of-phase and in-phase, respectively.

3. Data and Preliminary Data Analysis

In this chapter, we used weekly averages of stock market closing prices for a sample period from October 2005 to February 2021 for a total of 776 observations for each stock index. The stock market indices examined were the S&P500 (US), DAX (Germany), FTSE100 (UK), NIKKEI225 (Japan), CAC40 (France), FTSE MIB Index (Italy), S&P/TSX Composite Index (Canada), BIST100 (Turkey), ATX Austrian Traded Index (Austria), S&P/ASX AXJO (Australia), BFX Belgium 20 Index (Belgium), BOVESPA (Brazil), IBEX35 Index (Spain), JKSE Jakarta Composite Index (Indonesia), JSE All Share Index (South Africa), SP MERVAL Index (Argentina), MOEX (Russia), MXX Index (Mexico), and S&P BSE SENSEX (India). We extracted our data from finance.yahoo.com and markets.businessinsider.com. To remedy potential heteroskedasticity problems, we transformed stock prices into their natural logarithms. The following table (Table 1) presents summary statistics of the continuously compounded returns, which are calculated taking the difference between the logarithms of two subsequent observations.

Table 1. Descriptive statistics

	Mean	Max	Min	SD Dev.	Skewness	Kurtosis	JB
DL_SP500	0.1534	7.0566	-21.3966	2.055	-2.498	22.607	13220.11***
DL_DAX	0.1367	9.3659	-19.1404	2.598	-1.568	11.561	2684.01***
DL_FTSE100	0.0295	7.8487	-16.634	2.077	-1.597	13.965	4211.38***
DL_Nikkei225	0.1027	10.6081	-24.074	2.663	-1.451	13.663	3943.37***
DL_CAC40	0.0337	10.0608	-18.7992	2.497	-1.297	11.548	2577.05***
DL_FTSE_MIB	-0.0428	21.1143	-23.5289	3.152	-1.103	14.875	4710.54***
DL_TSX	0.0748	7.344	-24.5514	2.080	-3.433	36.087	36873.93***
DL_BİST100	0.2051	10.3358	-15.9185	3.176	-0.947	5.937	394.54***
DL_ATX	-0.0082	13.4168	-30.465	3.270	-2.067	19.071	8892.07***
DL_AXJO	0.0569	7.4495	-12.902	1.967	-1.385	10.420	2025.88***
DL_BFX	0.0209	9.7981	-20.5406	2.487	-1.659	14.641	4731.1***
DL_BOVESPA	0.1801	9.5748	-27.0304	3.054	-1.715	15.547	5463.6***
DL_IBEX35	-0.0327	12.6169	-20.0153	2.682	-0.727	8.449	1027.02***
DL_JKSE	0.2275	14.568	-17.4866	2.536	-1.217	12.014	2815.12***
DL_JSE	0.1806	10.2555	-17.322	2.265	-1.291	12.629	3209.18***
DL_MERVAL	0.4490	17.3518	-33.4793	4.463	-1.160	9.834	1681.94***
DL_MOEX	0.1853	16.3281	-43.4124	3.610	-2.704	33.176	30349.42***
DL_MXX	0.1361	7.6485	-19.8693	2.272	-1.267	12.744	3273.35***
DL_SENSEX	0.2421	15.956	-18.0518	2.759	-0.674	9.219	1307.44***

Note: *** indicates rejection of the null hypothesis of normality at a 1 % significance level.

Table 1 summarizes the descriptive statistics of stock market returns. All stock indices yielded positive mean returns throughout the period, except FTSEMIB, ATX, and IBEX35. With an average weekly return of 0.449 %, the Argentinian stock market, MERVAL, displayed the highest weekly performance with the highest volatility (measured by the standard deviation) of 4.46 %, while the Australian stock index, AXJO, had the lowest variability of 1.97 %. By outperforming the stock markets in the G7 countries, the Turkish market index, BIST100, gave returns that varied between −15.92 % and 10.34 %, with a mean and standard deviation of 0.205 % and 3.18 %, respectively. Additionally, the Russian stock index, MOEX, achieved the maximum and minimum returns of 16.33 % and −43.41 % among the countries with the second-highest volatility of 3.61 %. All stock market returns exhibited right skewness and excess kurtosis, validating the Jarque–Bera test statistic result, and, therefore, indicating the rejection of the normality assumption at the 1 % significance level.

4. Empirical Findings

Before cointegration and causality testing, we employed the Kapetanios (2005) unit root test to identify unit roots in all the logarithmic transformations of stock prices. Following the procedure outlined by Kapetanios (2005), we computed the relevant test statistics allowing for up to five unknown structural breaks for Model C through publicly available GAUSS codes. The findings of the Kapetanios (2005) unit root test are reported in Table 2.

The Kapetanios (2005) unit root test suggests the presence of unit roots in all stock price series – it does not provide evidence against the null hypothesis and shows that the market shocks are permanent during the sample period. The test strongly rejects the null hypothesis for the return series at the 1 % significance level. Therefore, we assume that our variables are at a non-stationary level and become stationary with the intercept and with the time trend in their first difference, namely, integrated to the order one, $I(1)$, for Model C.

Having established the integration order of the stock prices, we test for any long-run relationship between the BIST100 and the other stock prices using the widely known cointegration test proposed by Maki (2012). The results of the cointegration test with multiple structural breakpoints are presented in Table 3.

Table 2. Kapetanios unit root test (2005) – model C (break in intercept & trend)

Indices	Logarithmic Series						First Differenced Series					
	Test Stat	TB1	TB2	TB3	TB4	TB5	Test Stat	TB1	TB2	TB3	TB4	TB5
LN_SP500	-6.26	'07-03-14	08-04-16	'09-03-04	'12-12-26	'20-02-19	-24.756***	'07-03-14	'08-03-12	'09-03-04	'19-05-29	'20-03-18
LN_DAX	-5.067	'06-08-09	07-09-12	'09-03-04	'12-06-06	'20-02-19	-24.239***	'07-03-14	'08-03-19	'09-03-04	'19-05-29	'20-03-18
LN_FTSE100	-6.047	'07-03-14	08-05-21	'09-03-04	'16-06-15	'20-02-19	-24.286***	'07-03-14	'08-03-19	'09-03-04	'10-06-30	'20-02-19
LN_NIKKEI	-5.391	'06-07-26	07-05-23	'08-03-19	'09-03-11	'12-11-14	-24.217***	'06-11-22	'08-01-23	'08-10-29	'19-06-26	'20-03-18
LN_CAC40	-5.087	'06-08-09	07-09-12	'09-03-04	'12-06-27	'20-02-19	-24.614***	'07-03-14	'08-03-19	'09-03-04	'10-06-30	'11-09-21
LN_MIB	-4.888	'07-03-14	08-03-19	'09-03-11	'11-07-06	'12-07-25	-25.953***	'06-08-09	'07-05-16	'08-03-19	'09-03-11	'11-09-21
LN_TSX	-6.058	'06-10-11	07-07-18	'08-04-30	'09-03-04	'20-02-19	-24.482***	'06-10-04	'07-07-18	'08-05-21	'09-03-04	'20-03-18
LN_BIST100	-5.621	'06-07-26	07-08-22	'08-05-28	'09-03-11	'20-02-19	-23.703***	'07-01-10	'08-02-06	'08-11-19	'09-08-26	'20-03-18
LN_ATX	-4.672	'06-09-20	07-07-11	'08-05-21	'09-03-04	'20-02-19	-24.896***	'06-09-13	'08-02-13	'08-11-19	'11-11-23	'20-02-19
LN_AXJO	-5.803	'06-09-20	07-08-15	'08-05-14	'09-03-04	'20-02-19	-22.842***	'06-09-20	'08-02-20	'08-11-19	'09-10-14	'20-02-19
LN_BFX	-4.737	'06-07-26	07-07-11	'08-04-30	'09-03-04	'20-02-19	-23.38***	'07-03-14	'08-01-23	'09-03-04	'10-06-30	'11-11-23
LN_BVSP	-7.793	'16-01-20	17-02-22	'18-05-16	'19-03-13	'20-02-19	-23.802***	'06-09-20	'08-01-23	'08-11-19	'10-05-19	'11-08-10
LN_IBEX3	-5.118	'06-09-13	07-09-12	'09-03-04	'12-07-25	'20-02-19	-23.869***	'06-11-08	'07-08-15	'08-05-14	'09-03-04	'10-06-09
LN_JKSE	-4.8	'06-07-26	07-08-22	'08-10-29	'09-08-05	'20-01-22	-24.569***	'07-03-07	'08-01-23	'08-10-29	'09-08-05	'20-01-15
LN_JSE	-5.716	'06-09-13	07-07-18	'08-05-21	'09-03-04	'13-06-26	-25.513***	'07-03-07	'08-01-23	'08-11-19	'19-05-29	'20-03-18
LN_MERVA	-5.681	'09-03-04	09-11-25	'10-09-15	'11-07-06	'13-06-26	-23.185***	'06-10-11	'08-01-23	'08-11-19	'19-04-24	'20-03-18
LN_MOEX	-6.388	'06-09-27	08-02-20	'08-11-19	'09-10-21	'11-07-27	-27.238***	'06-09-27	'08-02-06	'08-11-19	'10-08-25	'11-10-05
LN_MXX	-5.435	'06-11-01	07-08-01	'08-05-28	'09-03-04	'20-02-19	-25.412***	'06-08-09	'07-07-04	'08-05-28	'09-03-04	'10-05-19
LN_SENSEX	-4.629	'06-07-26	07-09-12	'09-03-11	'13-08-28	'20-02-19	-23.974***	'06-08-02	'07-08-22	'08-11-19	'09-09-30	'20-02-19

Note: *** denotes rejection of the null hypothesis that the underlying variable is stationary at a 1 % significance level. Critical values for "Model C" are -8.016, -8.343, and -9.039 for 5 breaks.

Table 3. Maki cointegration test (2012)

Dependent	Test Stat	TB1	TB2	TB3	TB4	TB5	Dependent	Test Stat	TB1	TB2	TB3	TB4	TB5
LN_SP500	-5.049	'08-09-24	'11-07-27	'13-04-17	'14-10-29	'16-07-13	LN_BIST100	-5.664	'07-07-18	'11-03-30	'14-06-11	'16-07-13	
LN_DAX	-6.239**	'08-12-10	'12-06-06	'13-12-18	'16-02-10		LN_BIST100	-6.018	'09-07-01	'11-06-01	'14-02-19	'17-01-25	'19-01-09
LN_FTSE100	-4.937	'08-09-24	'10-05-05	'12-03-07	'15-09-30		LN_BIST100	-5.289	'09-03-18	'11-09-14	'13-07-10	'15-05-06	'19-07-31
LN_NIKKEI	-5.09	'07-12-26	'10-01-20	'14-10-29	'16-07-13	'19-05-15	LN_BIST100	-6.073*	'08-10-22	'14-02-19	'16-03-30	'17-11-29	'19-07-31
LN_CAC40	-5.123	'07-07-18	'09-02-18	'12-04-04	'13-11-06	'15-06-17	LN_BIST100	-4.889	'07-07-04	'09-11-25	'11-09-14	'18-01-17	
LN_MIB	-5.959	'07-07-18	'09-02-25	'11-07-27	'14-09-03	'16-06-22	LN_BIST100	-4.607	'08-11-19				
LN_TSX	-5.263**	'08-09-24					LN_BIST100	-4.864	'08-01-16	'13-01-23	'19-03-20		
LN_ATX	-5.784	'09-01-14	'12-06-20	'14-07-02	'16-02-10	'19-05-22	LN_BIST100	-4.316	'08-07-02				
LN_AXJO	-5.192	'08-10-22	'16-04-13	'19-08-07			LN_BIST100	-4.875	'08-04-02	'19-03-20			
LN_BFX	-4.198	'07-05-23	'12-03-07	'13-12-18	'15-10-21	'17-04-26	LN_BIST100	-5.009	'07-07-18	'09-11-25	'11-11-23	'14-10-15	'16-06-29
LN_BVSP	-4.753	'07-07-25	'09-03-04	'11-04-27	'17-12-27	'19-07-31	LN_BIST100	-4.943	'08-10-22	'12-03-14	'14-07-16	'16-02-17	'17-10-11
LN_IBEX35	-5.35	'08-12-03	'11-08-03	'14-08-20	'17-09-27	'19-05-15	LN_BIST100	-4.099	'09-02-25	'11-03-30	'15-10-28	'17-05-17	
LN_JKSE	-5.525	'07-05-30	'09-04-29	'10-11-17	'12-06-06	'14-08-06	LN_BIST100	-4.277	'08-05-14	'09-11-25	'13-07-10	'15-10-28	'19-06-26
LN_JSE	-6.269*	'07-07-25	'09-04-15	'11-06-22	'13-01-23	'15-07-08	LN_BIST100	-5.2	'07-07-25	'09-04-01	'13-01-23	'16-11-09	'18-05-23
LN_ MERVAL	-5.77*	'14-01-29	'15-10-21	'17-08-09	'19-04-24		LN_BIST100	-5.061	'08-12-17	'11-08-24	'14-09-17	'17-07-12	'19-08-07
LN_MOEX	-6.106*	'08-09-24	'12-01-25	'13-08-21	'15-04-29	'17-11-01	LN_BIST100	-5.579*	'09-02-11	'11-07-27	'17-02-08		
LN_MXX	-4.98	'07-05-30	'09-03-11	'10-10-27	'12-12-26	'18-11-07	LN_BIST100	-5.341	'07-11-28	'09-07-29	'11-09-14	'17-07-12	'19-05-22
LN_SENSEX	-5.075	'07-06-20	'09-05-13	'14-05-07	'16-07-13	'19-05-15	LN_BIST100	-5.244	'07-12-26	'09-08-12	'12-03-14	'15-11-18	'18-01-03

Note: ***, **, and * denote rejection of the null hypothesis that the pair of variables is not cointegrated at 1 %, 5 %, and 10 % significance levels, respectively. The parameters are determined as m = 5, model = 2 (with exception for LN_CAC40 and LN_BFX with m=1 at the left-side), tp = 0.10 (the trimming parameter), and lagoption = 1 (GTOS). Critical values at 1 %, 5 %, and 10 % significance levels for m=1 and for five breaks are [-6.193, -5.699, -5.449] and for m=2 and for one, two, three, four and five breaks are [-5.524, -5.038, -4.784], [-5.708, -5.196, -4.938], [-5.833, -5.373, -5.106], [-6.059, -5.508, -5.245], and [-6.193, -5.699, -5.449].

Table 3 reveals the findings of the Maki (2012) cointegration test with multiple structural unknown breaks for Model C with regime shifts. The pairwise test findings report that the null hypothesis of no cointegration between markets could be strongly rejected for LN_DAX, LN_TSX, LN_JSE, LN_MERVAL, and LN_MOEX indices when LN_BIST100 index is included as the independent variable in the regression; however, in cases of the LN_BIST100 index being the dependent variable in the regression, we find that LN_BIST100 co-moves with the stock prices of LN_NIKKEI225 and LN_MOEX. These findings indicate that the prices of the Turkish BIST100 index are the forcing variable for each cointegrating vector pairs for the German, Canadian, South African, Argentinian, and Russian stock indices, indicating that when a shock hits the system, LN_DAX index, for example, will follow the LN_BIST100 index. As collinearity exists, the Turkey-resident (non-Turkey-resident) investors and portfolio managers cannot get advantageous portfolio diversification in both developed and emerging markets in the long run; however, the results also show the existence of individually international portfolio diversification benefits in the US, the UK, France, Italy, Austria, Australia, Belgium, Brazil, Spain, Indonesia, Mexico, and India for the investors and portfolio managers living in Turkey. In other words, the benefits of international portfolio diversification are available for the investors and portfolio managers of these aforementioned countries by investing in the Turkish equity markets in the long run. Our findings are consistent with the results of Kenourgios and Samitas (2011) for Germany.

Table 4. Granger causality test results based on VECM

Independent		Dependent	Dummy	Lag	χ^2 -statistics	ect_{t-1}
LN_BIST100	⇏	LN_DAX	[158, 335, 413, 521]	2	12.535***	-0.017**
LN_BIST100	⇏	LN_TSX	[148]	10	26.831***	-0.036***
LN_BIST100	⇏	LN_JSE	[88, 175, 286, 367, 490]	9	14.516	-0.018***
LN_BIST100	⇏	LN_MERVAL	[419, 505, 597, 604]	10	27.447***	-0.003
LN_BIST100	⇏	LN_MOEX	[148, 316, 396, 480, 609]	9	11.395	-0.019***
LN_NIKKEI225	⇏	LN_BIST100	[151, 422, 528, 613, 696]	2	5.874*	-0.004
LN_MOEX	⇏	LN_BIST100	[166, 291, 572]	9	21.217**	0.002

Note: ***, **, and * denote rejection of the null hypothesis of no causality between the underlying variables at 1 %, 5 %, and 10 % significance levels, respectively. The (structural breakpoints of Maki cointegration test) numbers in the third column as dummy variable indicate that the nth observation is equal to 1, and the others to 0.

Given that the existence of cointegration linkages ruled out non-causal relations between markets, we employed the Granger causality test based on the vector error correction model to confirm the causal direction in the short- and long run. Our results are given in Table 4.

Table 4 reveals that the VECM test provides evidence of short-run causality with the chi-square statistics, χ^2, and of long-run causality with the error correction term, ect_{t-1}. LN_BIST100 co-moves with and Granger-causes, and/or is caused by all cointegrated markets when including the structural breakpoints as a dummy variable in the VECM regression. The findings indicate short-run and long-run causalities from, for example, LN_BIST100 towards LN_DAX and LN_TSX. It similarly unidirectionally Granger causes LN_MERVAL in the short-run and LN_JSE and MOEX in the long-run at the 1 % significance level. Conversely, the movements of the Japan NIKKEI225, and Russian MOEX, equity indices can be used to predict the future movements in the Turkish market in the short run only. Our findings contradict Cevik et al. (2017), who found no causality between the Turkish and German stock markets through asymmetric and symmetric causality tests.

To investigate the lead/lag relationship between BIST100 index and other stock market returns during the periods of financial and pandemic crises and non-crisis, the wavelet coherency analysis is utilized and the results depicted through contour plots are presented in the following figures. Note that we execute a publicly available MATLAB code, *wtc(x,y,[,settings])*, provided by Grinsted et al. (2004) for wavelet coherence computations. Each plot includes three dimensions: the frequency dimension converted into time units (on the *Y*-axis), the time dimension (on thc *X*-axis). Thc last dimension, namely, the wavelet coherence power spectrum, is depicted by a color code in the right-hand of the plot and ranges from dark-blue (low) to dark red (high) values. Note that the thick and curved black contour indicates the 5 % level of significance against red noise and the cone of influence (COI) in which the region is subject to border distortions; therefore, one must be very cautious when interpreting outcomes.

Figure 1 exhibits the wavelet coherence between DL_BIST100 and the other six market returns of G7 countries. The left-top panel plot shows the existence of large islands of strong dependency, with an in-phase relation, for the pair DL_BIST100-DL_SP500 at the intermediate and lower frequency intervals over 2008–2010, at the lower frequency intervals over 2010–2016, and the higher and intermediate frequency bands in the 8~32 weeks band scale. Over 2008–2010, 2012–2015, and between the second half of 2015 (2015H2) and 2016H1 in the 64~128, 128~256, and 16~32 weeks band scale with the right-down arrows [↘], DL_BIST100 leads DL_SP500 and they are in-phase during the periods of the global financial crisis (GFC, 2007M8–2009M4) and European sovereign debt crisis (EUDC, 2009M11–2012M9), and a failed coup attempt in July in Turkey. Conversely, we observe that both stock market returns are in-phase with the right-up arrows [↗] in the 32~64 weeks band scale over 2008–2010 during the GFC, and the 32~64 weeks band scale over 2018H2-2020H2, during the currency crisis in Turkey (CCT) and the onset of the COVID-19 pandemic: DL_SP500 lags DL_BIST100, indicating a positive co-movement, with DL_BIST100 leading DL_SP500 during the crisis periods. DL_BIST100 has similar co-movements with the other G7 countries' stock returns as with the US SP500 index returns. For example, the right-up arrows [↗] show that DL_BIST100 leads DL_DAX over 2008–2010 (32~64 weeks cycle), 2015–2016 (128~256 weeks cycle), and 2019H2–2020H1 (8~32 weeks cycle) with an in-phase relation. Conversely, the arrows are predominantly turned down and to the right, [↘], indicating that DL_DAX and DL_BIST100 are in-phase, and BIST100 index lags DAX index at the medium (64~128 weeks cycle) and lower frequency (128~256 weeks cycle) bands over 2009–2010 and 2011–2013. Similarly, BIST100 index exhibits the same strong dependency with FTSE100, NIKKEI225, CAC40, and FTSEMIB stock index returns at the medium and lower frequency bands during the crisis periods (GFC and EUDC), and medium frequency bands during the CCT and COVID-19 outbreak.

Figure 2 reveals the wavelet coherence results between the six stock markets (TSX, ATX, AXJO, BFX, BOVESPA, and IBEX35) and BIST100. The Canadian stock market index, TSX, shows fewer regions of high coherency with the Turkish equity index than the rest of the G7 country markets. The stock market returns are in-phase, with DL_TSX leading DL_BIST100, at the long-run over 2009–2010 and 2012–2015 and in-phase, with DL_TSX lagging DL_BIST100, in the 16~64 weeks band scale over 2008–2009. For the other markets, except IBEX35, we found that all stock markets exhibit comparable cyclical and anti-cyclical patterns of dependencies during periods of crisis; however, the returns of IBEX35 index show a greater opportunity for capital diversification for intermediate and long-term Turkish investors over 2012–2019 as evidenced by smaller red islands compared to the other markets' strong dependencies.

Coherency plots in Figure 3 for the pairs of Turkish-Indonesian and Turkish-Indian stock market returns show strong coherency relationships within the acceptable zone (the periods inside the COI) over 2009–2010, 2011–2012, 2013–2014, and 2017–2018. During these periods, the direction of the relationship is positive, suggesting no potential diversification benefits for either country's investors and fund managers in the medium and long term. Contradicting the findings of the cointegration test, the indices of MERVAL and MOEX exhibit the lowest coherency dependencies with BIST100 during the period under consideration. Thus, there is a similar diversification opportunity with IBEX35 in the Russian and Argentinian stock markets during the same period and frequency intervals for Turkish investors over 2013–2019. In the case of the Turkey-Argentina pair, for example, both stock market returns are in-phase with the right-up arrows [↗] in the 4~16, 16~64, and 8~24 weeks band scale before 2008, over 2009–2010, and 2018–2019, with DL_BIST100 leading DL_MERVAL, respectively. However, although both market returns are in phase, with the arrows pointing rightward[→], over 2009–2012 in the 64~124 weeks band scale, there is no preferential stock return that lags or leads the other. For the BIST100-JKSE pairings, there is a strong level of wavelet coherence, with large red-colored islands, clustered over 2008–2014H1, with DL_BIST100 leading DL_JKSE, [↗], in the 24~64 weeks band scale and with DL_BIST100 lagging DL_JKSE, [↘], in the 128~256 weeks band scale, and with no lead/lag relationship [→] at the highest scale up to a period of 16 weeks. After 2018, and within the acceptable zone, both market returns are in-phase and co-move during the CCT and COVID-19 outbreak, with no leading/lagging linkages.

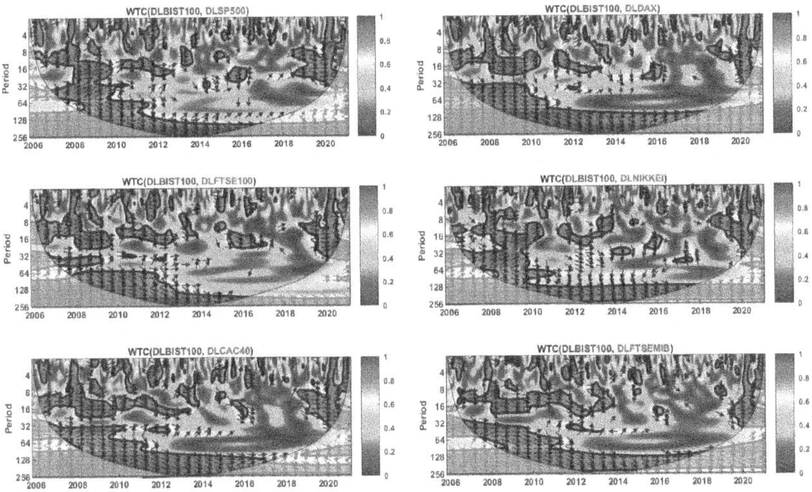

Figure 1. Wavelet coherence analysis of market stock returns (CWT)

Note: Each red island represents the significance at the 5 % level. The direction of the relationship is represented by the orientation of arrows. For details, see the "Methodology" section.

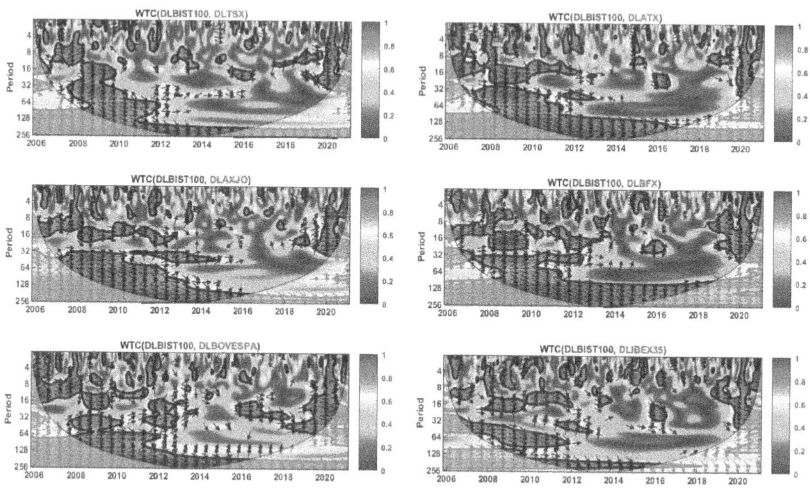

Figure 2. Wavelet coherence analysis of market stock returns (CWT)

Note: Each red island represents the significance at the 5 % level. The direction of the relationship is represented by the orientation of arrows. For details, see the "Methodology" section.

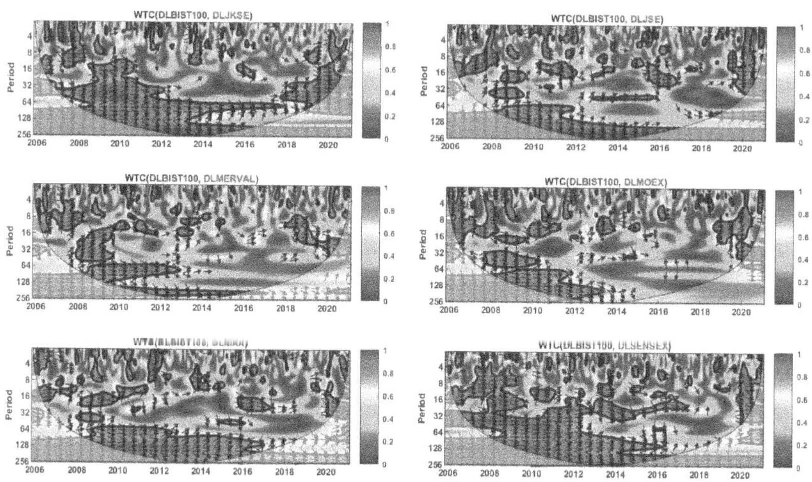

Figure 3. Wavelet coherence analysis of market stock returns (CWT)

Note: Each red island represents the significance at the 5 % level. The direction of the relationship is represented by the orientation of arrows. For details, see the "Methodology" section.

The various WTC-based findings indicate that the BIST100 index had strong (weak) coherence relationships with both developed and emerging markets during the periods of (non-) crisis, indicating destructive impacts from the financial and pandemic shocks perturbing equity markets. Combined with the evidence of high coherence, the strong market co-movements validate the financial contagion hypothesis at the intermediate and lower frequencies during the global financial crises, and at the higher and intermediate frequencies during the local currency crisis and the COVID-19 pandemic, for the Turkish equity index. These findings reinforce the findings of Akhtaruzzaman et al. (2021) and partially agree with the results from Dimitriou et al. (2013), which indicate, from the perspective of Turkish investors, an absence of international portfolio diversification benefits available in both the developed and emerging markets during crisis periods. Further, the results demonstrate that the Turkish stock market index displays a relatively weaker interdependence with the MERVAL, MOEX, and IBEX35 indices, suggesting a presence of significant diversification benefits and providing abnormal return opportunities for the Turkish investor with varying significance and magnitudes at different wavelet time scales and periods.

5. Conclusion

This study examines stock market co-movements between 18 stock markets of both developed and developing countries and the BIST100 index, using weekly average observations for the sample period 2005–2021. BIST100 is found to be cointegrated pairwise with DAX, TSX, JSE, MERVAL, and MOEX indices while NIKKEI225 and MOEX co-move with the BIST100 index in the long run. BIST100 unidirectionally Granger-causes the indices of DAX, TSX, JSE, MERVAL, and MOEX in the short-run and/or long-run while the reverse causal relationship holds for NIKKEI225 and MOEX in the short run only. The findings of wavelet coherence analysis provide strong evidence for co-movements and lead/lag relationships between the returns of BIST100 and the other markets during the financial crisis in the long run (lower frequencies), and during the COVID-19 pandemic in the short run (higher frequencies), indicating an absence of portfolio diversification benefits and arbitrage opportunities for Turkish investors. The results, overall, provide evidence for the validity of the contagion hypothesis in Turkey during crisis periods.

The results provide insights and have significant implications for investors in building international portfolio diversification, hedging, and arbitrage opportunities as well as for policymakers in constructing monetary policies to attain financial stability. From the portfolio and risk management point of view, the cointegration test results suggest investing in the stock markets of SP500, FTSE100, CAC40, FTSE MIB, ATX, AXJO, BFX, BOVESPA, IBEX35, JKSE, MXX, and SENSEX, as these markets individually provided opportunities for international portfolio diversification benefits for Turkish investors. Moreover, the findings of the causality test showed that variations in the BIST100 index could be used to predict the short-term and long-term stock price movements in DAX and TSX; the short-term changes in MERVAL; and long-term movements in JSE and MOEX, providing abnormal return opportunities for Turkish investors investing in these markets. Similarly, the changes in NIKKEI and MOEX are significant predictors of the movements in the BIST100 index in the short run, providing useful information for international portfolio diversification strategies, as well as achieving better risk-return tradeoffs in Turkey for these countries' investors. These results are fully or partially consistent with the findings of previous studies, such as Yarovaya and Lau (2016). The corresponding results of wavelet coherency show that the indices of MERVAL, MOEX, and IBEX35 have a relatively lower coherence linkage with BIST100 during the whole sample period, providing evidence of significant portfolio diversification benefits and abnormal returns for Turkish investors and portfolio managers. Accordant with existing theory, the co-movement is weaker during tranquil periods at all frequencies but becomes stronger over the medium- and long-term during the crisis periods, including financial, local, and pandemic crises. From the policy-making perspective, it is crucial to consider that equity markets are more sensitive to intermediate and long-run fluctuations than short-run movements during the periods of crisis, to reduce adverse contagion effects of crisis across stock markets. To obtain more robust results, there is a requirement to investigate this relationship by including global financial and economic variables, such as oil, VIX, US government bond rates, as control variables in the model, which is a potential topic for future research.

6. Data Availability Statement

Our data supporting the findings were derived from the following resources available in the public domain: https://finance.yahoo.com/quote/ and https://markets.businessinsider.com/index/historical-prices. The data set is available from the corresponding author upon reasonable request.

References

Akhtaruzzaman, M., Boubaker, S., & Sensoy, A. (2021). Financial contagion during COVID–19 crisis. *Finance Research Letters*, 38, 101604. https://doi.org/10.1016/j.frl.2020.101604. Accessed 14 March 2021.

Albulescu, C. T., Goyeau, D., & Tiwari, A. K. (2017). Co-movements and contagion between international stock index futures markets. *Empirical Economics*, 52(4), 1529–1568. https://doi.org/10.1007/s00181-016-1113-5. Accessed 14 March 2021.

Alkulaib, Y. A., Najand, M., & Mashayekh, A. (2009). Dynamic linkages among equity markets in the middle east and north African countries. *Journal of Multinational Financial Management,* 19(1), 43–53. https://doi.org/10.1016/j.mulfin.2008.03.002. Accessed 15 March 2021.

Aloui, C., & Hkiri, B. (2014). Co-movements of GCC emerging stock markets: New evidence from wavelet coherence analysis. *Economic Modelling*, 36, 421–431. https://doi.org/10.1016/j.econmod.2013.09.043. Accessed 14 March 2021.

Al-Yahyaee, K. H., Mensi, W., Al-Jarrah, I. M. W., & Tiwari, A. K. (2019). Testing for the Granger-causality between returns in the US and GIPSI stock markets. *Physica A: Statistical Mechanics and Its Applications*, 531, 120950. https://doi.org/10.1016/j.physa.2019.04.186. Accessed 15 March 2021.

Baele, L. (2002). Volatility spillover effects in European equity markets: Evidence from a regime switching model. *Journal of Financial and Quantitative Analysis*, 40, 31–43. https://doi.org/10.1017/S0022109000002350. Accessed 25 March 2021.

Benli, Y. K., Basci, S., & Degirmen, S. (2012). Common stochastic trend and co-integration in the stock exchange markets: European countries and Turkey. *African Journal of Business Management,* 6(7), 2565–2577. https://doi.org/10.5897/AJBM11.664. Accessed 25 March 2021.

Cevik, E. I., Korkmaz, T., & Cevik, E. (2017). Testing causal relation among Central and Eastern European equity markets: Evidence from asymmetric causality test. *Economic Research-Ekonomska Istraživanja*, 30(1), 381–393.

Dajcman, S. (2013). Interdependence between some major European stock markets – a wavelet lead/lag analysis. *Prague Economic Papers*, 22(1), 28–49.

Das, D., Kannadhasan, M., Tiwari, A. K., & Al-Yahyaee, K. H. (2018). Has co-movement dynamics in emerging stock markets changed after global financial crisis? New evidence from wavelet analysis. *Applied Economics Letters*, 25(20), 1447–1453. https://doi.org/10.1080/13504851.2018.1430307. Accessed 12 April 2021.

David, S. A., Inácio Jr, C. M. C., & Machado, J. A. T. (2021). The recovery of global stock markets indices after impacts due to pandemics. *Research in International Business and Finance, 55,* 101335. https://doi.org/10.1016/j.ribaf.2020.101335. Accessed 14 March 2021.

Demiralay, S., & Ulusoy, V. (2017). How has the behavior of cross-market correlations altered during financial and debt crises?. *The Manchester School*, 85(6), 765–794.

Dima, B., Dima, Ş. M., & Barna, F. (2015). A wavelet analysis of capital markets' integration in Latin America. *Applied Economics,* 47(10), 1019–1036. https://doi.org/10.1080/00036846.2014.987917. Accessed 5 March 2021.

Dimitriou, D., Kenourgios, D., & Simos, T. (2013). Global financial crisis and emerging stock market contagion: A multivariate FIAPARCH–DCC approach. *International Review of Financial Analysis*, 30, 46–56. https://doi.org/10.1016/j.irfa.2013.05.008. Accessed 14 March 2021.

Forbes, K. J., & Rigobon, R. (2002). No contagion, only interdependence: Measuring stock market co-movements. *The Journal of Finance*, 57(5), 2223–2261. https://doi.org/10.1111/0022-1082.00494. Accessed 14 March 2021.

Gallegati, M. (2005). *A wavelet analysis of MENA stock markets.* In Working paper presented at International Conference on Middle East and North African Economics, University of Brussels, Belgium. Retrieved from https://econwpa.ub.uni-muenchen.de/econ-wp/fin/papers/0512/0512027.pdf. Accessed 25 March 2021.

Graham, M., Kiviaho, J., and Nikkinen, J. (2012). Integration of 22 emerging stock markets: A three-dimensional analysis. *Global Finance Journal*, 23(1), 34–47. https://doi.org/10.1016/j.gfj.2012.01.003. Accessed 25 March 2021.

Grinsted, A., Moore, J. C., & Jevrejeva, S. (2004). Application of the cross wavelet transform and wavelet coherence to geophysical time series. *Nonlinear Processes in Geophysics,* 11(5/6), 561–566. Retrieved from https://hal.archives-ouvertes.fr/hal- 00302394. Accessed 14 March 2021.

Hatemi-J, A. (2012). Is the UAE stock market integrated with the USA stock market? New evidence from asymmetric causality testing. *Research in International Business and Finance*, 26(2), 273–280. https://doi.org/10.1016/j.ribaf.2012.01.002. Accessed 11 April 2021.

Kapetanios, G. (2005). Unit-root testing against the alternative hypothesis of up to m structural breaks. *Journal of Time Series Analysis*, 26(1), 123–133. https://doi.org/10.1111/j.1467-9892.2005.00393.x. Accessed 14 March 2021.

Kenourgios, D., & Samitas, A. (2011). Equity market integration in emerging Balkan markets. *Research in International Business and Finance*, 25(3), 296–307. https://doi.org/10.1016/j.ribaf.2011.02.004. Accessed 14 March 2021.

Lee, H. S. (2004). International transmission of stock market movements: A wavelet analysis. *Applied Economics Letters*, 11(3), 197–201. https://doi.org/10.1080/1350485042000203850. Accessed 12 April 2021.

Lucey, B. M., & Voronkova, S. (2004). *Linkages and relationships between emerging European and developed stock markets before and after the Russian crisis of 1997–1998*. https://doi.org/10.2139/ssrn.625581. Accessed 5 March 2021.

Lucey, B. M., & Zhang, Q. (2010). Does cultural distance matter in international stock market co-movement? Evidence from emerging economies around the World. *Emerging Markets Review*, 11(1), 62–78. https://doi.org/10.1016/j.ememar.2009.11.003. Accessed 23 March 2021.

Maki, D. (2012). Tests for cointegration allowing for an unknown number of breaks. *Economic Modelling*, 29(5), 2011–2015. https://doi.org/10.1016/j.econmod.2012.04.022. Accessed 5 March 2021.

Mandaci, P. E., & Torun, E. (2007). Testing integration between the major emerging markets. *Central Bank Review*, 1, 1–12. Retrieved from https://core.ac.uk/download/pdf/6462845.pdf. Accessed 14 March 2021.

Markowitz, H. M. (1952). Portfolio selection. *Journal of Finance*, 7, 77–91. https://doi.org/10.1111/j.1540-6261.1952.tb01525.x. Accessed 14 March 2021.

Neaime, S. (2006). Volatilities in emerging MENA stock markets. *Thunderbird International Business Review*, 48(4), 455–484. https://doi.org/10.1002/tie.20105. Accessed 14 March 2021.

Okorie, D. I., & Lin, B. (2021). Stock markets and the COVID-19 fractal contagion effects. *Finance Research Letters*, 38, 101640. https://doi.org/10.1016/j.frl.2020.101640. Accessed 22 May 2021.

Rua, A., & Nunes, L. C. (2009). International co-movement of stock market returns: A wavelet analysis. *Journal of Empirical Finance*, 16(4), 632–639. https://doi.org/10.1016/j.jempfin.2009.02.002. Accessed 22 May 2021.

Salisu, A. A., Sikiru, A. A., & Vo, X. V. (2020). Pandemics and the emerging stock markets. *Borsa Istanbul Review*, 20(1), 40–48. https://doi.org/10.1016/j.bir.2020.11.004. Accessed 14 March 2021.

Tiwari, A. K., Mutascu, M. I., & Albulescu, C. T. (2016). Continuous wavelet transform and rolling correlation of European stock markets. *International Review of Economics & Finance*, 42, 237–256. https://doi.org/10.1016/j.iref.2015.12.002. Accessed 14 March 2021.

Topcu, M., & Gulal, O. S. (2020). The impact of COVID-19 on emerging stock markets. *Finance Research Letters*, 36, 101691. https://doi.org/10.1016/j.frl.2020.101691. Accessed 5 March 2021.

Uddin, G. S., Yahya, M., Goswami, G. G., Ahmed, A., & Lucey, B. M. (2020). *Stock market contagion of COVID-19 in emerging economies.* Available at SSRN 3573333.

Vuran, B., & Türkay, K. (2017). Emerging markets stock exchange linkages: Evidence from BRICS and MIST countries. *International Research Journal of Applied Finance*, 8(1), 1–11. Retrieved from https://search.proquest.com/openview/2353e70b9adb2a1a17372d236cd613a6/1?pq-. Accessed 19 March 2021.

Yarovaya, L., & Lau, M. C. K. (2016). Stock market co-movements around the global financial crisis: Evidence from the UK, BRICS and MIST markets. *Research in International Business and Finance,* 37, 605–619. https://doi.org/10.1016/j.ribaf.2016.01.023. Accessed 5 March 2021.

Yilmaz, A., & Unal, G. (2016). Co-movement analysis of Asian stock markets against FTSE100 and S&P500: Wavelet-based approach. *International Journal of Financial Engineering,* 3(04), 1650033. https://doi.org/10.1142/S242478631650033X. Accessed 5 March 2021.